Armchair Alchemist

Alexandria E. Walsh-Roberts

Armchair Alchemist

Mastering The Alchemy of Balance

Alexandria E. Walsh-Roberts

LIFEOFLIGHT
MEDIA

Published by
LifeOfLight Media

www.lifeoflightmedia.com
info@lifeoflightmedia.com

ISBN: 0-908807-67-8

© 2009 Alexandria E. Walsh-Roberts

All rights reserved. No part of this book, either in part or in whole, may be produced, transmitted or utilised in any form, by any means, electronic, photographic or mechanical, including photocopying, recording or by any information storage system, without permission in writing from the publisher, except for brief quotations embodied in literary articles and reviews.

For my beloved, my father, Mother Earth known as England and Australia, and all the Armchair Alchemists who have supported this book into being -

White Lunar World-Bridger, Yellow Resonant Warrior, Red Rhythmic Sky-Walker, Yellow Self-Existing Warrior, Yellow Self-Existing Human, White Planetary Wind, Red Resonant Sky-Walker, Red Lunar Dragon, Yellow Galactic Human, White Overtone World-Bridger, Blue Overtone Hand, Red Cosmic Earth, Blue Rhythmic Monkey, Red Crystal Serpent.

TABLE OF CONTENTS

1.	The first act	1
2.	Uniting opposition	3
3.	Changing focus	14
4.	Falling into place	21
5.	A state of cooperation	26
6.	Going with the flow	35
7.	Opening doors	41
8.	Be my guest	55
9.	There's plenty more where that came from	60
10.	The chaos of creation	67
11.	The Curve Of Ascension	75
12.	The honesty gap	85
13.	A natural state of being	91
14.	Hide and seek	99
15.	By invitation only	106
16.	Critical observations	117
17.	Momentary learning	124
18.	The Creation Code	127
19.	Servings of expansion	146
20.	Making a meal of it	158
21.	Healing acceleration	162
22.	Hark who's talking	171
23.	Stepping back through lack	186
24.	I am heart	198
25.	Overturning assumption	216
26.	Your money or your life	220

27.	The root of all evil	232
28.	Assimilating abundance	239
29.	A fan of creation	246
30.	Inner vision	255
31.	Crossing the line	262
32.	A tale of two cities	272
33.	Juggling with possibility	284
34.	Fast food	291
35.	It's all relative	296
36.	Charlatans or visionaries	301
37.	Embracing nourishment	322
38.	Balancing with Now	328
39.	Baby steps	334
40.	Wayshower	341
41.	Servings of wisdom	348
42.	Unconditional change	352
43.	The space in time	356
44.	Fellowship of chaos	361
45.	Come together	377
46.	The return	397

The First Act

A swarm of whispers hummed behind the scenes.

"It's time to go on," they prompted.

I struggled with a reply as words tumbled through my mental fog and the reality of the situation began to condense around me. "But how can I go on? I don't know what I'm doing!" came my urgent plea as my feet stuck to the floor with resistance.

A gentle wave of encouragement moved towards me, arriving as a flow of words. "There is no rush. You have all the time in the world. An eternity, as a matter of fact, filled with an abundance of unlimited opportunity. It is all there for the choosing."

"Is that all?" I replied, feeling nervous at what appeared to be too much choice.

"*Is-that-all* can easily become All-that-is. Perhaps a shift of perspective would help," continued the voice, transforming my scarcity into abundance in one short sentence.

"Simple then. So no pressure!" I replied defensively with nervous humour.

"None at all. It is your mind that tells you creativity is a pressure when really it is the making of you. Let it be; allow the flow. Exercise the power of choice that continues your journey on the road of expansion and helps you to carry on growing into the real you. Words soon become lines and then lines become the paragraphs that become your speech. Each breath fills your lungs with the flow of truth and the flow of change. Choice is simply your next step on the journey of expansion. There is always a next step; it is a natural flow. You have just forgotten how easy it can be."

"But how can something I've never done before be natural?" I protested. "I've never given a speech before, I don't know what to expect and I have no idea what I'm going to say!"

"But this is no different to any of the changes that you have already undergone. Your new speech is just a different kind of flow, a different kind of creativity. That is why there has never been a better time to listen to your heart. There are always words in the heart, it is your most natural form of expression."

"But it's so unpredictable," I protested, continuing to nurse my apprehension.

"All expansions are unpredictable, that is why they are expansive. All the knowledge in your world cannot change that. Deep down you understand that the heart is the doorway to all you seek. Deep down you understand that there is no need to worry."

"But what else can I do in this situation? Knowing nothing about the next ten minutes of my life makes it stretch out before me like the longest of ordeals. It's normal to worry about something you've never done before, isn't it?"

"It is one choice, but not the only choice. Is it helping you take a step forward?"

"No. Quite the reverse. It's holding me back while I think of what could possibly go wrong."

"Why listen to your limited ego self? Ego just tells you that you know nothing about what you are facing. So why consult your ego? There are no answers there."

"Okay. If you put it like that, perhaps it's time I was open to something different."

"Wonderful."

The voice paused as if waiting for me to step over the threshold into my heart.

"One last prompt?" I asked. I hesitated and glanced behind.

"Embrace your new perspective instead of looking behind you into your pasts or way beyond yourself into the future projections of your mind, look in your heart. It might not be what you expected but all of you is in your heart. You can always find yourself there!"

I could feel a momentum building within me as I relaxed into the promise of what I could do rather than holding onto what I had been. I took a step closer to the stage.

"Trust is all you require," encouraged the voice. "Trust is the step that bridges the gap between the limited and the unlimited."

I was now close enough to glimpse the stage and the auditorium. "Trust you say?" I whispered.

"Yes, trust. Trust brings forth realisation—a response to an understanding that enables self. Trust begins and ends with your heart. Such is the infinity of creation."

"Very well," I decided. "There's no point in being an outsider looking into your own life! Here goes..."

And with that I walked out in a sudden flood of lights towards centre stage, just in time to hear, "And without further ado, please give a warm welcome to an explorer we all know and love... I give you... yourself!"

Uniting Opposition

I felt a sense of liberation as I came out of my meditation. I rubbed my hands together and positioned them over the keyboard ready to write. But my electronic page remained blank.

"Embracing flexibility," came an observation from both within and around me.

"Is that you, Higher Self?"

There was no reply.

I looked up at the clock to confirm I was indeed back in my physical world. Its reliable hands were pressed together at almost 8:45, the second hand hovering gently above them.

"What's the odds of all three hands stopping at the same place?" I questioned rhetorically, astonished at how they'd all stopped at once.

"Not the end," came the promise of a discussion. "Nothing is running out."

"And it appears there isn't a beginning either!" I protested. "And how am I going to write if I've got no time, no sense of productivity and no way of measuring what I've achieved?" I asked, throwing my hands up in the air feigning a creative tantrum.

"Creativity has no measure, only flow. There is no point in defining infinity. There is no end, only cycles within cycles. You don't require time to measure your achievement, you require allowance so it may come into being. This is a new cycle within the cycle of your greater development."

"I beg to differ," I protested, confused by the lack of definition.

"Indeed, and that is your choice. But why beg when you have such resources at your disposal? Why not give yourself space so that you can invest in creative expansion, step by step? Creative scarcity is an illusion. There is no separation, it's all in your head, not in your heart." The voice paused as if waiting for my answer.

"Well, layers and cycles might be fine in your world," I began, "but you don't have to do physicality. And you don't have limitations like time, structure and, I might add, a finished novel to produce. Thin air may be full of genius but it's no good if it doesn't introduce itself to the page... make itself known, as it were."

"And so it is to allow your inner genius and infinite creativity. It is to allow your no-time, your newness and, of course, your process. You can magnetise anything when you are in your heart, united with yourself. There are no gaps—just flow."

The front entrance door slammed, appearing to emphasise what'd been said.

"Sounds like we're back to trust again," I observed as remnants of my meditation floated through my inner-net.

"Did we ever leave it?"

Uniting Opposition

"No, because you always trust. It's a way of being for you. As for me, it's more of a scattered experience of trust. Here then gone, gone then here," I replied as my frustration began to rise. "And if this is *so* simple, why do I feel so fragile? As though pieces of my life are cracking and chips of my world are falling off?"

"You're just chipping away at resistance, waiting to break the next mold of conditioning so you can step beyond this layer of ego and discover your next tale. It's all part of the path, the continuing path that reunites you with your true self, your unlimited nature. You've experienced the completion of your last cycle and now this is your initiation into your latest new."

"Okay, so what you're saying is to stop wobbling and get onto this new portion of my creative path. And to do that I've just got to try that bit harder to break through."

"It is more a case of concentrating your efforts through centeredness, not forcing yourself. If you concentrate yourself, you don't pressure yourself. Concentration comes from being centred in your heart. Be open. You can't force creation but you can widen your creation stream; expand to embrace the new."

The voice was encouraging and yet I still felt disconnected, unwilling to contribute but incapable of reacting.

The voice paused, waiting patiently for my resistance to pass.

"Don't expect the same mechanism. All creations are unique, not repetitive. Never two flows the same. That's the beauty of it. You are unique. No one can create like you so be at peace. You aren't spiralling off into the obscure, you're flowing into the new. Allow the flow... allow the flow."

"But *what* flow?" I answered my inner companion out loud. "There isn't any. That's my problem. Can't you see I'm frustrated because I've got nothing to write?"

"There is always flow," began the voice gently, "but it isn't the flow you expected. Nor is it the flow your ego recognises. But it *is there*. It never leaves. It's all a matter of learning to work with greater and greater degrees of the unlimited flow. This is the expansion you seek."

The door slammed again, right on cue as if the voice was using my physical world as punctuation.

"How come I never normally hear the door and yet today it's a sound that's slamming right through me?"

"You hear it because you are becoming more sensitive. You are deepening your relationship with all that surrounds you and with all that is within you. You haven't allowed it yet; your ego is still trying to repel it. But these reactions will pass. It's all in the shift. Coming or going, it all just keeps on flowing," enthused the voice, enticing me further with a hint of progress.

"As one door closes, another door opens?" I suggested.

"Yes. This is an illustration of the flow that is your world," it continued. "Everything is connected; everything is part of the unlimited flow. Expansion is always on offer and you are joining in, albeit a little reluctantly."

I pictured ego slumped behind its power-hungry desk in the office of my mind. I ignored its projections, instead surrendering to the feeling of my heart. Our flow of conversation became pulses of truth throughout my body culminating in a long shiver.

I felt compelled to look behind me but there was no one there. The space fizzed at me as if charged with the potential I was growing into.

My companion returned. "Yes, there is flow all around you," pointed out the voice. "It's all part of you. These waves of energy make up your world and your experiences. You are a droplet in a tropical rainstorm, a ripple in the rivers of unity, a wave in the ocean of the unlimited."

"Hold on, I'm beginning to feel seasick."

I felt a wave of humour, my frustration tempered by the loving flow of guidance.

"All part of the process. You are just adapting. And was that a small ripple of expansion as you opened your heart?"

Uniting Opposition

"Perhaps," I replied begrudgingly.

The voice continued to tip-toe around ego, keeping the possibility of confrontation to a minimum. "And so it is. You are releasing your resistance and you are crafting that very same energy into your next step of personal alchemy.

"You are beginning to relate to your world and your creations differently. You are feeling what goes into your doing and being and what comes through your doing and your being and what comes out the other side. Your comings and goings are beginning to unite in purpose and in balance. You are starting to understand the reflections of your world. You are seeing that your internal environment is linked to the external. These are not two separate flows, two separate places you can create, they are all part of the process. It is only ego that protests, not your heart. It is ego that tries to resist this process of unification. Ego tells you that you are blocked because ego is blocked. Ego is surrounded by love and that love is growing as you deepen your commitment to your healing process."

"So, listen to my heart and my guidance? If ego tries to butt in then it's to remind ego that two's company, three's a crowd?"

"Yes. Heart and guidance are two halves of balance that create unity. Ego can never change this sacred truth no matter how hard it tries. But you are not excluding your ego, merely choosing to love it and to dissolve its opposition into loving alternatives."

"But ego wants control, not love."

"And you now know yourself well enough to understand that what really matters is what your heart chooses."

"So this is why I'm having a hard time believing that having nothing to write is actually supportive?"

"You are beginning to realise that all parts of your process are supportive and all are productive, just in different ways. It is difficult for ego, it is not difficult for your true nature.

"But as you see past your ego, you are beginning to

understand that everything you do with loving intention makes a difference. Just because there is no 'doing' at this point in your creative cycle does not mean there isn't anything going on. You are changing the way you relate to your world. You are opening up and it is ego that finds this difficult. Ego struggles with anything that is not limited. Ego doesn't want to understand the unlimited, nor does it want to relate to the endless nature of the greater Universe. Ego wants to be separate; off in its own limited world."

"Then ego is trying to hold me back?"

"Try not to see ego as being against you. Choose to believe you have a choice in each of your moments. One of those choices might be from ego but there will be many, many more from your heart. If you put your ego conditioning aside and choose to live abundantly, not through the scarce limitation of ego, you will benefit from this new flow. Stop your trying and allow your writing."

"So what's ego going to do if I keep on relating differently, exploring this next step in my alchemy?"

"Ego will do what it always does—keep on reinforcing limitation. But you don't have to listen. It's all a matter of choice, flow and how you experience it."

A spark of hope was igniting within my heart. The unfamiliar wasn't so overwhelming or frustrating. I didn't have to rush to label it, I could choose to flow with it, see where it lead. This was, after all, the unfolding path of alchemy.

"Not wrong, just different," I said, summing up my realisation.

"Quite so... an expanding sense of 'different.' You are easing yourself into a more expanded experience of the flow and your true nature. What is now is always flowing, always growing and it doesn't serve you to get stuck in one experience over and over again."

"Where's the learning in that?" I pondered. "Just makes ego feel secure because it can keep reinforcing limitation."

Uniting Opposition

"Indeed. Welcome to your expansion."

I could sense a smile guiding my words. "There's something else happening too. I can feel it, I just don't know how to describe it."

"Allow yourself to feel in the heart. The words are secondary; a means to trace your path, but not essential. Energy has many different ways to describe itself. What is important is that you are choosing to embrace this expansion, you are in allowance. You can dot the I's and cross the Ts later."

I relaxed as best I could with the feeling of both disturbance and expansion.

"Keep going," observed the voice. "You are beginning to feel the flow. Rather than thinking it through, you are *feeling* it through. You are beginning to relate to the infinity of which you are part."

The voice continued its observations. "Outgoing energy doesn't 'do something' then leave and never return, nor does this flow mean loss or less. Incoming isn't good, bad or *separate*."

The voice accented the word separate as if hinting.

"No it doesn't feel separate, just all sloshing around together in my heart space. It's odd because there appears to be less direction and more unity. But I'm stabilising and I'm happy to say I'm still here; I haven't drowned yet. On the contrary, I'm beginning to feel quite buoyant!"

"Wonderful. You are embracing your true nature. Imagine yourself in a bubble bath of energy, floating on your back, realising that creation can be a joy when you allow it. Why not inhale some relaxation and peace?"

"Interesting imagery." I picked up a handful of the imaginary bubbles. "And these are just like the unending flow. Burst the bubbles and they change into something else, still flowing, just not in form. Ego would say no way! But the unlimited is all ways right, with or without physical form."

"Precisely. There is always more than one way for everything. Always another choice, creation and perception. All you are required to do is recognise the loving way, the neutral way; the way of the heart."

"But what do you mean when you say *neutral*?"

"The flow doesn't judge what you want, it supports you in creating learning. It doesn't, for example, give you more flow if you appear good and less if you seem bad. Those ideas are just limitations of ego. The flow simply keeps on going and it's up to you to co-create with that flow through conscious choice. If you choose to be fearful, you create fearful experience. If you choose to be loving, you create loving experience. The way you experience your world is your choice. The unlimited flow might be unlimited but it isn't going to choose for you."

"So how I experience my creations depends on my choices and also the recycling of my ego conditioning that says everything is a struggle?"

"Yes. That is the great experiment—the exploration of limitation and then the return to the unlimited. You are in an equilibrium that keeps on changing with each choice you make. More love, more recycling, less fearful experience. More light, more awareness, more potential for expansion. Ego has appeared natural and right for so long but now that is changing."

"Changing to wrong?" I asked, letting out a sigh. "As ego's world gets turned upside down?"

"Try to perceive this whole shift in perspective as simply 'different'. It is a place of neutrality and balance that doesn't discredit what has gone before. It is simply an alternative to ego interpretation; a 'different' that now seems relevant in your experience and your world. And so the return to loving unity continues."

The voice paused just as what it was saying began to sink in deep within me.

"And it's always been there, it's just that I was immersed in ego research previously so I didn't notice the alternatives?"

"Yes."

Uniting Opposition

"So keep on believing in that loving flow, that unending flow, even if my experience here seems to be temporarily interrupted in the sense of disconnected from love?"

"Most certainly. Love is your true nature. Ego is the part of you that wants diversion... the illusion of separation. It isn't real."

"Meaning?"

"To experience limitation, you have allowed mind and ego to condition you to separation and imbalance. Now, though, you are choosing to return to your unlimited nature. To restore balance, you will go back through the resistance you created during your 'research.' You are not able to recycle your limited habits unless you go back through them, recycling as you go and as you flow. Your transmutation ability is increasing and this is why you are creating deeper transmutations for yourself and, as a result, greater accelerations. Also, the temporary impression that you are hitting your head against a brick wall."

"It has felt like that some days. But it's up to me to embrace this different perspective; to dunk myself in this flow of light and understanding so that the brick wall of resistance can dissolve and become support, right?"

"Yes. The dissolving is under way."

"No more standing in the shadow of my former self, then."

"No more believing in the shadows and gloom of your limited self."

"So ego tries to divert the neutral unlimited flow so that it can keep building on my limited conditioning and sooner or later I could believe that it's natural?

"Yes."

"And ego says change is bad, painful... even wrong."

"Yes."

"But I can choose differently."

"And three-fold yes! Now do you understand why you think your writing is going nowhere?"

"Because ego's telling me that change is going nowhere; change is a waste of time. And that's why I think I'm going around in circles."

"Precisely."

"I'm seeing the dents left behind by my research into limitation. Some of them are so deep that I fall back into that conditioning from time to time; I get caught in an ego blind spot. But I don't have to go around and around in ever-decreasing circles of scarcity."

"No you don't. You can go around and around in ever increasing cycles of creation!" replied the voice in celebration, as if we'd now successfully crossed our dark room of resistance and I'd reached up to find the light switch.

"Ah, now I get it. It's ego that's cornered. Ego's the one going around in circles telling me that I'm chasing nothing or receiving nothing. It's ego telling me I haven't got the words and I'm wasting my time."

The voice took up my realisation. "And it's ego that tells you that understanding is pinned to one static definition; one right or wrong, as ego sees it. But there is really so much more to understand, so much more to understanding."

"Ego is really the one in lack, then, trying to force its definitions through my mind?"

"Indeed. Ego is in lack because it has isolated itself in its static world, desperate to nail down everything through expectation and assumptions. Ego's world is either ego's way or no way; right or wrong, black or white. There is no multicolour, there is no different, just what ego likes and what it doesn't like. And what it doesn't like, it resists. And if something is different then ego is only too willing to label it as bad rather than become more flexible and understand what that difference brings, the expansion that makes the difference."

"So ego always wants to repel what it doesn't understand because it doesn't know how to control it."

Uniting Opposition

"Yes. But through your commitment to meditation, allowance and understanding, you are discovering that it doesn't have to be like that. This is why your writing is expanding too. And it will keep on changing because you are not static and nor are your creations."

"So it's to be patient and wait for different, not to be frustratingly distant?"

"Indeed. Allow the process."

"But that's just it. Hanging around this long in allowance makes it tempting to forget the whole thing and just give up; stop meditating because it isn't giving me the breakthrough I want."

"But are you really giving up in your meditation or merely standing in front of an unfamiliar scene? You do want to be there, don't you?"

"Of course I do! That's why I keep coming back for more!"

"Then why not just allow your position to be? Ego might say you are exposed but really you are still learning. Just because you can't do anything doesn't mean you aren't achieving anything. Achieving is both doing and being. Allowance is the way you will magnetise your next creative step. See this phase as supporting you in rearranging yourself into your next you, your next expansion."

"So just because I'm uncomfortable on that stage is no reason to say it's wrong and reject it. It's just waiting to be understood and integrated into my writing process. It's ego that's uncomfortable with something I didn't expect, something my mind can't explain."

"And so why give up when what you seek is right in front of you? You don't need lines, an audience or a director to be yourself, to allow the flow that is knocking at the door to your heart."

"But that's easy for you to say because you... well, you understand. I thought I understood but... I don't know if it's impatience or frustration creeping back in but... I'm getting confused again."

"Put it this way," suggested the voice, making a change of direction. "Do you journey to find what you already have?"

"That would seem rather pointless."

"So let everything rearrange before your very eyes. Your next step is there, even if you don't know what it is. To discover what's different and step into another part of the greater flow, you will always have periods of disturbance; of what your ego and mind calls annoying, irritating, frustrating, not-worth-its. But you know in your heart such 'differents' *are* worth it. They are the expansion you seek. And sometimes you are required to be patient and dissolve resistance. Then you find the gems you want; the wisdoms that encourage and support you. And then you realise your alchemy—turning ego into expansion; the silence of separation into words; resistance into support."

"Fear into love," I added.

"Always."

"And necessary disturbance is challenging the defined limits of my mind?"

"Most certainly. But it doesn't necessarily have to be a struggle. It can be fun if you allow it to be."

The voice stepped back as if giving me room to embrace the inner space I'd now cleared of mental attachments.

Meanwhile, ego was squirming in my mind. It knew that what it didn't expect had now happened—I'd realised a change. My mind prepared to project its irritation.

"But I still don't have any words. How long is this allowance going to take?" I insisted.

"As long as it takes."

"But after all this meditation... all our discussions... I thought that would make things easier; maybe give me a bit of a head start."

"A head start?" challenged the voice.

"It's an expression. What I meant to say was, I thought

I knew what all this was; I thought I'd broken into true self and an expanded relationship with the Universe through my Higher Self. I really thought I'd done that."

"And you have. A part of it, that is. And so this is another piece in the jigsaw of your true nature. All you are required to do is focus."

The word focus ignited all my ego opposition in one short sound.

"But that was what I was trying to do—focus!"

Ego had filled my reply with as much anger as it could until my voice turned to a croak, followed closely by a painful sore throat.

"Well, you know what I mean," I added apologetically.

The front entrance door slammed once more. Our conversation was at an end.

Changing Focus

My outburst had now reinstated ego and it seized its opportunity to flood my mind with sensations of abandonment, failure and isolation.

"Well, you're not going to do that again," it began. "Just count on what you know, don't waste your time with what doesn't work. You don't need all the frustration that change brings. You need to stick to what you know, not go on these unreliable meanderings that never amount to anything."

I could feel ego pushing me to return to my mind and end my path of expansion in a cul-de-sac of resistance.

"But what I know isn't working," I replied defiantly, "so I'm going to have another go at this. I don't believe that voice has gone, it's just gone silent while I deal with my resistance. I'm feeling strangely encouraged, ego, so I won't be joining you to weigh myself down with piles of commiseration! I am choosing differently,' I affirmed. "Voice... are you still there?"

"Just breathe and relax." The voice had returned. "Then you will create the breakthrough you seek. There is no need to fight for expansion, just remain in your heart. Allow and it will open up."

I let out a breath I didn't know I was holding.

"You are letting go," continued the voice, as if offering an upgraded flow with a new angle of explanation. "Your mode of perception is changing, opening out like a lens gaining a wider and wider angle on your world. Don't look through the eyes of judgement, it can only lead you back to your mind. Ego belongs to the limited world, not the greater Universe. Allow the expanding perception of the heart. These new pathways, new alternatives are all flowing into a higher way that leads to change and a greater flow of Love. Do not ask yourself if you are right or wrong, ask yourself if your intention is loving; if you are contributing to balance; if you are relating to love or fear in your surroundings."

"So if I can rephrase this, do you mean that when I hear that voice saying *I know, I know,* that's really ego saying it knows?"

"Correct. Ego is attempting to reinforce your conditioning by telling you that what ego knows is all that matters. But you are beginning to see and feel the difference. This path is part of your developing awareness; understanding when you are relating to your world through ego and when you are relating through heart. Ego has been the norm for your experience in limitation, but that is all changing now, moment by moment.

"You used to think that *I know* meant it is fixed and certain within your world. But now you are beginning to see a difference between this fixed definition that resists change and the knowingness of your heart that allows you to understand your expanded nature and keep on embracing change."

"So the ego 'I know' just knows about the limited world and it doesn't want to develop any other alternatives, any other understanding?"

"It certainly doesn't because, for ego, there isn't anything else!"

"Then if I'm going to carry on working with my heart, understanding is going to get fairly elastic. No more static definitions?"

"Certainly."

"And no more mind. Only heart from now on."

The voice appeared to pause. "Logic would tell you that the mind is no longer useful to you from this moment on because the heart is the true interface with the greater Universe. But remember, you are becoming a unity, not a polarity."

"Wait a minute. I don't understand. Isn't it more loving to stay in the heart rather than the mind?"

"But are you choosing heart and pushing mind away? Do the heart and mind have to be poles apart?"

"No, I suppose not."

"Are you trying to be in your heart by rejecting your mind?"

I began to recognise my black and white conditioning but nevertheless continued with my belief that I was right.

"But I thought the mind was the home of ego and so it was the home of limitation and so, in a way, it's completely opposite to the heart because the heart is the interface for the unlimited."

"How can you become reunited with the unlimited if you're polarised within yourself?"

I paused to absorb what was said. "I've fallen into an ego trap, right?"

"Let us just call it conditioning; jumping to ego conclusions—mind *or* heart, limited *or* unlimited rather than a unity between heart *and* mind; a flow of Love embracing your mind and dissolving resistance. There is nothing wrong with mind, it just depends on how it is used."

The voice was gaining momentum.

"Look on the bright side. Every time you recognise ego

conditioning, you are gaining awareness. The more awareness you have, the easier it is to change."

"So I was analysing, not feeling. And my outburst earlier was my ego reacting to my choice to gain awareness. I released all that pent up energy, that limitation, and managed to put some of it into anger. But the rest I reapplied into creating this conversation, having another go in a different way."

"Yes you did. You took another step into your expansion instead of rebounding off it or running away. You are beginning to learn in your transmutations that being able to go through them is one aspect, but what is also important is that you reapply the energy that is released, applying it to creating more choices in your world. Value what you are achieving rather than polarise it and let ego take control of what you have worked hard to free."

"So no more thinking mind is wrong and heart is right," I mused.

"Because if all is reuniting in Love, then..." The voice was prompting me to fill in the blanks.

"...Then as my mind frees up from ego, it'll flow more and more until there won't be any definitions left; no more attachments to scarcity and control. And then the mind will be free, empty of attachment but full of space for flow. Heart and mind will reunite. Ego has never been the enemy, just the part of me that helped me experience limitation. The more judgmental I become, the less allowing and the more polarised I can become. So let go of judgment and stay in my heart."

"Progress indeed!" encouraged my Higher Self. "And in this return to love, this recycling, what appears to be poles apart will come together in the unlimited flow of love. Wrong may appear right and right appear wrong but, really, they are two sides of the same story and they will be recycled into love. Ego will never help you become unlimited; it cannot because it does not understand how. Yet do not assume it is against you. Remember that your mind is an integral part of yourself and will reunite in love, as will all parts of yourself that were once fully immersed in your research into the limited world.

"Your mind has enabled you to draw energy into such concentrated limitation that it was sketched into form. The more experienced you became, the more dense the form and your experience of form. This convinced you that the limited world was solid. Mind and ego cultivated physical senses, perceptions and definitions so that you could focus exclusively on form, even to the point where the invisible—the *no-form*—was considered impossible. Quite a remarkable feat! Then you joined all your experiences in limitation end to end and wrapped them up in linear time, convincing yourself that there wasn't an unlimited eternal flow but only a flow defined through the four corners of limitation—fear, control, lack and loss. You were thinking inside the cube."

The voice paused, having completed its journey through limitation to the expansion of our Now. "And so now you are undergoing the process of reversing your perception out into the unlimited. But you are not leaving your mind behind, you are simply emptying it of the attachments that have made your limited nature seem so real. You are returning to building your life from love, not fear. And all the flow that has been compressed into the conditionings of a limited world will become your fuel; the fuel for your alchemy of change. You are dissolving the outlines of form so that you can embrace the endless flows of the unlimited. Call it a liberating lack of definitions."

"I certainly feel more liberated. I just wish I hadn't blasted my way through that resistance!"

"Quite. But as you will see in your coming moments, all is learning and with learning comes practice and with practice comes focus."

"Oh, that word again. Don't worry, I'm not going to blow things out of proportion again. At least, I don't feel I am." I paused as if checking. "But maybe it's about time you helped me understand why I seem to have so much resistance to the concept of focus? What's focus in the bigger picture?"

"Being open hearted and open minded to the best of your ability and capacity in each moment."

"But that's the complete opposite of the usual focus which is sticking to what you're doing!"

I paused as I got a sudden flashback of what had been said earlier. "So this is one of those *right-becomes-wrong* moments, I suppose?"

"Yes and no. Actually it is simply that one understanding comes from ego and one from heart. And so, now that you are choosing from the heart, the ego perspective appears to be wrong. But it's just another perspective."

I was beginning to see why the voice was encouraging me to perceive in terms of love rather than the limiting polarities of right and wrong.

"So basically, ego has been defining the limited world from within my limited perspective. If I turn those definitions inside out then they're explained in terms of the unlimited. And that's why I often feel wrong because when I talk to you, everything is the opposite of what I thought it was."

"It is ego that thinks it is wrong. Ego is the one taking it personally, not your true nature. Ego is the one that doesn't know any different," the voice chuckled.

"So now I'm taking it lovingly, not personally! That way I can keep my focus?"

"Correct. It is one thing to create what you are looking for, but to embrace it is another matter."

"You are joking, right? People actually create what they want and then don't embrace it?"

"This can be the case. That is part of the cruelty of ego; one of the ways it keeps you down, as it were. It reinforces the impossible. It tells you that you cannot embrace Love, that you are not Love, and that you cannot embrace yourself."

I was taken aback. "So a person goes through all the

detachment and recycling to get more love and then they don't know what to do with it?"

"In simple terms, yes. A soul creates a path to embrace greater love, choice and awareness but then it is required to appreciate what it has created so that it can embrace it."

"So that's why we require practice?"

"Yes. An abundance of practice so that when an abundance of love arrives within your world, you are able to deal with the shift it creates."

"Make room for all that flow, all that love?"

"Yes."

"I know humanity isn't all that evolved but I didn't think we were that stupid or self damaging."

"It is more an issue of ignorance. When you are aware of alternatives then it becomes cruel to constantly limit yourself. But when you are not aware then it is just existing in limitation; just doing what you know and being who you think you are."

"So it's all related to awareness. Who am I? What am I doing here? What's it all for? Those big questions?"

"Yes. And your awareness is related to whether you ask these questions and whether you explore where these questions lead you. Do you dare? And do you care?"

"As a matter a fact, I do. And I'm choosing the daring and the caring that builds a path of expansion."

"And so it is. Limitation, like all aspects of your world, is of course relative! Ego has taken the infinite and put it into limitation. So you have infinite ways to be limited. If you are unaware then this is easily done. And as we have mentioned before, just because you know something doesn't make you intelligent. It is only now that the humanity is waking up to what is truly intelligent."

"And this is why we need to practice our choices so that we can work out whether we are coming from love or fear, create learning and then find those gems of wisdom. All part of the alchemy?"

"Yes. Just another day in the life of a wizard."

"So I AM choosing to transmute my ignorance and expand my awareness so that I can become truly intelligent."

"Now that is an intelligent choice; one made through self observation," the voice appeared to applaud. "And as your loving responses become natural, you will see an endless flow of moments designed for you by your higher nature so that you may return to your expanded self. No more fleeting scarcities of the mind."

The voice and I paused simultaneously as another cycle of wisdom completed itself. I felt a growing acceleration, full of encouragement and empowerment. I wanted to gather up as much of this feeling as possible and store it for the days when inspiration eluded me. But this time, when I wanted to reach for ego, I recognised my conditioning. If I was going to believe in the unlimited flow then it was time I started letting go of the fear of losing it. And the time to start was right here, right now.

Falling Into Place

The voice appeared restless, as if preparing to tie up the loose ends of our conversation.

"The mind is much more fragile than you understand at this time. Therefore create your path with balance at all times. Dismantle your attachments gently, don't rip them out in your rush to change. Honour your path. You want to free your mind, not go out of your mind."

"Okay, I'll try to remember that!" I laughed. "But I'm curious... What happens if you go out of your mind?"

"Then you are in no-man's land, unable to expand; in limbo between heart and mind. This is why balance is so important in your process."

"Fine. Then I'll be careful how I go."

"Yes, be gentle with self. You are already beginning to

understand that fighting ego and trying to make it wrong—or right, for that matter—will yield nothing. You are seeing that your recycling can only happen through love and not through force. Seek what is supportive, not what is strugglesome. All will come together, it is in the making."

I could feel another wave of resistance growing. "So what do I do now?" My voice was filling with demanding ego overtones.

"Flow. Remember, coming and going is all part of the flowing," replied the voice, beginning to fade.

"But I need a next step. What do I do with all the space we've been clearing?"

"Trust and you will see and feel differently. It's simpler than you think, much simpler. The nature of the Universe is simplicity. It's the mind and ego's insecurity that makes it complicated."

The voice seemed to stabilise but ego was trying to rush me to a guaranteed conclusion.

"Fine. So how do I open up to the infinite? Do I go with the flow, trust and get there? Alright, I know the infinite isn't a destination... I'm talking in terms of realising the connection."

"You're getting warmer. Keep going," the voice said, waving me along on my energetic treasure hunt. "It is almost where you are now, almost right in front of you. Keep going."

I looked in front of myself, half hoping there would be something both magical and tangible.

"No, not outside of yourself. And not where you have been *trying* to be lately," the voice said, completing its trail of hints.

I felt like a chick trying to hatch, suddenly filled with an urgency to break out. But I was pinned in my chair under the weight of what my ego told me was impossible.

"So where have I been trying to be lately?" I paused,

asking myself the question out loud. "Have I been *trying* to write?"

My ego was fanning my growing impatience into a destructive outburst as it challenged each of my questions but offered no alternatives.

The voice returned in support of my stream of clarification. "And has the *trying* been relating to the infinite? Has it been flowful and fulfilling?"

"No, of course not," I snapped, my ego resisting the guidance and recoiling back into my mind.

The voice waited patiently for my realisation to flow into words.

"Oh, I get it. I've been in my head, not in my heart. I thought I was being creative because I was trying to write but I can't relate to the infinite because I was in my head, unable to expand. Hence why I've been *trying* and not creating."

"Bingo!" the voice filled with enthusiasm.

"So if I try and focus then I'm forcing from the mind and I'm not creating from the heart."

"Indeed. So your creation, your writing, will flow when...?"

I took the hint. "When I start in Heart Central and I focus on keeping an open heart and an open mind."

"Wonderful," replied the voice, seeing whether it was time for me to hatch.

But I obviously hadn't finished pecking through a hard shell of self doubt. "But how do I do that?" I asked, stalling once more.

Silence was the reply.

"I think I understand, but then I don't know how to apply this."

I felt like I was fumbling with the key to my creative relief, like searching for that word that is always just on the tip of your tongue.

"Magnetise your answer from your heart flow. Cooperate with the unlimited, don't try and control it, then you will find what you seek. And sooner than you know. Effortless creativity is simple—force less, flow more. You don't want to struggle any more."

"I agree with that!"

"Wonderful. So flow. Just because energy is going into dissolving ego attachment doesn't mean it stops flowing through you. Limitation is, after all, a bit of a cosmic joke if you can learn to laugh with yourself and your ego!"

I had a strong feeling the voice had used up all its hints observing the desperate antics of a juvenile mind. I slapped the arms of my chair. I was becoming agitated as my frustration built once more. I knew I knew, but something was missing. Ego had jumped to its feet in the office of the mind, pounding a fist on an imaginary desk, demanding results and reactions. Why couldn't I follow through? What was I waiting for?

I rose to my feet in provocation, wanting to rush out of my flat and get away from my discomfort. But as I stepped forward, I tripped over the computer power cable and landed face to face with the loud pattern of my aging carpet. The sudden shock stopped my ego and mind in their tracks. I finally understood it was time to surrender.

Gathering my shaking limbs to stand, I heard a faint voice saying: "Hello? Hello? Is that you?"

For a moment I thought my inner world had come out to meet me until I realised it was my phone. I'd pressed my speed dial as I'd fallen. I dug in my pocket to answer but they'd already hung up. Struggling to my feet, I shuffled towards the armchair and sank into its reliable comfort.

Stretching my legs out before me, I began to laugh. My body hurt and my head hurt, but my heart was laughing with more joy than I'd experienced in the whole of the last two weeks. I wanted to open up and ego wanted to shut me down. Nothing was working and, fortunately, I now realised it was high time I accepted help.

I pressed redial.

"Good morning," came the cheery tones of Erica, the editor with a ten tonne stockpile of enthusiasm. "What happened to you? I heard a muffled sound, then nothing. Are you alright?"

"Yes Erica. I just tripped over my computer and ended up ringing you!"

I could hear her trying not to laugh. She always felt like laughing at the slightest hint of mishap.

"Go on laugh! I did!"

"Oh, come on," Erica chuckled, "it *is* funny! And it could even be a sign. Were you actually falling over yourself to reach me?"

"Oh ha, ha, ha," I cringed. "But I think you might have stumbled upon something there. I did want to talk to you, I just didn't know it. The Universe has a funny way of helping you magnetise exactly what you need, even if you refuse to see it."

"Great. So how can I help?"

"I'm your struggling author traversing the desert of doubt and beating myself up. Literally, I might add. So it's high time I stepped back and asked for help. I can't see the wood for the trees, Erica."

"But you're in a desert. There aren't any trees," she laughed.

"This is no time for editor's continuity." I paused to change my metaphor. "Well anyway, I thought a bit of your fire could burn off some of my confusion; create clarity; stimulate some new growth. You walk me through what appears to be normal, just like you always do, so I can conjure up something completely different."

There was a theatrical silence that almost had me worried.

"You are still there, Erica?" I glanced at my phone to check in case I'd lost reception.

"Yes. What you're saying sounds completely insane but there is a fine line between genius and madness. But what concerns me slightly is that I thought we'd been through this before. Tell me I'm not going senile. We did have a follow up meeting three weeks ago in which we discussed the vision that was your second book. Or was that just a shimmering promise you've been chasing across your desert of doubt?"

"Yes and no. The meeting did happen, it's just... nothing has happened since then," I admitted. Stretching Erica's good humour as far as it would go, I continued, "So I come bearing no pages and grovelling for an audience with Erica The Wise! I've got a bad case of scribus blockus maximus. I want some of your double espresso fire to help me spark."

Erica took a deep breath, inhaling a temporary silence. I felt nervous.

"Of course," she began, "your timing is perfect, even if you didn't know it was. My morning is pretty quiet and coffee's approaching on the horizon as we speak. I've got a few calls to make. Shall we say, in the office in forty-five minutes?"

"I'm desperate but not *that* desperate. Shall we say an hour and a half so that you've got time for your espresso worship?"

"Do you dare to defy your master?!" she boomed, trying not to laugh. "Just kidding. The door is always open. But don't keep me waiting. You know how I hate waiting, particularly after a double espresso!"

A State Of Cooperation

I arrived on the last stroke of ten. Pushing open a slab of executive tower, I was greeted by a very tidy space. The reception was empty. It felt strange. Where was Linda? She was always here. I had a feeling that a long term familiarity was dissolving into the past, right before my eyes. I was just about to go in the direction of Erica's office when a man in his early twenties tapped me on the shoulder.

"Can I help you?" he said, moving around and sitting behind the reception desk.

"Sorry, I was just going to see Erica. I thought there was no one in. Is Linda off sick?"

"No, she's off pregnant. Make that very pregnant, due any time now. I'm John, her replacement."

"God! Linda's been here for years. I just can't believe I didn't know. Where have I been these past seven months?"

"Not here?" he smiled.

"Quite. Please give her my best when you hear from her."

"I will. She's due to return to work in two months. You're the author of *Magician from the Masses*, right?"

"Yes, that's correct."

"You know Erica—always refers to books, not names."

"Yep, that's Erica. All work, work, work. Unless, of course, that's changed too?"

"No, that part is still present and correct," he smiled. Go straight through. She's expecting you."

"Thanks."

I smiled to myself. The outline of my world was coming away at the seams as each certainty was released. It felt as though one day Linda was there, part of the familiar fabric and the next she'd dissolved, birthing a whole new world. I tried to think back over the past seven months but everything was a blank. Was I really that disconnected?

I arrived at Erica's open door, out of my comfort zone and in search of a very necessary next step.

I knocked gingerly, hearing Erica in full flow. She beckoned me in.

'I'll only be a minute,' she mouthed, offering me a seat while skillfully tailoring the conversation to a close.

"Oh, if you enjoyed the spiritual theme then there's plenty more where that came from," she said. "It's a complete departure from the usual stuff but, what can I say... It brings out the faith in me and that's a miracle in itself!"

She beamed a smile across the desk as I acknowledged her enthusiastic review.

"Must dash. Keep me posted." She hung up and brushed an auburn curl from her glacier-blue eyes.

"Tea? Or should I say, chai?" she smiled, gesturing towards her mini coffee lounge.

"No chai, thanks. Not in India now. Just water, please."

Acknowledging my choice and without taking a breath, Erica went straight to business.

"But your sequel is. In India, I mean. Just a heartbeat away from your next monsoon magic, right?"

"Well actually, my monsoon of inspiration isn't flowing. Not failed, just postponed."

"But I thought we'd discussed all this. It's simple now—you just continue the Indian theme of your previous novel. Same setting, different characters, new insights, etcetera etcetera into your best selling sunset. You know how it goes."

"I thought I did, but knowing how it goes and actually getting it going appear to be a subcontinent apart. It's like I'm stuck in a recurring vision. I want to move ahead but I don't have the words to reach the vision I've already embraced. And then it starts all over again from the same place. Does that make any sense?"

"Not really. But when in doubt, go back to basics. That's what I always say. What's not working in the formula? Is it the setting? The characters? The message?"

"If you put it like that... all of the above."

"You mean the formula isn't working?" Erica looked disappointed. "But the formula is what you've worked so hard for. Now you have it, that's what allows you to write easily. Stick to the formula and you've got guaranteed sales, over and over again."

Something inside me groaned.

"Erica," I leaned forward, "I didn't go to India to miss the point, I went through India so I could remember the point. That became my turning point."

"That's a lot of points and you aren't making much sense."

"Sorry. So much potential, just too few words."

I sat back in the chair, stabilising myself in what I realised was a breakthrough in the making.

"Let me go back to the beginning. Before India, I was trying—not so convincingly towards the end—to prop up the old flagging formula of my writing. I was churning out the same-old-same-old. But those cycles were closing in on themselves. Less and less expansion only produced dissatisfaction and it started to hang around like a thin fog. Everything looked greyish."

"So something had to give?" suggested Erica, joining in my journey of explanation.

"Yes, you could say that. When I went to India, that whole structure of my existence imploded. I woke up. I got out of the box my ego had tried to keep me in. I moved in with my Higher Self and my heart and started expanding my heart space. I gave myself room to create. I can't go back now, I just don't fit. Trying to write to a formula makes me feel claustrophobic. Besides, the last book isn't a formula, it's a flow of creation sketched into words."

Erica was listening intently with a mixture of curiosity and concern. "But you can't afford to go off on some artistic rebellion, there's simply too much at stake. This is your editor talking. Remember? The one who sells your work? You can't be a writer for the people and an intellectual snob all in the same sentence. There's got to be continuity."

"But Erica, originality doesn't necessarily imply one-offs or flash-in-the-pan fads."

Erica began to realise she was reacting rather than understanding. "Okay, I am being a bit dramatic," she admitted.

A State Of Cooperation

"But I've also been in the business quite a few years and I've seen many writers come and go. Sometimes people get so wound up in their work that they end up producing something that only works for them and then I'm left with a book with a potential market of one! This is why I'm cautious. Originality needs balance if it's going to flourish."

"I agree, Erica. But the market of one, as you call it, is when ego is running the show. But that isn't the case here. I'm digging deeper because there's more to come. I'm just finding my bearings at the moment, so I can understand where this is going. This is why I've been really frustrated these past few weeks. It's like working with a new material and I don't quite understand how to flow with it. This sounds really old fashioned but... I just don't know how to fashion it."

"Well you're obviously not reacting and trying to be different for the sake of it. Good. I trust that deep down feeling. I believe you. So how does that flow turn into a book?"

"I was hoping you could tell me that. Just keep on talking through it and then sooner or later all this clarity will make it obvious."

Erica took my lead. "Okay. So if you don't have a formula behind your book, what *is* behind it?"

"Purposeful intention," I replied immediately, surprising myself.

"Well that sounds like flow!" she enthused.

"It's got chaos, I know that much," I replied, breaking into laughter.

"You're right on track then," said Erica laughing with me. "So you could call this new writing process a type of flexi-structure rather than a formula?"

"Right. You don't have to worry, there is some structure but it's the intention that counts. And it's to take the spiritual adventure to the next level but to allow the flow of creativity to guide me to that level. This way I keep it light, say what I want to say, and I don't get caught up in expectations. Some of the characters will be there but the setting is probably going to change."

"Okay," agreed Erica, out of her mental comfort zone and willing to explore.

Our momentum of understanding was building as we were giving each other the confidence to feel where the book was flowing, rather than organising it logically and stunting its growth.

"So you can be original and balanced," she continued. "This isn't a situation of *safe formula* versus *man-seen-dashing-into-ideological-maze*. There are obviously many other forms this book can take. That actually feels encouraging. After all, what's life without breaking moulds and taking risks?!"

"Lifeless?" I ventured.

"Exactly. But this feels different. It's got sparks of inspiration," she mused. "I love it when I feel this because it means it's a worthwhile project. I call it resonance; that 'something' that strikes a chord in your own heart. Excitement is so important, just as long as it connects with here and now. People love dreams that they can learn to touch. Those are the ones they bother to nurture and bring into the mundane and lighten it up by making a permanent difference. They don't want the dreams and ideals that stay on pedestals, out of reach for the whole of their lives."

She sat back as if writing a promotional blurb. "Adventurous and purposeful. That could work." She paused, settling into her new perspective. "So now we've got the foundation of the book, how are you going to download it into words? Do you need to go back to India?"

"Funnily enough, no."

Erica seemed visibly relieved.

"I've got a feeling," I added, "that this might be the travel book that goes everywhere but never leaves home."

"That's a relief! I thought you were going to ask me for big expenses!"

We both laughed out loud.

"No, Erica. Travelling is wonderful but this book is about the other journey... the one most people forget."

"Well I'm obviously one of those *most* people. Where is this journey? From A to B?"

"In a way. It's from the mundane to the extraordinary. It's that journey through 9 to 5. It's the journey through the normal that so many people take for granted rather than take for wisdom. Let's face it, this book has already had me at boiling point and flat on my face and I haven't even left my living room! You don't necessarily have to get away from it all to find it all."

"I'm all for finding the extraordinary in the mundane, so three cheers for originality! The changes of perspective it creates and its economic efficiency!" she winked.

"Don't get me wrong, Erica, India is fabulous. The West appears so proud of being in charge of its civilisation and yet it's so often totally in control of what's mostly insignificant. I love the feeling of endless flow and simple genius that makes the East so amazing. India has that. It enables the heart because it hasn't forgotten love and the liberating feeling of being part of something greater."

I paused.

"Perhaps I'm talking myself into going back there after all," I smirked.

"But you can't go back, you said it yourself!" Erica jokingly raised her eyebrows and flared her eyes into blue laser beams.

"Okay, okay. Yes I was only joking! No travel budget required. Honest. Please don't laser stun me with your piercing blue eyes or I'll... I'll sing!" I grabbed the arms of my chair for dramatic effect, preparing to launch into full volume.

"Okay let's call a truce. After last year's karaoke, that's a legitimate threat!" smiled Erica, leaning back in her chair. "I don't know about you but I feel great. Something's changed since we started talking. Nothing tangible yet but I can definitely sense we're making progress. This discussion is a breath of fresh air. Almost as good as caffeine."

I felt a tightness let go inside of me. Ego had been stretching me further and further out of balance and into stress, but now I was back in my centre. Words began to flash past with images from my meditations.

"Are you alright?" asked Erica, sensing a shift. She waited as I shivered from head to toe.

"And that's why I haven't got any lines when I'm on stage," my answer burst out of my mouth.

"I thought I was with you for a moment but you're babbling again. What's this about being on stage?" She smiled at her inability to control our discussion.

"My recurring meditation at the moment is that I'm about to do an audition but when I walk out on stage and look down at my script, there isn't one. The page is completely blank."

"So make it up as you go along. Isn't that what writing's all about?"

I felt a wave of euphoria move through the centre of my body.

"What was that?" she frowned.

"That was a truth rush, Erica. And you're a genius. It's so simple. It's all completely clear now. I've got to go!"

"I am? It is? Stop making cosmic sense and explain before you leave," enthused Erica, impatient and delighted all in the same breath.

"I can't play anyone's part but my own. I write my own script. Somewhere inside of me I was still ambushed in my head, trying to fit with the formula; expecting something or someone outside of me to tell me who to be and what to write. I was juggling the past and the future; spinning my wheels, unable to touch down and put both feet forward because I was still in my head, far from the heart of Now."

"So now you've found yourself, where is that taking you?"

A State Of Cooperation

"To another layer of creativity and another layer of self," I clarified.

"Yes, yes the eternal onion of self... always unravelling, hopefully without too many tears."

"Exactly, Erica. So each time you get to the next layer, you find reminders of ego habits. Ego says you should go back to what you know or what you have known or what ego has been projecting. But then you create from expectation and all you get is frustrated or disappointed. If you create, hoping to reinvent past foundations, then all you get is the past. So I'm just experiencing that resistance; that sense of walking waist-deep through metaphorical treacle that you encounter before ego lets go. And, more importantly, before you realise that you're capable of expanding more; capable of getting to the next level and allowing the heart to continue instead of reinstating the mind."

"I can't say I understand all of this," replied Erica, throwing her hands open, implying one big question mark, "so I'm not going to try to sum it up in words. But the feeling is a breakthrough in itself. And that's a genuine expansion; a breakthrough that has momentum and has maintained its purpose... whatever that may be."

"Yes, I've stopped *making* it work. And with your help, I've begun to *allow* it to work. The heart is never short of flow, no matter what ego tries to tell us. But if you force it then you block it and let ego get between you and what you really want. There is always flow, it's just a matter of realigning with it. When you expand, there's always a period of realignment, assimilation and adjustment. That's it. I knew you could help me. You held the key to this process and you were kind enough to show me the way."

"So what key do you see? Because I've got no idea!"

"The key is trust, Erica. You always trust when it matters. You didn't try to convince me to go back to the past to confirm what you know, you helped me get back into balance. You listened to the journey into the creative Now. You trusted me with me. It's just that I have trouble trusting me with me!"

"Well, I wouldn't be much of an editor if I didn't trust, would I?"

"No, you wouldn't."

I sat up in my chair preparing to leave. "So... do you trust me to write you a journey spiralling out of control all over again?"

"Yes, I do. Like you said, it's not in the lines, it's in the waves; those ripples of inspiration."

"That's brilliant, Erica! Do you mind if I use it?"

"You already have. That's what being a magician is all about—recycling the old into the new; discovering and seeing afresh."

"I bow to your brilliance. Are you sure you don't want to start writing? This could be the beginning of a beautiful collaboration."

"It's already as beautiful a collaboration as it's going to get," she smiled. "I think I'll stick with being a magician's apprentice. And now you're flying again, you're going to wave your magic wand and deliver me a book in four months time, right?"

"Yes I am."

Erica smiled, relaxing back into her chair. She'd completed her journey.

Going with the flow

Now that my blind spot was disappearing within an expanding view, I had a new perspective and was all fired up, ready to put the flow into words. Hurrying towards the Underground, I bought an Evening Standard and was just about to disappear into a sea of passengers when I turned around to glimpse a bus slowing down behind me.

Going With The Flow

"Now, that's what I call going with the flow," I muttered to myself, knowing this bus would take me almost to my door. I jumped on and found a seat at the front of the top deck. The bus joined the flow of its migrating herd as it curved down Regent Street. Double deckers had always been the hippo-giraffe hybrid of the London transport system; ever ready to wallow in a traffic jam and tall enough to gain a higher perspective on anything.

I unrolled the paper and went straight to the astrology column. No sooner had I found my sign than the bus lurched forward suddenly and the momentum had me on the edge of my seat, chasing the words off the page.

"Enjoying yourself?" came the familiar voice of my Higher Self.

"Yes. I see I'm not the only one to be late to the office today! I was wondering when you'd make an appearance."

"I did when you were on stage in your limelight. Didn't you see me? It was a bit of a cameo role, I must admit."

"No I didn't see you. I was all alone out there. All I saw was no script and no help." Ego was managing to goad me into a small amount of petulance.

"The perfect reflection then?"

"Okay. As it turned out, you're right. But why weren't you more obvious? I'm a little disgruntled. If you're meant to be my guide then surely, at times like those, a bit of guidance would come in handy. You could've helped me find the words instead of leaving me stranded."

My Higher Self appeared to pause, as if selecting an angle of approach.

"Oh, you mean rescue you and do it for you?"

"No, that wasn't what I meant at all." I was surprised at my indignation.

"But there would be no guidance if you were told what to do. No path; no discovery; no learning. And that would mean no real progress. You'd be sourcing your innovation from the limited conditioning of ego. Ego says 'Say this' and you say it; ego says 'Do this' and you do it. Where is the expansion in that? Is ego going to encourage you to do anything that will bring a genuine change?"

I began to come down to earth as I recognised the loving honesty in my Higher Self's words, even though my ego was busy taking it personally.

"But today," my Higher Self continued, "was full of conscious choices. You went through your healing instead of expecting someone or something to do it for you. And you were rewarded with a genuine breakthrough."

"Yes, that's true. If you put it like that, it was quite fulfilling to work it out myself."

"Aren't you forgetting something?"

"Okay, with the help of Erica, that is," I replied with a hint of reluctance.

"Aren't you forgetting something?"

"Alright, with your help too. Because you're never really gone, just silently helping."

"And so, we aren't here to spoon feed you, just to guide you on your way; emphasis on the *your*. Perhaps it would be helpful to see help as multi-directional and multi-formed; tangible and intangible. Silence is, after all, golden."

"You're right, as usual."

"Oh yes, everyone wants to be right; fighting for ego but falling out of the flow of love."

"Alright. Not *right*. But it's difficult to find another word."

"Perhaps *supportive* or *loving* would be more accurate."

"Okay, no right and no wrong from now on, only supportive in a loving way. I might be going backwards if I ask this question but I'm going to ask anyway: If you of all people—and I use the word people very loosely—don't know what's going to happen, who does?" I looked down at my paper. "The astrologer?"

"Guidance and knowledge are very different. *Knowing it*

all comes from the limited perspectives of ego. Ego thinks that if it can know everything then it can control everything. But still the world keeps on changing and evolving. Ego continues to chase the projections of its own limitations. Knowledge isn't wisdom and it isn't empowerment. Understanding and wisdom are what you seek. You will create understanding from trying out what you think you know. Wisdom will then follow when you realise what's loving and what's limiting... the true nature of your learning. And if you create that then you can find love and support in every aspect of your world and in every moment of your experience.

"Struggle isn't natural, it's just ego. The more you stay in your heart and listen to heartfelt truth, the easier it becomes. It's a little unfamiliar at first because you've been listening to ego for so long that you think you don't know what else there could be. But your heart truth can always give you alternatives. Your ego might not like them but that doesn't mean you can't make progress with them."

My Higher Self paused as if checking how much was sinking in.

"So I suppose when and if I follow my heart truth long enough, I'll forget about ego, struggle, pain and limitation and I'll have no inclination to know it all?"

"You will understand there is no point, no purpose in knowing it all because you are rejoining the unlimited. So you will have less and less inclination to control it all. You will understand how you can embrace it all and be a part of everything, All-That-Is. And if we can return to your question, do you think the astrologer can guide you or lead you through a destiny with no choice?"

"It's up to me. It depends on how I see it."

"Quite so. And...?"

"The astrologer can guide me because I'm learning to cooperate with the creative flow of my surroundings as well as what I think of as my resources. This kind of guidance can help me look at the choices in my life, teach me how to cooperate with the flows of energy that are the planets. If I think that I have no choice and my destiny is fixed then I simply don't have a choice."

"So now you can answer your own question."

"Yes, the astrologer can help me. No, the astrologer doesn't know it all because everything is a choice and so nothing is set in stone." I felt at ease with my newfound clarity.

"And so it is. Also, try not to forget that many of the sacred wisdoms of your world have fallen into disrepair. A bit like Chinese whispers, they started out as Universal wisdom but gradually became misunderstood until they are now mere shadows of their former selves and ego has sought to redefine them. Destiny is one such wisdom. Earlier in your world, energy moved slowly; so slowly that the conscious cycles of evolution appeared to be defined. They could be mapped out, 'foretold' as it were. But then they became linked to time, not to intention, and so they appeared to be a path of destiny with no choice. Now, the energy and conscious change within your world is moving at such an increased pace that each conscious shift you make can happen in many, many different ways and in a much shorter time."

"So as we become more aware, the conscious acceleration becomes more obvious and the changes of one hundred years can fit into a morning?"

"You said it." My Higher Self paused, preparing to take up the general theme of our conversation. "When we walk with you as your guidance, we walk along side you. We never stand in front of you like your ego seeking to blur your vision. But ego always wants to crowd you; to eclipse your true nature so that it can distort your perception and limit your choices. Ego wants you to look through ego's eyes and, in so doing, see a limited, fearful existence rather than the unlimited love that is your true nature. You thought you had no words but in truth ego was simply blocking your view. Ego was blocking your source of inspiration, saying it did not exist. For a while you fought with your ego and made it stronger until you surrendered, asked for help and welcomed in an alternative so you could recycle resistance and move forward."

"Yes. All that frustration and conflict seems like months ago now," I acknowledged, agreeing with what my Higher Self had said only moments before.

"And so we are together in cooperation once more; side by side. And gradually, through this next part of your journey, you will see guidance everywhere in your world—editor, friend, stranger at the front door. Everyone and everything is a reflection of you. How you choose to see that reflection..."

My Higher Self paused.

I sensed a stream of words beginning to follow from within.

"... Depends on my choice. It depends on whether I let ego stand in front of me and block my perception or I allow you, my guidance, to talk honestly and help me stand in my heart truth." I took a long breath.

"Indeed. And today you began to feel the value of guidance through help and you acknowledged how you have struggled with your resistance to help. It was even amusing in parts."

"That depends on your standpoint. Or fall-down point!" I felt a wave of humour move across my face. "Alright. Looking back on it now, it was quite funny."

"A real heart opener," said My Higher Self, as though delivering some kind of punch line.

There was a flash of different forms flowing through my inner vision. My heart room was crowded.

"What's out there is in here," replied my Higher Self, answering my rush of realisation.

"Wait a minute. Let's rewind a little. You said *we* back there and the voice this morning wasn't you. And there's now loads of different beings in my heart room, not just you."

"If your limited world can come up with more than one way then the unlimited, unending flow of your heart can surely have more than one guide."

"So it's not just you?" I felt astonished and over-joyed.

"We are always here and now, and we welcome you to your new awareness."

"Is there anything else all of you can tell me?" Suddenly I wanted as much guidance as I could get.

"It's time to go. And don't miss your stop!"

I snapped out of my inner conference just as the bus turned into my street. I rang the bell and slid down the stairs.

"Now that's what I call guidance!"

Opening Doors

As I crossed the street from the bus stop, I saw Mrs Daley digging in the dark recesses of her handbag.

"Good afternoon, Mrs Daley. How's your archaeological dig going?"

"Well, put it this way—I've got 'istory in this bag."

"A deep and dark history?"

"Well, it 'as more depth than shallow humour!" replied Agnes as she tried not to laugh.

"Ouch, Mrs Daley. I think I might be mortally wounded!" I stumbled about on the step behind her as if dying in one of Shakespeare's tragedies.

"Oh, stop dying, you fool, or I'll give myself a heart attack trying not to laugh."

"Allow me," I said, producing my key as if it were a rabbit out of a hat. "We would do well to remember that one man's lack is another man's fortune."

I bowed ceremoniously as I pushed open the front door. Mrs Daley played along, acknowledging my manners and waiting until I'd closed the door and returned to her side.

Opening Doors

"Well, you've turned out to be quite the philosopher since you came back from India. I knew you'd catch something there, just didn't expect it to be wisdom." She looked me deep in the eyes as if searching for my secret.

There was an awkward silence as we arrived at my door.

In that moment it occurred to me that I'd never actually invited Mrs Daley into my flat, she'd only experienced my hospitality in absentia. I'd leave, she'd arrive. But now something was different. Why not go with the flow and invite her in? Embrace some of the unknown I was always writing about; make my life up a bit as I went along.

"Would you like to join me in an afternoon cuppa? Or something stronger, perhaps? Can I tempt you with a little stout?"

Mrs Daley's face lit up with surprise and what I liked to think of as delight.

"Tea would be lovely. And, I might say, it's about time!" she said, smacking my arm affectionately. "Thought you'd never ask. Invitations are rare at my age and it's the only time I get to leap at anything. Figuratively, you understand."

"Tea it is then."

Mrs Daley hesitated two paces through the door. She seemed to sense a change; my flat was no longer how it always was. There was a welcome.

"Please have a seat," I said, gesturing towards the armchair. "Do you know, I don't think I've had any guests since I moved in, and that must be all of..."

"Six years," said Mrs Daley, completing my sentence.

"Yes, you're quite right. Six years. Is it really that long? I suppose that makes me a recluse!"

"No, to be fair you've been coming an' going an awful lot with your travel writing, so recluse isn't accurate. You're just antisocial!"

Mrs Daley tried to keep a straight face as she settled into the armchair. "Being a recluse takes a lot of effort. You've got to actively avoid people and the way London's going, that isn't easy because there're so many more people these days."

She paused.

"But getting to that place where 'ardly anyone knows you and no one's likely to miss you... now that's some achievement," she smiled wryly.

I gave Mrs Daley a fake round of applause then filled the kettle.

"You sound like you're a bit of an expert," I teased.

"Maybe you've got me there. Not really what I'd intended. Being a recluse isn't all that it's cracked up to be. So be glad that we've both graduated to antisocial so we can meet on a whole new level! You know what they say..."

"No. What do they say, Mrs Daley?"

"A change is as good as a rest. It's just working up to that change; getting up to speed so you can break through your perceived ceiling of self; go beyond the beyond bit. You could fall off your world; you could find that there's nothing to fear. But d'you dare and do you care? D'you carry on listening to the fear outside that says there's no point because you'll be disappointed or because it's too hard? Or d'you go and 'ave a look for yourself; stop taking other people's word for it? Limits... they're all self imposed y'know, every single one of 'em."

"So have you ever fallen off your world, Mrs Daley? Or perhaps hit your head on a self imposed ceiling?"

"Well, I've 'it rock bottom and fallen through it if that counts. An' I'll tell you, I knew what it was like to exist under a self imposed ceiling. The insurance company were proud to tell me that I'd reached my 'ceiling of potential'. Then they made me redundant. Who were they to tell me about my ceiling of anything?"

She paused. "Then Albert died and I 'it rock bottom. I was shattered. Couldn't make a list or string a sentence together for what seemed to be months. Everything stopped. I was adrift; so far away from joy that I was numb, floating towards an endless 'orizon of depression."

Her description hung on the edge of grief. Tears welled up in her eyes. She brushed them away self consciously.

"Can't stop 'em. They come out when you least expect. Every time I think they've dried up, there's more," she sobbed, reaching into her handbag for her handkerchief.

"But you're here, now, Mrs Daley," I began, "and maybe it's time to set a whole new course. Treat this as a friendly port; somewhere you can get your bearings; a chance to let the past finally dissolve into the present. What have you got to lose?"

"Well, I'm a bit of a gambler myself and I agree with you." She blew her nose. "I could do a lot worse than gamble my past away in this conversation. We might be the most unlikely pair but who said you 'ave to be logical to be friendly? It's just got to feel right and have a cuppa included." She raised her eyebrows, throwing a glance and a nod behind me.

"Oh, sorry," I said, realising I hadn't turned the kettle on.

"So everything comes down to fear an' love," she continued. "Fear makes you separate, love brings you into unity. Heart keeps you in unity and ego takes you out of the flow of life. An' that's quite easy when logic tells you you're on your own an' all you 'ave is what you can control."

Mrs Daley was getting into full flow. "Ego makes excuses instead of changes, an' before you know it you're isolated, investing in what you know and building 'abits that end up stopping you doing what you love. The mind can find a hundred different reasons why we shouldn't do something different. Take our meeting today. We both jumped through that window of spontaneity. We didn't know what was on the other side but we were willing to 'ave a look. I could've analysed your invitation and thought you were feeling sorry for me. Or maybe you were just bein' polite. But instead, I felt the moment. A simple yes or no. My heart said yes."

The kettle saluted Mrs Daley's choice as it came to the boil.

"And I'm very glad you did, Mrs Daley. Milk and sugar?"

"Call me Agnes. I've cried in your front room so I don't mind bein' on first name terms. No sugar but lots of milk, please."

I served her tea and settled on my bar stool, ready for the flow of insight. I was beginning to see just how guidance was present in all situations.

"I'm not stopping you writing, am I?" Agnes looked concerned. "You writing types can really get wound up if what you want doesn't come down, if you know what I mean. Got to keep the drainpipe of inspiration flowing or you get blocked up. And that'd never do, eh?"

"No, you're not stopping me writing. I think you're actually helping me. But I do have a concern… Have you been spying on me, Agnes?" I asked jokingly, "Or are you just a mind reader? Until this morning I was suffering from writer's block."

"Well it's all there if you look. Take the time just before you went to India. You started to change. You might not've known it, but y'did."

"How do you know that?" I asked, intrigued by her observations.

"You threw out those old pot plants."

"I don't quite follow, Agnes. What've pot plants got to do with change?"

"In this case, everything. To create expansion you've got to create space. Sometimes we do it like my example, by our whole world changing all at once. Sometimes it's more subtle; a collection of small details, all adding up to a bigger change. When you threw out those plants it was as if you'd stopped trying to make something in your life work. You surrendered to the fact that those plants were never going to grow any more because they didn't 'ave any space. They were pot-bound an' already 'alf gone. It was only a matter of time before they'd die. There was no space in those pots for expansion an' no way you could transplant them."

"You are truly amazing, Agnes. It's astonishing how much our surroundings give away the person that's within; even reflect the cycle of creation that we'd benefit most from if we bothered to look."

"What's even more amazing," she continued, "is that reflection is seeing an' doing combined. So many people see reflection as something they might consider when they haven't got anything better to do. But really, reflection is a vital part of life. It keeps us balanced because we can see 'ow our intentions are panning out in front of us in our physical world. An' we can see the impact we have on our surroundings. These are two sides of the same coin. If our intentions are loving an' we cooperate with the unlimited flow that runs through all our experience, then we've got unity for 'owever long we choose to stay in balance."

"So what you're saying is that if what's in here," I said, pointing to my heart, "matches what's out there," I pointed around the room, "then we're living our truth and reflecting that truth in a loving way, in that moment?"

"Yes. An' if it isn't loving an' flowful then we can still learn because it'll reflect the unloving part of ourselves that we need to change. If it's loving, abundant and flowful then we're aligned with the greater Universe; we're being fulfilled by a greater flow, not just the flow of the limited world. That's why there's no more struggle, no more pain or conflict. An' when that happens, you feel like you're on cloud nine or you can do and be absolutely anything."

"Let's drink to that!" I said, walking over to Agnes to clink cups. "If I let it, that nagging voice of logic in my head would say I should be writing. But the truth is, I'm really enjoying your company. And I'm feeling the difference between listening to my heart not my head. Besides, Agnes, you've got so much wisdom to share, I want you to keep talking. You never know, you might end up reading yourself in my next novel! A little snapshot of Agnes. Salt of the Earth; a grounded Goddess!"

"Well it'd better be flattering. Take my best side!" she chuckled.

"Of course. That won't be difficult. So... back to your story, what happened to get your world back on course? What did you do?"

"I stopped waiting for Albert to come 'ome an' I began to trust in a journey that goes beyond 'abit an' what you think you know."

"And...?"

"Well, it's quite an irony, really. At the grand age of sixty-four, it was time to learn about timing. I thought the insurance company had no idea of timing. In fact, they couldn't've been more wrong. They knew nothing of that place where cosmic cycles overlap with linear experience; a glimpse of the unlimited, the eternal, just for a moment, flowing through the cracks in our world. But that was just ego talking. The corporation ensured my biggest break!"

"Which was?"

"I stopped believing in an unjust world that took my Albert from me and gave me the sack. When y' lose everything that you think is important, its easy to think you've got nothing left. But that only becomes a reality if you get stuck to what's gone. Living in the past just drains the life out of you. So I stopped looking out there for a fix an' started to listen to my heart. It told me to start listening to everything. I listened to the bus driver. I listened to the dog in the park an' the wind in the trees. I listened to buskers an' stockbrokers, cousins an' even telemarketers! I practiced getting back into my world through listening.

"Don't get me wrong," she frowned. "I didn't believe all of it but I was prepared to let it in. Until one day I stopped rejecting my world an' started living again. A bit like when you welcomed me in today. You let me in because you wanted to change. I accepted because I've never forgotten to listen. There's meaning in everything an' every meaning is a journey of change that 'elps you arrive at your next level of self."

"And then?" I was completely enthralled by Agnes' words.

"Well, when it'd gone completely quiet one day, I 'eard the almost deafening sound of the rebirth of my heart. I felt rushes of euphoria. Maybe they were truth. Whatever they were, they created a beginning. I was all charged up. I realised that the only way to start was to... well, start! Connect one choice after another until you've got learning; one foot in front of the other an' begin. So I did. But this time was different. I didn't do what was logical, I decided to trust myself an' be open to anything and everything. After spending nearly twenty-five years in one industry, I suddenly realised I wasn't creating, I was just working. So I decided to create a joyous occupation an' get paid for it. I tried lots of different types of work so I could understand how work could expand into creativity. I ran an animal rescue centre for a while. I organised functions an' fund raising for charity an' I worked at the Citizens Advice Bureau giving financial advice. I made choices from what was right in front of me, not from the past or what could be."

"So where did the trail of experience take you?"

"Well the big day wasn't what I expected. The day I found what I love doing—and get very well paid for, I might add—started when I went to collect the newspaper. Sounds boring, mundane, even irrelevant but often we don't see our turning points. Perhaps we wouldn't make 'em if we did. What's significant is that in that moment, we turn our spiritual corner by committing to change. My intention to change was there, it was just that the form was a mystery. I'd never 'ave got to my 'paper day' without all the other days and jobs before. So I got up at 6:30 a.m, as I always do. You wouldn't know 'cause you're never up that early unless you're jet lagged."

"Agnes, you should be a private investigator. Or maybe you already are?"

"Oh, that's only my 'obby," she winked. "Anyway, when I collected my paper I found that they'd delivered the Financial Times instead o' the Times. I was really angry. How could they make such a mistake after delivering for twenty-seven years?"

"How indeed?" I feigned astonishment.

"Well, I decided to read it anyway and complain t' the news agent later. But as I leafed through the share options and investment pages, I 'ad an idea. Why didn't I invest in me? I'd always been good with money. Why not make it a business?"

She paused, her mouth dry. "What about another cup of tea?'

"Coming right up." Cleaning the cups and refilling the kettle, I asked "So do you mean to say I've got a blue chip analyst living in the basement?".

"Yes, I suppose you 'ave."

"Agnes, you're full to the brim with surprises. And I suppose you're going to tell me that you've got a fast broadband connection, and you don't actually meet clients just send them reports by email."

"Yes, that's right. People don't really want to meet these days an', 'aving been a recluse, I don't want to see them either!" she smiled, "just have fun making money for them and for m'self."

"You are incredible. My editor, Erica, insisted I get email even though I'm the worst technophobe. And here you are, learning completely new tricks at a time in your life when most people would be holding fast to the habits of a lifetime."

"Well, that just goes t' prove one thing," Agnes shrugged.

"What's that?"

"Never trust assumptions. Never think that old people are wise and that young people are flexible!"

"That's your tip on assumption—don't buy into it?"

"Definitely not! No futures in it and hardly any options!"

"Ha ha, Agnes, very witty! But now I'm going to ask the sixty-four million dollar question. With all you have to offer, how come you haven't invested in another relationship?"

"What did we say? Heart makes alternatives an' ego makes excuses? Well, I agree. When you love your work it's easy to stop there; t'say 'That's enough love for me,' an' carry on with what you've got rather than think of it as an endless flow that just keeps on expanding throughout your whole being."

"But don't you want some company?"

"Do you know, you're the first one to ask me that since Albert died," she pondered. "An' he's been gone nearly ten years."

"Maybe I'm the first to ask because of assumption, again. Perhaps everyone you knew just thought you were too old for another relationship. Or maybe that you simply weren't prepared to replace Albert."

"In part, that may be true. But it's much simpler than that. I never wanted to. I didn't choose to dig that deep inside myself. Found it too painful. Besides, I didn't see myself as 'aving a whole heart, I saw myself as having one heart for work, one heart for family, one for relationship... One for every situation."

"So your relationship heart was broken?"

"Yes. An' I thought—emphasis on thought, not feeling—I didn't 'ave what it took to rebuild it. So there wasn't a hint of relationship in the outside world because there wasn't a hint of it from within me."

"But what about now?" I asked, digging a little deeper.

"Well, now you've asked me, I find the question quite disturbing. It's like that feeling you get when you risk a bit of yourself you thought you could avoid; go somewhere ego doesn't want you to go. Perhaps it's time I started listening to that part of me, too?"

Tears welled up in Agnes' eyes but this time it wasn't a flow of grief but a sense of joy. Something new and wonderful. "Maybe it's about time I put a light in a corner of myself I thought I'd shut down forever."

She took a moment to compose herself.

"But what about you?" she smiled. "You don't get away with this so easily. You're an antisocial workaholic like me. Or do you have a mystery partner that's slipped past my surveillance?"

"Well, if I do Agnes, they're indeed deeply mysterious because even I haven't met them quite yet," I grinned. "And, in my defence, I have been doing a lot of leaving."

"But 'ow does that stop you arriving?" Agnes enquired, unwilling to let my ego run away with me.

"Okay, you've got me there," I admitted. "No excuses when you believe in the endless flow. If we haven't experienced it, it's because deep down we haven't chosen it."

"Or," Agnes added, "we've spent so long avoiding it. We've piled up so much in our way that we've got to tunnel through all of the resistance before we can get going."

"Absolutely. It's often easier to justify why you haven't done something rather than put your energy into clarifying what you really want. Look at me; I just did that very thing. I let ego apologise for my lack. But look at us. We've found a strange unity. In this moment, Agnes, we're the perfect reflection of each other. We both love our work and have let our egos excuse us from relationships."

"That's very true. But as we're jointly expanding into the new, do we want this to be a permanent state of affairs?"

"No," we said in unison.

"So why don't we launch O. R.?" I asked, honouring a flash of inspiration.

"What's that?"

"Operation Relationship."

"What a great idea." Agnes sat up in the armchair as if

Opening Doors

she was standing around the roulette table of life and a new game was calling for new bets. "I'm in. So 'ow do we start?"

I paused for a moment so I could keep balanced with the flow. "If we want effortless creativity then we require to be in balance and in the centre of our hearts: our I AM Presence. That's always connected to the unlimited flow."

"Remain in balance an' constant contact with 'eart truth. Check," replied Agnes with military discipline. "Next?"

"We need to form an intention that clarifies what we want. What about this? I am attracting loving, joyous and abundant relationships. I am expanding my awareness of relationships."

"That sounds appropriate," Agnes agreed, and repeated the statements of intention.

"So all that remains now is to understand the reflections of ourselves as we journey to our creative destination. No waiting for the Universe to deliver what we want, we need to cooperate with the unlimited flow in the Now. So, if our hearts say listen, we listen. If we are disturbed or uncomfortable, we look into ourselves and see what we're changing rather than thinking everything is going wrong. If our hearts say to go out and meet people, we leave seclusion in search of expansion. If we don't go on the journey we expected, that doesn't mean we won't succeed. Everything we do and feel is part of our final destination."

"Received an' understood," said Agnes. "No waiting for the Universe to fix us. No forcing the Universe to create what our ego thinks we need. Learn from Now so that we can stay there an' create with ease."

"Well put," I replied, acknowledging Agnes' practical simplicity.

The initial foundation felt complete. Agnes appeared to be drifting away from our conversation, distracted. She was looking over my left shoulder.

"Well this has been really inspiring," she enthused. "I'd better be going; start on that cosmic homework. High time I cleared out some emotional clutter so that I can make space for the new."

"But you don't have to go just yet."

I was surprised at what appeared to be a rather abrupt ending to our discussion.

"Oh, but I do," Agnes replied. "Your next guest—or should I say, reflection—is here."

"What do you mean?" I asked, turning around to look.

There was a black cat sitting perfectly still on the window sill.

"Oh *that* guest," I said, completely at a loss as to where this feline magician had materialised.

"Well created," acknowledged Agnes. "You've just got a brand new relationship. Not bad going for a Magician From The Masses."

"Thanks, Agnes." I was surprised at her reference. "Did you read my book?"

"Certainly. All part of the surveillance, y'know," she smiled, flaring her eyes with a hint of stalker. "I'll bring it up here one of these days so you can sign it. Might be worth something!" she said.

"Surprised, eh?" she questioned. "Surprised that a little old lady like me would read your book?"

"I just didn't think you were the type." I cringed as the conditioned assumptions of ego fell out of my mouth.

"So, if I'm the last person on Earth you'd think has read your book then 'ow is it going to fly?" she smiled. "Are you going to control everything until it fits your assumptions? Even an outside chance like me?"

I winced. "Thanks for the reminder of my limited vision! If I believe in what ego thinks, that isn't going to let my book distribute freely anywhere, let alone everywhere."

"Exactly. So believe in your work. Your heart is in it an' that's the most important step."

"Step?"

"The step we can take from work to creativity. The step that combines two into one, heart an' mind."

"Received and understood, Agnes. Invest in the unlimited and unending support of the ever-expanding Universe. There's no point in investing in ego! Look where it gets us—more ego and more limitation. So it's time for a change. I'm investing in the unlimited and the unending. What about you, Agnes?"

"Snap," replied Agnes as she rose to leave. "I'd rather bet on the unlimited any day than the ponies!"

"But that's made me curious. Just before you go… Do you really bet on the horses, Agnes?"

"Oh, no, far too complicated. Too much 'form' for me."

"Very funny, Agnes. A play on words! Too much *form*. I get it. You don't need the form from the bookies! You don't need form at all. It's the cosmic and the comic you love."

Agnes' wit had arrived long before me. She winked her acknowledgement.

"So instead of form, you prefer the immaterial?" I suggested.

"Oh yes, any day," she laughed. "Immaterial, unlimited, inspirational or imaginary. All of those are much more powerful than anything form can offer."

She smiled. "Thanks for the tea. I'll see myself out."

"See you sometime soon," I replied, feeling unwilling to relinquish my newfound friend.

"Well, I'll see you," she replied, kissing me on the cheek. "Whether you see me is another matter. Until our next enlightening," she chuckled, closing the door gently behind her.

I lifted the sash window thinking the cat would come in but it remained motionless, all except one flick of the tail.

"I'm sorry, I don't speak Morse Tail. Are you coming in or not?"

The cat took one step towards the kitchen then sat across

the window sill, half in and half out. It blinked as if to say 'Your move'.

"If you don't mind, I'm going to have what's left of my tea. If you decide to grace my humble abode with your presence, I'll be over there," I said, gesturing towards the armchair.

No sooner had I sat down than the cat was on my lap in the flick of a tail and three elegant bounds. It purred contentedly as it kneaded my legs into a satisfactory resting place.

"Quite an entrance. I can see what all the purring is about," I said, blinking my approval.

I looked at the kitchen clock; it was nearly 4 p.m. Time seemed to have evaporated. I yawned as if I should be tired but really I was simply relaxed and, like the cat, I was lapping it up. I became cosier and drowsier as my guest settled, tucking its feet under a fur skirt while continuing to hypnotise me with the steady rhythm of purr. I surrendered to an all-embracing feeling of fulfilment, falling through layers of space, sound and warmth.

Be My Guest

The day's events were swirling into a vortex of unity, mixing without definition or interruption. Lack and frustration were dissolving quickly as I embraced my inner journey. A voice began to emerge from the flow of energy until it became a sound, and then words.

"Do you swirl here often?" said the voice beside me.

"I'd say yes, but this feels different. I have no memory of this place; not a photograph in my heart nor an imprint of feeling. It's all new."

"Indeed. A new perspective brings new vision. The old limitations dissolve effortlessly when you allow the magic of the Universe. What was, is no longer."

"Where is this place?" I began, with a hint of concern. Surrounded by a vast landscape with no signs of wildlife or human life, my ego was pestering me for answers that might restore security.

"Oh, just a moment. Your mind is stirring," replied the form, as if dealing with a troublesome detail. "Take a few long deep breaths through your heart before we set off."

I felt my whole body expanding while the form of the voice came into sharper focus. I took a step back to get a better look at my companion. He was a rather bedraggled tramp in a three piece sack. A chunk of disappointment collided with my heart, scraping reluctantly past as it dissolved.

"Who are you? You aren't my Higher Self." Predictably, my mind was clutching at definition.

"Can we forget about a name for now?" suggested the tramp. "It is, after all, only a flimsy label. Could fall off without a moment's notice."

"I understand. Be in the feeling rather than trying to analyse it," I replied while my mind continued to protest, *Honestly, what kind of person doesn't know their own name?* "I'm..." I tried to introduce myself but no name would form. "Oh, I see. In this place there's no need for definition?" I was beginning to catch on.

"Indeed. No need at all," replied the tramp. "It slows everything down and that would be going in completely the opposite direction; working against yourself. Unless that's what you want, of course. It's all up to you."

"I'm here to go with the flow. I am choosing to go with the flow. So let's not call each other names!" I said, attempting a joke. "But can I ask where this acceleration is going?"

My companion paused before his answer. My mind told me he was preparing for a burst of disapproval. But it didn't arrive. Instead, a gentle yet commanding nature flowed into words. It was a voice that was asking me to respect my process and the changes I was now undergoing; a voice that reminded me deeply of the power of honesty and love.

"Be with your journey. Embrace your beginning and

don't look for a destination because, as you are beginning to see, it's never what you think."

Shuffling away, the tramp paused and turned back, looking deeply into me.

"How does it look?" I enquired, feeling a little less uncomfortable but a lot more ignorant.

"You are with yourself," he said, "but just getting to know the other dimensions of you; the real you, the extended, expanded version. Not really a linear question of going from A to B. Think more of travelling out in all directions at once. That should keep your mind occupied for now. Suffice it to say that you've just found a whole new level within you. So the idea of travelling somewhere to be more of yourself ends up splitting geometrically, conceptually and sensorially. In simple terms, it ends up splitting you between your heart and your mind. That can be most inconvenient, not to mention uncomfortable. So let ego get lost, as it were, so that we can have our adventure. Your mind can only offer a shattered fragment of what you really are. It is the distortion that limits your view, not the lens that magnetises, bringing what you wish into your Now."

"So when I expand into this dimension, I'd be well advised to release the preconception that I'm leaving somewhere to go somewhere else?"

"Indeed. Simply expand beyond your limited mind. Realise that you are so much more than the self that resides in your limited reality. Leave the limited clutter, the facts and definitions that mind thinks are so important in limitation. You are beyond those now if you allow yourself to be. That is why we talk to your heart, not your mind. Heart has the capacity to flow with the greater you. It was built for the job. Mind was built to manage the fearful separation of ego that, as you are beginning to understand, is not your true nature."

I was sure I looked puzzled but I surrendered to the tramp's commentary and tried my best to step away from the mental bombardment of ego.

Be My Guest

"Wondrous times," he mused. "You're shining brighter. Here and now, all around. Expansion and progress are such troublesome concepts in your world because they are always thought of as being outside of yourself, rather than the genuine expansions and progress that always starts within."

"So it's all a matter of direction then?" I replied surrendering to feeling my way.

"Indeed. The direction of your perception. Are you in your heart, reuniting with the unlimited? Or is your limited mind trying to make the new, the unknown and unlimited fit back into limitation?" He paused for my response.

"So stop thinking I'm coming from the limited and trying to adapt to the unlimited?"

"Exactly. Ego likes to tell you that you come from isolation and separateness only because ego comes from that. But it is a falsehood, trying to isolate you from unity."

I was beginning to make space for my new perspective. "Yes... I used to seek refuge in the familiar and the repetitive. Now I realise I've come away from that conditioning and I don't want to get back in the limited box ego used to put me in. I believe that's what allowed me to get here."

"Well recognised. You have become a seeker. You are searching beyond what ego says is fact to find the real you, the expanded you of which you have always been a part. Ego told you it was just a dream of the impossible; a vapour that disperses on the air; a sound that is stolen by the wind; a purpose that is lost to habit..."

I finished the tramp's commentary. "But now everything is different. That's why I've come to this place. Truth is expanding to meet me?"

"Expansion is relative, as is understanding. Let's say that truth is like standing at the point where two lines diverge. The more you allow your experience and release limitation, the more your view opens out before you. Ego will try to obscure your view at the beginning, jumping up and down right in front of you shouting 'I have all the truth you need to know.' But, as you detach and embrace loving consciousness, you will see that truth flows with you as you expand your perception. When the desire to control tells you it is all known, you step back to gain a detached view, then step through ego into a new experience of yourself, one that allows you to reclaim more of your unlimited self. No comparisons or measurements required, just go with the flow and with the sense of expansion."

"But my ego would say that this is all too convenient; that I'm making up truths that I like, not the reality that I face."

"And what would that be reflecting to you?"

"I suppose if I'm genuinely experiencing expansion and newness then it would reflect my ego trying to hold me back through self doubt and fear."

"Indeed."

"So truth isn't fact. The way I experience truth depends on how willing I am to listen and act upon my inner heart truth."

"Bingo! There is no one truth, only an ever-expanding truth. As you experience more of your unlimited nature then your experience of truth will expand according to your perspectives. That is why your Higher Self encourages you to describe your learning in terms of love, support and abundance, not in the judgmental terms of right and wrong. Judgment just reinforces your attachments to a limited truth and your limited self. Judgment puts barriers in the way of flow; it doesn't allow flow."

"So if I'm fitting in with myself differently, where do you fit in? What's your role?"

"I am a neighbour come to teach you about your new surroundings."

I was caught in a mixture of anticipation and expectation. Ego wanted precise answers and my heart wanted to learn. The division within me was showing signs of strain. "I don't really understand. Can't you give away any more information?"

Be My Guest

"Why?" said the tramp, suddenly standing still.

I halted at the edge of my reply. "I thought that was obvious... Because I'd understand more."

"But to realise, you are required to choose allowance. Trust. Be in the flow so that you can expand beyond those limited truths."

I was feeling frustrated. Ego was beginning to needle me.

"But isn't it the other way around? You understand, then you allow?" I was now knee-deep in the limitations of logic.

"How can you realise if there is no discovery? Where's the expansion? Your mind has you going round and around in circles. Ego is thinking you out of learning! It reinforces your assumption of your own inability. You are chasing your own tail and making it into a drama! Drama is the exaggerated way of ego, not the journey of discovery you seek. Ego clings to drama to make you think something is really going on. When you are in your heart you realise ego has just been dragging you around on a fool's errand trying to maintain attachment."

The tramp began to fade.

I rubbed my eyes hoping I'd see more clearly but he continued to fade. I felt a mild panic, as if I was losing something precious.

"Please don't go!" I cried, desperately raising my voice.

The tramp appeared to take no notice, now just a mirage of purple dust.

"Wait! I can recycle this panic. Look, I am centering in my heart."

I was choosing to repair my fading connection with centeredness and commitment. "I am prepared to do what it takes, even if I don't know what it is. I am prepared to trust that this is supportive and meaningful. I am letting go of the need to work it all out."

My heart was now emptied of words. I closed my eyes and waited.

There's Plenty More Where That Came From

After what seemed an eternity, I opened my eyes. The tramp was in front of me just as before.

"Well done! You reached into your heart instead of running back into the safety of what was. Congratulations! You've confirmed your commitment to this resonance. We are on the same wavelength and there is now a bigger part of you prepared to trust the unknown. Keep on digging below the surface of yourself. There's more to come."

"Okay. So, trust and I'll discover that this journey is supportive, loving and abundant. Even if I don't know what it's going to be like."

"Keep going. There are plenty more gems available apart from trust."

"So you're my guide to help me feel my way."

"Ye-e-es..."

"Observing my reactions and responses will help me see if I'm being loving or fearful. Analysing my experience doesn't help because it fractures my world into meaningless pieces. The more trusting I become, the more expansion I create but also the less logical everything will appear to be. Scary and liberating all at once. All part of the coming and going, I suppose."

"Wonderful! Your digging is going rather well. It's amazing what resources you have if you are prepared to disturb your conditioning to find them."

With that, the tramp set off walking, quickly leaving me behind.

"But wait! I've got another observation," I added quickly, out of breath as I hurried after him. "You aren't going to spoon feed me because then I won't learn."

Suddenly we were shoulder to shoulder.

"Precisely," he said. "We can always lead you through

There's Plenty More Where That Came From

your learning but we cannot make you learn. Nor can we predict just when you realise what you have learnt. But if you trust, you will learn to allow the guidance of any moment in your world; you will learn to be at peace with what your mind cannot limit."

"You will see that nothing is too early nor too late but exactly when it is required in the unlimited flow. If it is there in the Now, you can connect with it no matter how remote or irrelevant your mind may think it is. You explore your path with increasing depth and share what you learn with your guidance and your greater world. You're a bit of a story teller yourself, we understand."

"Yes, but sometimes it's difficult to convey all of this flow when I'm back in my limited part of self. Words sometimes can't capture that flow. They don't seem enough. For example, everything in our world is lines. I can't arrange words in lots of different directions or in a new order. Words only have one direction."

I tripped suddenly, taking my struggle out on a stone I kicked randomly.

"Just remember your intention," said the tramp. "That is what matters most because that is what keeps your meaning together. There are many layers to your language, many ways the sound of words can be understood. Just concern yourself with the words flowing from your heart. That is what is important."

"You make it sound so simple."

"It is simple. Just your mind finds it so complicated. So you are learning not to consult your mind but to stay in your heart. That is sentience."

"What is?" I looked all around myself thinking I'd missed something.

"Sentience is a state of being; a capacity to consciously feel your world rather than limit it or react to it. It is within you, not outside of you. You are sentient when you are in your I AM Presence. You feel the unlimited self that is truly you. It's a sense of unity and connection with the greater Universe rather than the isolated physical senses that you have in your body."

I was embarrassed about my conditioned reaction.

"Oh, don't bother yourself with that passing assessment of self, that's just ego illusion. Just continue recycling the misunderstandings of self and you'll get closer to the real you."

"So don't get caught up with what's leaving?" I replied.

"Precisely. There will be plenty more veritable crowds of the old you's leaving as you move forward," the tramp smiled. "All part of the dissolving illusion; what you thought you were; what you thought you could do. Call it spiritual exfoliating! All of these layers are simply the ego image of yourself. But once you learn how to do and be differently, you won't be stuck to a limited experience of yourself."

"So sentience is going to replace sight, touch, taste, smell and hearing?"

"More a case of those senses being absorbed into your sentience; all senses reuniting within your greater sensitivities. As your consciousness grows you will feel more because you are choosing to be more unified. You are not seeking to separate yourself from your experience, you are unifying through allowing learning. You have always been capable of sentience but during your research in limitation, ego conditioned you to feel through your physical senses and become separate from sentience."

As the tramp was explaining, I began to feel curious sensations all over my body. The top of my head was tingling, my hands and feet were pulsating and my body appeared to be oscillating like a collection of waves. I wanted to make elliptical movements with my head and upper body as if I was orbiting around where I was standing.

"Breathe," said the tramp. "Breathe."

I responded to the request and took deep breaths, connecting each one to the centre of my heart. The vibration decreased until it appeared to have disappeared.

There's Plenty More Where That Came From

"I'm fine now," I announced.

"As you have been all the way along. There is nothing wrong, you are merely adapting."

I felt annoyed with myself that I'd again fallen into the trap of judgment. I refocused in my heart and let the immature conflict subside in my head. All went quiet.

The tramp smiled and walked through my mind and out the other side.

"Empty," he observed in a long lingering tone. "Progress, indeed."

The pendulum of my internal balance swung from over-confident to insecure. It soon settled at encouraged.

"Good. That is of service," said the tramp, registering my choice to rebalance.

He looked into my eyes and I began to feel a growing energy all around me. I could barely believe that he was magnetising the whole landscape tightly around me.

"Wowaaaaaaah. That's some lens pull! How on Earth do you do that!?"

"This isn't a cheap trick," snapped the tramp abruptly, "this is genuine magnetism."

"You mean you've got some kind of super-high-powered magnet?"

I cringed at my response.

"You're thinking again," said the tramp with a very serious expression.

"I didn't mean to say that. Ego just had to get in there with the thudding sound of limitation. I really do feel that this is the genuine article, it just took me by surprise. You're so balanced and in such harmony with this world that you're magnetising it to yourself, not from control or fear but from love and allowance. That's what's so amazing."

Silent and surrounded by air that was charged with belief, I let the tension out of my body and surrendered. My mind was overloading with the weird and the wonderful. There was nowhere to file such daring, such unknown, it just didn't fit into anything I'd experienced. Ego wanted to take this whole scene and screw it up like a huge sheet of paper but I remained in my heart. I wanted to stretch out in all directions as the charged atmosphere created a huge bubble of pearlescent blues, greens, pinks and purples around me.

The tramp smiled, keeping an eye on my process; never interrupting or commenting, just allowing my belief to combine with the sphere. "Do you want to take your expanded self for a spin?"

"Okay," I replied, trying not to think at all.

"Be in your heart, embracing all the being you can be."

I breathed into the very centre of my heart.

"Now look into your landscape and unify with it," said the tramp, as if it were the most simple of tasks.

I looked towards the horizon and willed myself to join with it. The bubble burst and I landed flat on my back on the ground.

The tramp laughed heartily. "Interesting. A mixture of force and creation. But as you can see, at higher frequencies of energy, force can bring you back to Earth with a thud."

"Is that why I burst the bubble?"

"Indeed. But that was just an introduction, not an ending. There will be plenty more opportunities."

"But why couldn't I join with the horizon?"

"You are magnetising, remember? Cooperating, not forcing. Be the quality that you want rather than trying to make the quality in your world come to you. If you are what you seek, you will find it."

"But it's so difficult to merge with something so large as the horizon. I couldn't decide whether to relate to it as form or space. Then I started thinking how I was going to flow with something so large. And then... Oh, okay," I acknowledged, understanding how my mind had taken over.

"This is why there is a process. The process allows you to build your sentience. Remember, it is ego that says 'either/or,' not your heart. You are used to being tripped up by your ego but this will not always be the case. Feel the horizon as energy and then you will merge with it. Labels are limiting. The nature of form is a spec in the flow of the greater Universe. This is why labels bring limitation and they make you try and force flow into form rather than dissolve form within the flow."

"But I knew all that so why couldn't I complete it?"

"Ego thought it knew. Your heart learnt. That is what is significant. You are undergoing the process. There is no need to undermine your efforts. Knowing is not feeling and experiencing. There is often a gap between what you think you know and what you feel you learn. Don't be so harsh on yourself, you have made learning. And your guidance has gained a greater insight into how you can be supported."

"Two way learning?"

"Multi-way learning. All you are required to do is believe in your progress and build upon it."

"Since you mention learning observations, I'm beginning to realise just how attached I am to my limited senses. They certainly aren't as much of an asset as they are in the limited world. More of a distraction, actually. So can I try again, this time with my eyes closed?"

"Certainly," replied the tramp with a hint of optimism, as if I'd picked up on some of his silent teaching hints.

I wobbled gently as the skyline disappeared. Once I regained my balance, I settled into the pulse in front of my eyes. I was amazed that it wasn't dark. There was light and the sense of lots of different colours.

"Now this might sound really bizarre, but..." I began.

"Go on," encouraged the tramp.

"I can sense a helter-skelter; fun fairs; a sense of rising up, jumping upwards. There's this huge acceleration. I'm in a racing car going round the tightest of bends... but I'm determined not to spin off the spiral... And yet I'm not controlling the car,

I'm cooperating with it. It's so freeing, so gentle and smooth... There's no real effort at all. This is fantastic!"

I felt a vortex spinning around and around in my heart. I was freer with every turn. Just as I aligned with the sensations, the vision began to dissolve into purple.

"Maybe I should close my eyes more often. This inner sight is amazing!"

"A veritable magical mystery tour!" observed my companion as my temporary blindness revealed the deepening nature of my inner vision.

The Chaos Of Creation

"Open your eyes and tell me what you see now," began the tramp as we started a new cycle of learning.

I opened my eyes to a dazzling view of the horizon. A small mountain range of crystal and chalk curved like the scales on a dragon's back, sculpting the elevation. On one side appeared to be a sheer drop into the glistening promise of a sea and on the other a small peak with a path carved around in ever tightening spirals. Buildings crowned its top, piercing the sky dusted in clouds. I stared for what seemed to be an age. I wanted to ask where all this had come from but instead I magnetised its feeling towards me just by opening my heart.

"Is that where you and the other neighbours live?"

"It's really the other way around. They are your new guests. You did invite them, after all."

"I did? Oh I get it. My next exercise is to merge with the neighbours because really, through this journey, I'm expanding so I can invite them into my heart space?"

"Well done. You're getting the hang of this; relating from lots of different directions, not just one."

"So shall I close my eyes and try the merge again?"

"What does your heart truth tell you?"

The Chaos Of Creation

The word *map* stood out clearly in my heart. The tramp was waiting for me to ask.

"Can I have the map then, please?"

"Certainly," he said. "Just close your eyes and rebalance in your heart."

I blinked quickly, hoping I'd see a caravan of supplies and a weather-worn piece of cloth with an ancient map. But everything was as before.

The tramp looked at me, assessing how I'd detoured with my ego.

"Why not?" I asked, sensing he'd already seen my vision. "It could've been like that," I grumbled, reluctantly letting go of my expectation.

The tramp ignored ego and refocused on the ground, resting on his staff as if calling the dust to order. "All that you require is right here, right now. That is the creative infinity," he replied firmly.

"That may be true," I smiled, "but you just can't get the staff these days... Get it?"

He smiled with me. "Humour opens the heart," he observed, gesturing towards my chest. "And all the help you require is in there, as you are finding out."

The tramp stepped back and with one movement of his staff he sketched a horizontal line with a parallel one about a hand's width below it. He looked at me as if searching for some sacred proportion that I was unaware of. Then, with another sweeping movement, a third line glanced the first, curving up sharply, rising into an exponential climb to merge with the vertical. He took a step back.

"Not bad for drawing upside down," I remarked.

The tramp raised his eyebrows to indicate that his teaching style had shifted from informal practical to formal lecture.

"And now to the important matter of turning things upside down." There was a smile under his serious veneer but I knew it was time to concentrate on listening.

He reversed the map to face him, checking all was present. Then, in one flash, it turned back to face me. I was silent, recognising his stroke of genius.

"So where are you on this map?" he asked. "No thinking, only feeling."

I hesitated. I didn't have an answer and didn't dare complicate matters by straying into my mind.

"I'm not getting anything at the moment. Can I close my eyes again?"

"Certainly."

As I did, the map appeared before me traced in gold. The areas where the curve rose up from the horizontal line flashed in dark blue. I opened my eyes, walked forward and marked the same position on the map.

"X marks the spot," I said, attempting a joke. I wanted to ask if it was the right answer but stopped short of the words.

"There are no right answers here, just honest ones, conscious ones, loving ones," the tramp smiled. "But a sense of humour is always handy for all those moments when everything isn't what you think."

"So what's the purpose of the map? Obviously there's a lot more to it than just my next step."

"Never underestimate your conscious next step for it keeps you in the flow. But, yes, your feeling confirms your ability. You are, from this point on, stepping differently. Shall we say, stepping in a multi-purpose, multi-tasking way. One step in this place is an expansion out in all directions, not just the direction in which you see yourself moving. And so this map describes your general progress and process as well as this moment."

"That's efficient!"

"The Universe always is. It is only ego that limits your experience of the ease that comes from one hundred per cent efficiency," replied the tramp as a purposeful momentum began to build.

He returned to the diagram. "The space between the

two parallels is where you used to keep all of your awareness when you were immersed in your research of limitation. But through your more recent explorations you have discovered some of the aspects of yourself that aren't within those limited vibrations. We shall call those your *other selves*. Also, you've decided you are less keen to fit within the classic ego square which is marked out by Fear, Control, Lack and Loss."

He drew a separate square on the diagram with a word at each corner. "As you move forward on your spiritual exploration you are finding out just how much of you is anchored to these core limitations and how much of you is detaching so that you can embrace your natural unlimited state of being."

"So as my awareness expands, I'll spend less of my experiences within a limited perspective? That means less existing through ego and more living through heart."

"Indeed. You will also continue to rebuild your I AM Presence that will coordinate the balance required to keep on your path."

"That means now I'm at the beginning of the curve that's rising up?"

"Exactly."

"What does the curve represent, though?"

"Your path of detachment, out of limitation. Your return to balance, to your true unlimited nature."

"That's great! That's what I've been working on."

"Indeed."

My mind projected forward, reaching out of the now. "So what happens when I get to the end of the curve? Am I a Master of Alchemy?"

"How are you going to receive your reward, as you think of it, if you have not been creating the path from here..."—he pointed to my cross at the beginning of the curve—"... to here?" he asked, pointing to the vertical portion at the other end. "Always a destination in the mind but never a path. How can you arrive if you create no path?"

Armchair Alchemist

I sat down with a huff in a cloud of dust, realising that once more I'd simply let my mind take over and jump to conclusions that took me away from what I really wanted. I lowered my head in self pity but the tramp ignored my ego sulk.

"All is learning. It wasn't so long ago when coming here would have caused you so much mental distress and anguish that it would have been impossible. Your mind and ego would have resisted this process to such a degree that you would not have been aware of the learning that was before you. But now you can see the difference. You are becoming aware of when you fall from your heart to what ego tells you is the security of your mind."

"But there isn't any security in my mind. I know it. I just keep falling back into the habit. Why can't I just feel and stop trying to think?"

"Because you still have parts of your unlimited nature attached to the patterning of ego and fear."

"They seem like boulders that are blocking my way."

"But you don't really feel that in your heart because the strength of your unlimited nature is returning. You are beginning to believe that you are always flowing; flowing in all directions. You are beginning to reach for conscious action rather than the scattered reactions of ego conditioning. You are learning to flow through your ego resistance and reclaim your power rather than flowing in the opposite direction in search of denial. You are recognising what you build for yourself in each moment and you are willing to learn from it.

"Don't concern yourself about the aspects of limitation that are still rattling around in your unity. With each loving step forward on your unique path, you are able to see through obstacles that have appeared so solid for so long. Trust the progress that you feel, not the aberrations that are the passing imbalances of ego."

"So I suppose the reason I feel disappointed in myself is that I don't always flow smoothly through these changes.

They often lack the grace and efficiency that seems to be second nature to you."

"First nature," the tramp corrected me. "Always remember that unlimited nature, ease and effortless creation are your first nature. Limitation is a research experience. Admittedly, it's perhaps gone on longer than you ever imagined it would but it is the greatest illusion you will ever experience."

"So to return to first nature, as you call it, I'll create my path, this curve rising up..."—I pointed to my X— "...and return progressively to an experience of life that's less fearful and less limited."

"Indeed. You will recognise the attached patterning that you embedded in your unlimited nature and, through conscious action, you will detach and recycle those knots of limitation into unlimited flow... just as you are doing here and now. There will be no more time line to follow, no more extreme imbalances, no more trying and struggling. As you move up the curve you will return to the unlimited being you really are. You will return to the state of being where you will not search for an end because there is no end, only flow."

"Again you make it sound so easy, so simple."

"It is. For simplicity is the nature of the greater Universe. It is only your limited nature and ego's desire for separation that expects struggle, pain and difficulty. But they are not natural to you."

"So how can I keep going up the curve? It looks pretty steep."

"Chaos. You require chaos."

My mind was close to exploding with rejection. I felt flashes of anger and an outburst simmering on the tip of my tongue.

"Breathe, please," said the tramp, peering into me. "You can transmute this. You are capable."

I did as I was told. The pressure began to recede. I closed my eyes and allowed my ego's outrage to pass straight through

Armchair Alchemist

me. I shifted position so I could refocus on our discussion. I felt a gust of purple blow through me and the transmutation was completed. I sensed a new question forming.

"One question," I began, feeling awkward as ego reminded me how ignorant I was.

"Only one?" the tramp asked, smiling to ease the tension.

"Well it's hard to ask a question because you always seem to know what I'm about to say. That makes it seem so irrelevant."

"Learning is never irrelevant. Nor is your choice to learn. And your ego is just risking disapproval, that is all. Your words that form your intentions are the most important aspect here. What is the foundation of your intentions? If you can feel the origin of your creations then you can return to your unlimited nature. Questions are the beginning of any healing cycle."

"Okay, here goes... Why chaos? To keep on the curve, I feel I require balance, not extremes that wreak havoc!"

The tramp took a step back. I looked into his kind eyes and realised there was no judgment. He was doing his job, gently working around my ego so he could teach the real me.

"The mind will always tell you that chaos is bad, that it is harmful and it could destroy your satisfaction and security when, in truth, ego has labelled the unlimited Universe as chaos. Anything ego can't control into limitation is seen, of course, as chaotic."

"But when you're in the limited world, it's the other way around."

"And who gives you the impression it runs that limited world?"

"Ego."

"Precisely. So ego sees chaos from its own perspective, the perspective which only sees one way—the way of ego."

"So the next time I hear someone say 'You can't do that, it'll be chaos!', it's really their ego saying not to rock the boat, not to go and choose expansion because that threatens ego's limited state of being.

"Indeed."

"So if chaos is unlimited energy, how am I going to work with that to keep moving up the curve?"

"Practice. You are going to practice."

"Practice creation?"

"Yes. And also what a magician does best."

"Alchemy?"

"Bingo! You are your path. Each conscious change you make reminds you of the unlimited being you truly are. Each conscious change puts your heart back in the centre of your world. Each time you cooperate with chaos, you practice transmutation and greater and greater degrees of balance. Chaos strengthens your I AM Presence. It is the fuel you seek. Whether you are rejoining with the unlimited flows of the Universe or recycling limited attachments into flow, it's all chaos."

"That's the complete opposite to what ego told me. But chaos is growing on me. And now I think I understand when my Higher Self talks about necessary disturbances. Those are small bursts of chaos; unlimited energy that help me see my attachments so I can understand what's really holding me back."

"Your command of change does you credit," the tramp smiled encouragingly. "It is also important to understand that the greater the disturbance, the greater the resistance. So you only get what ego calls chaos in your experience if you've been heaping avoidance on top of avoidance, fear onto fear and attachment onto attachment. The unlimited flow never stops, so when it meets such a multiple pile up, what do you think happens?"

"The attachments get broken?"

"Yes. And the structure of fear begins to dissolve. Picture chaos as a beautiful winged horse. If you respect the horse then it will carry you everywhere your heart chooses to go, to learn what you are required to learn. But this relationship is built on cooperation. You can lead a horse to water but you cannot make it drink. Force the flow and you will block it. Avoid the flow and the structure of denial your ego is building will repel the very fuel and freedom you are seeking.

"Remember, chaos is your companion, not your adversary. It is an unlimited flow that is always supportive and always loving. It is the part of your unlimited nature that always reminds you to keep flowing through your experience rather than becoming stuck in it or falling away from your path. It is constantly supporting you in expanding your perspective, your heartfelt truth and your return to unlimited nature. Chaos holds empowerment within it. It can support you in the **C**-onscious **H**-eartfelt **A**-spects **O**-f **S**-ervice."

The tramp's last sentence hung in the air, the word chaos illuminated in gold.

"That sounds like a bit of a mouthful."

"You yourself said it is difficult to put these concepts into words."

"True. But what about **C**-ourageous **H**-elp **A**-iding **O**-ption **S**-eekers? There can't be just one definition."

"Quite so. Chaos is unlimited. There is never just one definition and no one has the last word!" His face unfolded into a broad smile.

He waved his staff and my definition appeared in the air next to his and he blew a ring of gold that gracefully floated towards the letters until it encircled all.

"Chaos is really the unlimited flow—all part of the unending unity," said the tramp, and took a long luxuriant breath of fulfilment.

I felt a gasp echo through my heart. Oh to be that fulfilled... to be as detached as my companion.

"All in good time. Oh yes... and space," smiled the tramp. "We mustn't forget the space. It's the most important part."

The Curve Of Ascension

Our discussion was now completely soaked in chaos. All I wanted to do was fall into these layers of unlimited potential. I felt a gust of relaxation blow through me and in a moment I was lying flat on my back in a gesture of complete surrender.

What a magical mystery tour this expanding truth and freedom was turning out to be. The parts of me that had been folded in on themselves, stuck and forgotten were becoming accessible once more. I was now beginning to appreciate that the pathways of change were infinite but such a chaos of creation was no longer daunting, it was now reassuring. I knew in my heart that everything I discovered on my path could be supportive, it all depended on my perception and the choices I made.

The tramp waited, rocking back and forth with what appeared to be unlimited patience. A slight breeze danced through his long white beard. I was sure that beard had grown through many, many lifetimes.

"Tell me," I began, sitting back upright, "just how old are you?"

"Old enough to know your question requires no answer," replied the tramp.

"Go on! You can tell me! I won't tell another soul."

"No you won't because age is a limit and there are no limits here, just expanding horizons. If you want the wisdom that you perceive comes from age, if you want to hear the echo that resounds in the unlimited depth of the heart, then absorb the wisdom of Now and you will learn never to leave it. All is within Now just waiting to be discovered. As you apply your Now learning you will be supported by wisdom rather than be defined by the expectations of age."

The tramp paused, checking how much I was absorbing. I felt my heart prepare to expand once more. "And now let us return to the sketch. What shall we call this curve?" he asked.

I took a moment to consider my answer. "The return to unlimited nature?" I suggested.

"That describes it very well. How about the curve of ascension?"

"Catchy. It has a certain uplifting quality!" I enthused.

"Catchy and uplifting is appealing then?"

"Yes, that would encourage me to move upward and inward."

"Excellent. So let us continue to describe this upliftment," the tramp said, gesturing towards his diagram. "If this is the curve of your ascension, what do you do to get started?"

"To get on the curve, you mean?"

"Yes."

"First..." I was reluctant to trust as memories of school came flooding back. There I was, daydreaming about what I wanted to do rather than what I was supposed to be learning.

"First... last... it's all the same progress," reinforced the tramp. "Unleash the meaning that you feel. This is heart learning. There are no rights or wrongs. Embrace your loving truth. You aren't at school now." He was enticing me away from my fear of making a mistake.

"I really want to make progress," I confided.

"Then do it. Take the steps that will create genuine learning. There is always learning. How your ego judges your learning is of no consequence here."

"Okay... I believe that for everyone there comes a time in life... maybe fleeting or maybe it's so obvious you can't ignore it... but you feel the momentum of change. Everything makes sense and nothing makes sense... but regardless, you're dislodged from the world of conditioned ego. And at that moment, with a bit of help from chaos, and of course guidance..."—the tramp inclined his head in acknowledgement—"...everything speeds up. The will to change combines with circumstances and realisations and then you can get on the curve; you start your ascension. Of course, each curve is different because everyone is unique... but that sense of upliftment, unfamiliar, release... whatever it feels like, it comes to us all when we make that choice to change."

"And how do you create that momentum?"

"Through detaching from fearful behaviour and making life choices from heart and intuition. Through developing a dialogue with Higher Self and guidance. And, of course, through trust."

"And," said the tramp, building on my answer, "through commanding the momentum of the guidance coming into your world by applying it to your experience. When you apply what you learn, you are practicing expansion. You are trying it on for size through adapting to the rate of change in your experience and through the allowance of your heart. You are feeling what it is to embrace your unlimited nature. This is the assimilation process, the part where you finally let go of your limited attachment and simultaneously confirm that you are committed to absorbing your change so your ego won't distract you or re-attach you."

"Oh is that all?" I joked as my mind filled with overwhelming why's as it tried to work everything out. "It's a good job I've got you to teach me. It seems so much all at once."

"That is just the unlimited flow finding its level within you. You are simultaneously adapting to that while reclaiming another part of your true nature. Your mind will try to lodge ego protests. Just let them pass. If you don't encourage resistance, it will transmute more easily. The unlimited flow will go where it can serve the most. Nothing is wasted, remember?"

"All of this feels right... I mean, correct... well, you know what I mean. However, the sense that there's always more takes some getting used to. Ego always conditions us to believe there's less and less—less time, less energy, less creativity."

"Well observed. But as you stay in your I AM Presence this scarcity will pass. Just because you are accelerating doesn't mean you lose the ability to choose. You can go step by step or

Armchair Alchemist

leap by leap. Or a mixture of those. There is no particular way that is best, just the one within which you feel balanced."

"But will that be enough?" I felt the words of scarcity once more. "What I mean is, if I go a bit slower from time to time, will that jeopardise my acceleration?"

"Not at all. Balance is the key, not speed. Acceleration is a function of expansion. You can choose how you expand. Contrary to what your ego says, you don't have to do everything all at once, rushing to your destination. Nor, for that matter, resist at full speed. Nor do you need to analyse your path, shattering it into pieces. You are simply required to understand the intention behind your actions, and to experience with an open heart, an open mind, and balance."

"That sounds simple enough."

"It is."

"But adapting to simplicity can be complicated," I suggested.

"Look at it more as complex. Simplicity has many layers and so it will require many adjustments. You are already realising that, as you expand, you are also faced with your passing scarcity. Ego shouts at you not to give up the scarcity because for ego, scarcity is security. Ego can only keep this illusion going if you believe in it."

"But I don't want security, I want to expand."

"Indeed. And this is why you are a seeker. You are looking beyond the mundane and through the past to discover the extraordinary."

"And now I'm on the curve, will I adjust to more and more unlimited flow by going through initiations that help me unstick from ego attachment?"

"Indeed. Your initiations support you in undoing the parts of yourself that have become caught up in ego. But it is for you to handle the process in a unified way. The parts of you that are wound up in attachment are not bad or a failure, they are simply part of your unity. The unlimited love of the higher aspects of yourself through your choices are dissolving the misunderstandings of ego. And so mistakes become learning and resistances become fuel. You embrace your mental, emotional and physical nature within your spiritual nature. You reunify within love. Since your physical body is the aspect of yourself with the most concentrated attachments, when you absorb more Light you can often feel the opposite to what you expected."

"Yes, that's what's got me confused. If I'm returning to my Light nature, why then do I feel so heavy, so tired from time to time?"

"You are really feeling your attachments as they absorb the Light. You are feeling the process of taking Light into these dense areas and the heaviness is the inevitable contrast. The heaviness or fatigue is just a by-product of the increase in Light. It is only temporary. It will pass."

"Do you mean that having a physical body is a handicap?" I interrupted.

"No, it is an added consideration. Through ascension, you are returning to your Light nature one hundred per cent. So you are required to recycle all the physical attachments related to your embodiment. This process takes into consideration all the experiences you have in limitation. Your return to Light is total when you complete your ascension. You will then have no attachments left."

"So... no stone left unturned then? Or in this case, no attachments left untransmuted."

"Indeed. Ego will have no dark corners in which to hide because there will be only Light."

"When you put it like that, I can see how extensive the detachment process is. No wonder change can appear to be so slow at times. But the overall picture is actually really encouraging when I consider what's actually being achieved."

"Indeed, it is magical and miraculous. Quite some alchemy! And as you re-express these parts of your nature that have been enmeshed with ego, it can take some moments in your world to untie these ego knots. So the path of ascension is a process that helps iron out the extremes and the polarities that could halt your progress."

"What do you mean?"

"Guidance works to support you as you move up the curve, encourage you on your way, inspire you forward. But it is also to help you integrate your change so that you don't shock your system and try to move beyond what your remaining resistances and attachments can withstand."

"So I can actually try too hard?"

"Oh indeed! Being completely resistant to change and trying to force change are two extremes that can knock you off your curve. They are two sides of the same extreme, one forcing with all its might and the other resisting. That's why the periods of adjustment are so important."

"So I could get up so much momentum that I could actually accelerate way beyond the finishing line? Well, you know what I mean!"

"Indeed. You could accelerate beyond what you wish and as a result be unable to complete your ascension."

"How?"

"You could take off with your Lightness; believe you are at the finishing line, as it were, but be unable to become ascended because you have not completed the recycling of attachments within your physical self."

"So I can get to the energy level that is required to be an Ascended Master but I won't become ascended until I'm completely Light?"

"In general terms, that is accurate."

"And what does completely Light look like?" Ego was busy trying to limit our discussion with mental constraints.

"Perhaps you will continue your detachment process long enough to answer your own question."

I realised I'd stepped back into my mind and felt a twinge of guilt.

My companion continued. "More importantly, this is why we always encourage you to remain balanced and in your Now. Then you have the joy of your process and can appreciate what you have undergone to attain ascension."

The tramp rested. The Light learning he'd built was completed, for now anyway. Each word was a beam supporting this elegant and brilliant alchemy. As we sat within it, I wondered if this was the real El Dorado; the city of golden architecture constructed out of pure Light."

"How are you feeling?" asked the tramp, sensing my vision.

"Light; full of the magic of legend and the truth of heart. I really want to embrace this state; understand what it is to be Light. My mind is less enthusiastic."

The tramp smiled knowingly.

I continued in my observations and wonder. "My mind is having a hard time with the empowerment of your teachings. It likes the kind of power ego used to exert in my life; the idea of power *over*—master/servant; winner/loser. All this expansion is highlighting how inflexible those polarities are. But I feel... arrived. I feel the fulfillment that shows we've created something together that I can build on further. Let's face it, if ego doesn't like it then it's probably worth exploring!"

"Quite so. And your willingness does you valuable service. Each time you reclaim another layer of yourself, your journey and capacity for learning will become greater, full of the abundance, awareness and realisation that you seek."

"Great! I'm all for that!" I enthused.

"Excellent. An expanding unity in the making. And what about your Light structure?" The tramp waved his staff and a building of simple grandeur shimmered around us.

"I'm settling in," I smiled.

"Wonderful. There was a time not too long ago when being within the walls of light would have been so suffocating for ego that you would never have been able to magnetise such a structure. And now look. You are embracing it as part of your natural beingness. And so the process, the progress and the purpose are aligned."

"What do you mean?"

"The process of ascension. Your experiences and learnings that carry you from what your ego likes to call A to B are of course the building blocks of your spiritual mastery. If you do not change along your way, there is simply no change. Ego would love to fool you into thinking you have travelled from A to B and therefore you have journeyed within yourself and transmuted your blocks. But if you have simply focused on your destination then you are unlikely to have achieved much learning."

"Apart from learning how to resist?"

"Indeed."

"So journeying is all about being within the journey, discovering which part of me needs to change and how I can achieve it"

"Yes. Spiritual mastery is made possible through the *becoming*—the journey you take to dislodge and recycle ego and reinstate your unlimited nature. As you build your becoming, you learn to value what it represents. You embrace the importance of your process and then you can understand what it is to master alchemy. Ascension is to empower self through the return to love and unlimited nature, and to maintain your embodiment in the process. And last, but by no means least, to maintain purpose."

"So in simple terms that means keep on opening up to love and change and don't resist or force change so that your physical nature doesn't get so stressed it can't take it. And always listen to the advice of your heart and guidance so that you can maintain purpose."

"A succinct Light summary. Yes. And as you embrace chaos you see that your attachments become your fuel of progress. You realise you are your path and the illusion of ego

The Curve Of Ascension

limitation dissolves. Ego will even try and tell you about its expectations for ascension. But only your heart can guide you. One of the most common misunderstandings of the ascension process is that purpose is one fixed deed or expression of self rather than a state of being that changes according to your process of learning. In any given moment, balance is part of purpose on your spiritual journey, as is dealing with what is right here and now."

"So I suppose, in a way, purpose brings to the surface of any moment what's ripe for learning, what's most supportive in the path forward and what's going to help keep everything balanced, the higher and the lower."

"Yes. Purpose is much more flexible and multi-layered than has been thought. And to become ascended, it is most supportive to remain as connected as you can to your purpose through your heart, your guidance, your sentience, your practice of alchemy and your loving commitment to embracing who you are becoming."

The tramp paused. We'd climbed far enough on our curve.

"Look at the view!" he exclaimed. "Would you have thought it would have so many layers, so much love and potentiality?"

"No. My mind couldn't have held this view," I smiled, "but my heart is now open to it, and to all the chaos it will bring."

"Bravo!" said the tramp, clapping. "And here endeth the lesson. Not the learning, you understand, just the lesson!"

I felt a wave of euphoria through the centre of my being that flowed out into the vastness of the landscape. And in that moment I was connected to everything. Energy flowed without resistance. Everything was making a difference and everything was worthwhile. I began to feel breathless as my physical nature caught up with the flow. My heart hadn't had such a workout since I couldn't remember when. I'd been sitting on the ground for most of our discussion and yet I felt like I'd been walking briskly up a steep incline.

"Breathe. There is no hurry here," said the tramp gently. "You go at your own pace here so you can feel what you achieve. All is feeling. All is flow."

I took the tramp's advice and lay down, extending my limbs as far as they would stretch. The sand was warm and soothing. My eyes began to close as I drifted away towards the horizon.

The Honesty Gap

"A bit of a transmutation nap, eh?"

I opened my eyes to find myself at the top of a high ridge, just below a collection of buildings.

"Yes, it was wonderful," I replied drowsily.

I reached for a logical question but began to dissolve it of my own accord. "I won't ask where we are but I feel much lighter so let's get this flow on the road!"

"As you wish," the tramp said, now wearing a different sack, more like a cloak. With one sweep, our previous diagram was drawn again before my very eyes.

"So, what's in the flow?" he asked.

I was silent as my respect for this wise vagabond and his teaching methods was now beyond flippancy. But I couldn't help wondering why we were repeating what appeared to be the same lesson.

"You are here," he said, pointing to the curve. "And we are not repeating the lesson, we are seeing how much was lost in translation. All part of the job."

"What do you mean, lost in translation?"

"The process is unique, as is the transmutation part. Each time you absorb unlimited vibrations, it's always helpful to see where you now think you are versus where you feel you are. Sometimes they are the same, sometimes a polarity apart. Call

The Honesty Gap

the difference the Honesty Gap. This opens up when your mind tries to tell you one thing and your heart realises something else. If sustained for too long, the polarity that opens up between your mental body and your emotional body can eventually tear you apart. This is why honesty in all your experiences is always the best policy. It is also why guidance will from time to time appear to ask you the same question but you may be surprised to hear yourself replying completely differently. Such is your expansion and such is the acceleration up the curve."

"So if my perspective has shifted then I'm choosing more alternatives, more love, less fear. So now, in this bit of our conversation, you are checking how I'm being with you and myself."

The tramp grinned and raised his eyebrows.

"Well," I continued, "ego illusion isn't standing right in front of me, if that's what you mean," and I swept my hands through the air. "See! Just space and flow."

I felt eager to prove myself to my teacher.

"Indeed," he said. "And so what are you feeling in your heart now?" The tramp was persistent, as if keen to recycle the smaller pieces of my residual resistance.

"I feel peace mixed with a little anxiety. The curve looks so simple but I know that simplicity takes a lot of surrender. And I'm still tempted to control or fiddle with my experience rather than detach enough to learn from it. I suppose my ego feels a little exposed because I'm walking away from the attachments that I've thought for so long were my life."

I pointed to the box created between the two horizontal lines. "Ego and being inside the cube aren't enough any more. I want to move beyond limited security into the joy of RealLife. But it's still really tempting to *make* it happen; to force and control rather than cooperate and allow."

"Wonderful!"

"What do you mean?"

"You are honouring your commitment with a new level

of honesty. This helps you keep up the momentum in your process. Commitment helps you apply what you have learned. That creates the wisdom which sustains you on your journey. Instead of fumbling around in the dim density of attachment, you are lighting your way forward."

"So you're saying to keep it light, keep it honest?"

"Yes, in a manner of speaking. And always remember to laugh. There is plenty of cause for amusement along your path. Taking ego seriously can be a bit of a drag, if you'll pardon the pun."

"No holding on, then. That way there'll be nothing to drag me down!"

"Precisely. The moment you recognise an attachment, you have the capacity to release it. How you do it is up to you."

"And so we come back to choice."

"But we never left. For there is always an abundance of choice."

"Of course," I agreed. "And the more we choose, the more choices we have. Choice attracts choice. All we're required to do is believe."

"And it sounds as though you are ready to receive your reward."

"Great! What is it?"

"Welcome to the fellowship of choice!" The tramp bowed towards me theatrically as if receiving a nobleman.

"So does that make me the chosen one?" I joked, my ego hoping to elevate me to separateness.

The tramp decided to play along. "You and all the other souls who choose choice... yes, you are all the chosen ones; all unique and special in your own way."

"Not so special after all!" I pouted theatrically, trying to get some sympathy.

"Not so separate," replied the tramp, stifling a chuckle.

"But seriously... why do we want to be special? What

The Honesty Gap

part of us wants to be a cut above the rest; someone set aside from others?"

"What part of you? Ego, of course!" He banged the point home with his staff. "It is ego that seeks to elevate itself out of the unlimited flow of love and distance itself from the loving purpose of the Universe. Oh yes... such is the precious accolade of ego."

"I walked right into that one, didn't I?"

"Put it this way. You walked off with ego into the detour that is separation. But you've caught yourself in a moment. And as always, there was learning, wasn't there?"

"Yes, there's always learning," I agreed, rolling my eyes at what seems such a rudimentary mistake.

The tramp continued, paying no attention to my self judgment.

"So what else can you discover on your curve in this moment? Remember, don't think what you know, feel what your heart's knowingness tells you."

"Well, I know it doesn't seem to make sense at first but... I'm sensing circles, like I did before in the bubble. That's the feeling in my heart: I'm in the bubble and joined with it all at the same time."

"Encouraging. Sit with that feeling and remember that these concepts are somewhat forgotten within you so they might appear a bit like an echo; like something that you hear about the Universe but it is blown around through the mythical rather than the practical. But odd will become different and then it will become possible and then it will become... well, present. So while you are undergoing your process, let me colour and shade in a little more detail."

I made myself comfortable for the next flow of teaching.

"Although the curve is a line, it is really a path that expands out in all directions. I AM Centre is connected to the centre of the path. As you and all those on the path of ascension become more and more aware of the way you create, you realise that you aren't rejecting ego so that you can run off into the sunset of another world, you are dissolving the conflict and pain that the limited part of yourself experiences. You are all transmuting your attachment to separation.

"So, if you look at the diagram... how do you keep your research in the limited world going?" the tramp asked with raised eyebrows.

"That's simple," I began confidently. "You get attached; hooked into creating more and more extremes which in turn create more and more imbalance and separation."

"And then what?" he continued, drawing me further forward.

"Then you become saturated and forget about your unlimited first nature. Ego takes over. You forget that you can be anything else in the Universe. Then you become your limited world until it takes over completely and the physical part of you can't survive because there's so much attachment that there's no more energy flow. And so you become so rigid that you die holding onto your attachments."

"Well explained. If I may recap... In our diagram," said the tramp, pointing with his staff, "limited experience is within the box between the two horizontal lines. In these frequencies you can experience limitation. In truth, you aren't really going anywhere, your awareness is what does all the travelling, as you would think of it. So your awareness has expanded into the vibrations of limitation but you are still unified with your unlimited nature. It's simply that your awareness that is in your limited experiences makes the biggest impression. So that is why you think you are limited."

"Is there more of me somewhere else?"

"In a way. But you are not separate. Picture yourself as a big sphere made from different layers of consciousness and awareness. You are fluid and can flow into lots of different expressions, some physical but, as you are now finding out, also some non-physical. That is why we refer to you as a unity."

The Honesty Gap

"But before I started my most recent spiritual journey, I was so engrossed in limitation that I didn't know I had a choice, right?"

"Yes. And you now understand how limitation can be so attaching. How exhilarating imbalance is. How used you are to the fearful and dramatic reactions of ego."

"Okay, yes. When we talk about limitation here, it's easy to see how attached this part of me can get and so..." A part of me was searching, following a feeling that the tramp was leading up to something.

"So when all the attachments in here," the tramp continued, pointing inside the box again, "...pile up and there is no more space for flow, your research stops and you die. Ego then replaces the rebalancing cycles of ease and unlimited flow with the imbalanced polarity of birth and death. Limitation leaves a big impression on you so, as your research in limitation happens over and over, you start to believe in birth and death as being normal, as being the only way to experience."

"So I... we... those in limitation... forget about the rest of our unity, allowing limitation to take over our awareness. And we start to define our whole nature through the limited perception of ego."

"But do you believe it always has to be like that?" asked the tramp in a lighthearted tone.

"I suppose not..." I stopped mid sentence as the implications of my words began to sink in. "Wait a minute! Perhaps I've misunderstood here. Have I talked myself into a dead end?" I asked.

"Oh, by the way, that wasn't a deliberate joke, I assure you," I added.

I fell silent. My mind hit a brick wall but curiosity kept my heart open. The guided discussion was opening out into a whole new dimension.

"But why shouldn't spontaneous humour be deliberate?" the tramp asked, encouraging the feeling in my heart.

"Doesn't your joke come from you choosing to keep your heart open to a whole new way of being?"

"Nervous humour, is more like it! But yes, my heart is still open and, if I understand correctly, I feel you're saying that if I return to my first nature, the true unlimited self that's in unity with the unlimited flow of love..."—I took a deep breath—"...then I wouldn't need birth or death? I'd just have life... A never ending flow of life, of energy. Perhaps you call it unlimited Life?"

"Of course," said the tramp, as if he'd spoken the most natural and ordinary of truths. "You seem surprised."

"Surprised?! That's one massive acceleration! It goes straight past death!" I spluttered as my heart raced and my mind bulged in all directions, ready to burst.

"Breathe," replied the tramp. "Breathe and you will find the connection within you."

I did as he asked and immediately felt returned to my I AM Presence.

"Death is, after all, only a choice," he explained. "It's just one that you've been conditioned to believe you have to make."

The tramp commanded the silence which followed. Merging with his surroundings, he patiently awaited my response as the sun rose high in the sky and rays of golden orange sparkled through the landscape.

A Natural State Of Being

I couldn't talk for a moment that seemed to lapse into hours. I was astounded. My mouth opened and closed like a goldfish as my mind screamed objections but could form no words. Suddenly, as if I was standing outside of myself, I heard my voice begin a reply.

"I can feel what you're saying, I just can't understand how that can be. And yet in my heart I know it's true. I believe it." My words drew me back together.

A Natural State Of Being

"Welcome to the land of endless life," said the tramp. "You have bridged your honesty gap, embracing the foundation of your true nature. In this moment you are remembering what the unending feels like. Keep feeling. There's plenty more; an unending abundance."

He rested on his staff, grinning from head to toe.

"Such a possibility is mind boggling," I began.

"Just allow your Now. When you allow, you give yourself the gift of expansion. You can feel the love and expansion, can you not?"

"I can certainly feel a sense of expansion... like I'm part of the whole landscape... as if everything and anything was all joined up, flowing together."

"Yes, yes. Unity and love is your nature. And you can always choose to continue that flow. You don't ever have to leave it again. You are not passing death, or cheating death, you are simply putting it in context. You are seeing it in a new Light... as a choice. Just as to live through love and in balance is a choice."

I stuttered my way back into the conversation. "So, if I chose not to die..." I could barely believe what I was saying. "Then... that would mean my physical nature wouldn't become congested with fear attachments. There'd be no imbalance to cause ill health, there'd simply be an endless flow of life."

"Indeed. And an endless stream of choice so that your life was built of love, not fear."

"So does that mean... I'd be eternal?"

"The return to the eternal is unique to all. What do you sense it means?" The tramp was picking his words very carefully.

"In all honesty, my first response would be 'Is that it?!' If I'm going to become eternal and get stuck in the world as I know it, I'd ask 'What's the point?' I don't want to live like some immortal being, century after century observing humanity fumbling on in everlasting cycles of conflict as history repeats itself. I thought the whole reason for expanding awareness is to get out of limitation, not be in it forever?"

"Indeed, there would be no point at all in that," replied the tramp. "But the state of eternal life is greatly misunderstood. And you are letting your mind extrapolate how you *think* this state of being would affect you, not how you really feel about being within it."

"So ego's also embellished the concept of eternal life?"

"Yes. It has created its own definition—an un-aging self left to roam from one century to the next, remaining in embodiment with ego."

"But that doesn't ring true. Surely, after all the detachments, there'd be flow; liberation from struggle and difficulty?"

"Yes. Eternal life is reuniting with the unending flow of love, balance, effortless creation and harmony. But as you are becoming aware, there is nothing to stop ego forming definitions of concepts and states of being that it actually has no experience of. Ego creates assumptions about your alchemy of change, your ascension and what it would be like to be eternal. But these definitions are all constructed from limited perception. If you choose to be eternal, you won't try to be immortal and live in form forever! Eternal life is not locked to form and time. When you are eternal you are just that—without limitation. There is no time, no measurement or definition, only flow. So eternal life is a flow within which you can keep on expanding. When you complete your ascension you will have the understanding of what it was to descend and experience limitation and you will also have the experience of what it was like to rise out of attachment and regain your true nature. And so when you become eternal, you have expanded beyond the limitation of ego, back into your first nature, your true nature which is love. What was once so impossible in limitation becomes normal in your return to eternal nature.

"You are finding it an interesting challenge," the tramp continued, "to control the unlimited within your mind. Your ego is desperately trying to attach form to the eternal so that it can say 'See, I know what it is.' But ego cannot embrace eternal life because ego itself is a product of limitation. And so this is why we ask you to allow. Allowance shows you the power of the heart and also the unlimited nature that you truly are. And so you are learning to feel, learning to understand and build your experiences from love, not fear."

"So ego will dissolve into love. My illusion of limited nature will be recycled completely. The story of research that was *Once upon a limited time* will have come full circle. The unlimited part of me will no longer wonder what it's like to be limited and I will be able to appreciate what it's like to be unlimited."

"In simple terms, yes. Welcome to the grand experiment!"

I could feel ego shrinking away from the feeling of love and the sensation of what I could be. It cast doubt and cynicism in all directions as it retreated. I couldn't help feeling some of it rubbing off.

"I do believe in what you're saying... in the here and now... but what about when I'm back in physical awareness? This potentiality, this alternative, this fantastic avenue of expansion can start to fade, particularly when I'm surrounded by the consciousness of limitation in which birth and death seem so tangible and so normal."

"But this discussion is not discrediting or judging your experience in limitation," explained the tramp. "Birth-and-death in the physical world is, indeed, a valid form of experience. And it is one of the polarities that you chose to research. This is why experience in limitation has continued for thousands of your years. There is nothing like it in the rest of the Universe!"

"So at the beginning of my research trip I could've said 'Just make it one quick trip into limitation,' thinking 'Oh I'll just explore for one lifetime and then ascend back into unity.' But what appeared to be a simple exercise soon got embellished by ego detours and attachment and before I knew it, I'd become caught up in it."

"Indeed. But here you are learning how to unravel your pasts and your futures so that you can return to Now and to Unity. All is a matter of choice and you are made of the matter of choice. This is why you have reconnected with guidance. And now, through choice, you have created your step by step tutorial as you transmute fear, control, lack and loss."

"So I'm dismantling ego definition?"

"Yes, so that you can live through love, not fear, by making choices that enable love, not fear."

"Then I can return to love, to the centre of my universe, and remember that the me here in physicality isn't the only me?"

"Indeed. It is to remember that Love is the centre and substance of all universes. It's just that ego, through the limitations of the mind, thinks fear and separation are the centre of the only universe."

"So eternity is living through Love. But if I live through ego, I limit my awareness of that Love. And then fear, control, lack and loss become my defining parameters. It's these attachments that separate me from Love. No wonder I require guidance to shine a light through those attachments to remind me there's a greater self in here," I said, gesturing to my heart.

"And thus you are discovering the greater you, step by step," encouraged the tramp.

"And you... guidance supports me in seeing my path back through attachment. And through guidance, everyone who goes on this journey of ascension can have the awareness to cope with these shifts out of limitation back into Love?"

"Yes. There is an unlimited flow of guidance for anyone who chooses to connect. There is more than enough for all. No one will miss out. The flow of guidance is as unique to each as their ascension out of limitation."

"And that means each individual gets the ascension they choose and each individual gets the guidance they choose?"

A Natural State Of Being

"Indeed. And as you move further on your path you will spot ego habits more readily and you will choose differently. You are replacing the structures of self gratification and *power over* with love and genuine empowerment. Imagine you are building a Light grid within yourself. As that Light grid grows, you are learning how to spiritualise your life and how to cope with greater and greater degrees of empowerment."

"So does that mean I'll accelerate into eternity?"

"More a case of learning to balance within your I AM Presence as you expand your consciousness, awareness and Light capacity. Let us take the example of eternal life. There was a time in your not-too-distant past when you would have reacted so strongly against such an idea that you would have ceased your spiritual development."

"And now?" I was curious.

"Now you have learned about a new focus—open-mindedness and openheartedness. You are more allowing. And so you can be with such alternatives; you can allow their possibility instead of reacting and resisting. You have come a long way on your journey of alchemy."

"So when I can create instantaneously, command acceleration and momentum of the changes in my experience, will it be like living in a magical world?"

"That is for the Masters in Light to appreciate and for you to find out!"

"What kind of an answer is that?"

"That is an answer of guidance—never doing it for you but always encouraging the seeker within you."

"Okay, always a journey, never a destination. Stay on the belief train as far as it flows."

"Indeed. Keep believing. There is an alternative to what you think you see. Recognise that all your changes, however insignificant they might appear, are contributing to a flow of conscious change that will enlighten your world. Ego might say it was a waste of time but when you are learning, nothing is wasted. And at some point you will cease to ask where you are on your curve of ascension, whether you're making any progress, or even whether you've finished yet. You will simply trust endlessly and begin to experience infinite change in a single moment.

"The more your heart is open and remains open, the more you will return to your true nature."

The tramp fell silent.

"That's a lot to take in, even here! I do believe in what you're saying, I really do, but why does eternal life seem like a mirage, an unobtainable vision that only a few have achieved in the forgotten tales of mysticism?"

"Because with increasing attachment, it becomes easy to replace genuine belief and experience with security and the promise, or appearance, of experience. To become eternal you are required to create, be and walk your path so that you rediscover your true nature. That is the process that you are undertaking now. Without experience you are unable to recycle aspects of limitation that have become embedded in your unity. Ego does what it can to fight the process but, in truth, with awareness you can see through the limited methods of ego as it tries to maintain its grip by appearing to know it all; by seeming to be an advisor that can help you make the right decision, stop you wasting your energy on the impossible, support you with logic. And, of course, guarantee your security, your attachment and your limitation."

"But I know ego can't guarantee anything because the Universe is always changing."

"Precisely. But, when you were deeply immersed in your limited state, you believed it could. And so you are retracing your steps back through such conditioning. You are an explorer reaching for the truth and seeing that the supposed facts and knowledge of ego aren't enough any more."

"So the seeker keeps on looking into the chaos of the weird until it makes sense?"

"Indeed. And, moment by moment, the seeker rediscovers their true nature and the unlimited flow of love."

I was beginning to fizz all over. "Well," I gasped, catching my breath through a wave of euphoria and turning to face the greater landscape, "that is one hell of a view!"

We both began to laugh.

"Okay, if I can rephrase that… This is one eternal view and one vast introduction to what we really can be."

I hesitated, sensing the tramp wanted to add something.

"What you truly *are!*" he added.

"Okay, the truly eternal beings that we are. That doesn't seem…"

The tramp finished my sentence. "So far fetched any more?"

"Well, if you'd just come out and said 'You don't have to die, it's just an ego habit!', I probably would've exploded. But you wouldn't do that because you are love. And you're here to guide me into a state that can allow such an expanded perspective. And you understand the precise recipe of alchemy that has a pinch of curiosity and a generous helping of Light. So in this moment, yes, I can begin to understand. It's not right or wrong, it's Light, it's love and it's support."

The tramp nodded in acknowledgement. "Nothing is forever," he replied, "but everything is for Now and that Now is love." His words embraced the strongest force of gentle that I'd ever known as his wrinkled face spread into a smile for all eternity.

I was compelled to return to his question. "So, is this far fetched? No. Is it far reaching? Definitely. And I'm glad to say I'm a part of it. And if I stay in the Now, my expanding perspectives can embrace the unlimited I seek and I can return to eternity."

"And is it forever?" enquired the tramp.

"No, it's for Love," I replied. "It's all for Love."

Hide And Seek

I jumped to my feet with surprising ease. Everything suddenly appeared to be just that bit brighter. The tramp was shimmering silently by my side.

"You're all of a glow, I see," I smiled at the tramp.

"Look who's talking. You are shining just like new!"

"Thanks," I acknowledged. "Seeker at the ready. I feel a journey coming on..."

"Indeed," he nodded.

As we took our first steps in our new direction, there was now a distinct path lined with small succulents leaning towards us like curious children. We covered the distance between our discussion and the distant buildings so quickly that I looked down at my feet to see that they were still on the ground. It was tempting to look behind to compare the distance I thought we'd covered, but the tramp was reading my mind again.

"No point looking back," he said. "Comparison is an ego habit that is becoming less useful by the moment. Believe in your progress and believe in the effortlessness of balance. Those are more than enough to absorb for now."

"Are they part of the perks included in my ascension package?" My lightness was becoming cheeky.

"No. They are part of your sentience package included within your humour," he replied as we arrived at the door of what now looked like an enormous mansion.

"After you," he said, extending out his hand, formalising his invitation. "Age before beauty."

"Now you're being cheeky!" I exclaimed. "There's no way you're younger than me!"

"Comparison! There you go again!" smiled the tramp, bowing and extending his hand once more.

"Okay, okay. I walked right into that, didn't I?" I slapped the tramp's arm as I stepped through the doorway. "Those ego habits," I muttered.

Hide And Seek

The house had a grand entrance that opened into a magnificent domed foyer. The sense of expansion was unlike anything I'd ever felt. The top of my head tingled as if reaching for the highest point of the dome. My limbs felt a pull in all directions, a pull to expand into the enormity of the space. I opened my mouth but no words would form. Like a butterfly, I flitted through a dictionary of superlatives but couldn't settle on any single one.

The tramp resumed his role as guide. "It's challenging when you first come to this space, these frequencies of energy, this architecture. Is it grand? Is it great? No, it simply IS... **I**-AM **S**-ervice."

The words 'I AM Service' floated before me. I reached out to cup them in my hands but they rearranged into the single word IS, evading capture."

"Attachment will never bring more purpose. You don't need to control it to experience it," whispered the tramp as he glanced past me. "Allow it to be. Allow the lovingness, the support and upliftment. Allow I AM. Onward and upward."

The words chattered as they spiralled around and around the dome chasing their own sound. I listened until they became dissolved in the grandeur of the dome.

I walked in the direction I thought the tramp had gone but as I rounded the corner, he wasn't there. I continued down a wide corridor into a courtyard garden with a central fountain and rooms laid out in a square around the central garden.

I called out, "I know you're in here somewhere. I'm going to count to ten and then I'm coming to find you. That was some disappearing act."

There was no reply to my attempt at hide and seek.

"I'm starting counting. One. Two. Three..."

I thought I heard a door slam off to the left. I decided to investigate.

I walked to the room in the left hand corner but when I turned the handle it was locked. I went to the next door, and the next, and the next until I'd been around the entire square. All the doors were locked. I felt rejected, locked out from my experience.

"What kind of guide are you, leaving me here without at least explaining the task at hand?"

I'd tried to remain in good humour, make a game of it, a bit of a joke, but... nothing. Absolutely nothing.

I retraced my steps, hunched over as if I were an upset eight year old walking home from school in the pouring rain. I'd just reached the entrance when I felt a tap on my shoulder.

"Looking for me?"

I turned around to face the tramp.

"Not any more," came my sharp reply. "What's the point of being a guide if you disappear on me like that? I don't understand. You're the one always talking about step by step. Do you call being left in the middle of the middle of nowhere easily digestible? There are a lot of steps between then and now and where were you? Nowhere in sight! You weren't even talking to me in my inner space. Plus there was no way out. And, for that matter, no way in. You tell me not to try and work things out, just be with them, but that's easy for you when you've got an ocean of expansion and hallowed halls of wisdom. How can I get in if I don't know where the entrance is?"

"Your response is your doorway in. Openness creates doorways in this Universe. Patience and centeredness are the tools that build your architecture of allowance. Work with them, not discard them in favour of ego habits at the first sign of change. Why did you choose to believe you were rejected? Why would the unending Love of the Universe shut you out?"

"Because you left me and then wouldn't answer when I asked you to rejoin me. That's fairly clear, I'd have thought." I was still holding on firmly to my conflict.

"Alas, it is not. Your perception is distorted with conflict. You are fighting your learning, not allowing it to flow to you. Guidance comes in many forms but these can change. It is not

Hide And Seek

to become attached to any single form. We can only show you the way, we cannot be there with you as some kind of guarantee of your progress. You were not left alone, we simply left you with yourself and the unlimited flow that you are growing into. It was ego that said you were rejected. It was ego that said you were unwelcome. You chose to come here. You were not forced, lead by the nose, or pushed. You chose. It is simply that now your ego is trying to talk you out of your choice to be with yourself, to come further than you ever have before; to create progress from what appears to be nothing, or less. If you can discern this to be true, you will see that it is your ego that is protesting against the chaos it faces."

As his words sunk in, I could form no more reactions.

"The inexplicable, the unknown and the unexpected. This was an experience of discernment, anchoring a foundation. That is why we allowed you your choices. You were dissolving the old structures of learning and only you can do this."

"I feel like I've let you down."

"That is your choice. But what about feeling learning; feeling the new tool of discernment? What about realising that you are capable of making your own choices and that guidance is present in and out of form and all you are required to do is look in your heart?"

"That all makes perfect sense, it's just these flash points when I'm handling a new layer of awareness. They catch me by surprise."

"So that you can catch the learning through your own choices. The inexplicable, the unknown and the unexpected are all great opportunities to use your newfound tools.

"Discernment is always in your heart. It ensures that your awareness expands in ways that maintain the unity within your mental, emotional and physical nature. Your mind only knows how to break things into parts until your ego sells them for scrap, devoid of purpose, in pieces of shattered unity. It is ego that says that separation has value and is worth fighting for.

You will not find your way through separation by employing more separation. You are required to feel unity; to rejoin unity; to allow yourself so that you can allow this separate aspect of yourself to reunite with your true self."

The tramp's words formed such an empowering flow of love that my eyes filled with tears. I knew he was supporting me but it was hard to let go of my conflict. I brushed away the flow of release, clearing a way to a reply.

"So you left me with myself, not on my own, to see how I'd cope with being with myself? A little bit of chaos in the middle of all my expectation... sounds awfully familiar."

"Indeed. Well done. You have returned to your I AM Centre." The tramp appeared satisfied with my observation.

"Sorry. Maybe it's a good idea if I repeat the bit in the courtyard; see it from another angle."

"Not necessary. You just did. In this case you don't have to reconnect physically, just observe your world differently."

I began to feel incredibly hot. "Is it me or has it suddenly become really hot?"

The tramp raised his eyebrows, showing me that, yet again, there was much more to this.

I continued to overheat. "Shall we go now? Get some fresh air?" I gasped.

"As you wish."

I was sure the entrance was some distance away but it was now just around the corner.

"You thought you would retrace your steps," observed the tramp, "but you have expanded beyond them already."

I stepped through the entrance but immediately wanted to go back inside as if there were some magnetic draw. Outside, the air, the space... it felt cool. Stepping momentarily inside, I felt a surge of heat. The tramp remained inside.

"That is astonishing... the difference between the building and the outside," I commented.

"Well discovered. Your sentience certainly is developing.

Acceleration can bring heat as your ego processes its resistance to your progress. Shall we move on?"

"Just one moment." I walked outside and back into the dome again. The effect was still there but it had lessened.

"A more obvious way of feeling how you are adapting," smiled the tramp as he overtook me, striding off down the path.

"Wait for me," I exclaimed, noticing a flash of purple as the tramp stepped through the entrance.

"Waiting is for those who have time," called the tramp as he continued on his way.

My perspective had changed again. As I caught up to the tramp, the path we'd come by seemed smaller, more familiar, as if I'd done the same walk a thousand times before.

My curiosity was growing as my fear was dissolving. Who was this tramp? I knew he could hear my thoughts but decided to bring them out into the open.

"Hey, you can hear my thoughts. So why don't I come out and ask you in words, the old fashioned way? Why are you wearing sacking? Surely you aren't wearing that because it's part of your true nature."

"That's for me to know and you to discover," he smiled mysteriously. "Do you listen to a man in finery because you are impressed with his attire or because you sense learning in his words?"

"Well, appearances can be deceptive, as you've said, so I suppose I listen because I sense learning, and what you're wearing really isn't that important. It's just... something doesn't add up."

"Indeed," replied the tramp. "But for many, that is not the case. For many, appearances are all they require to build an illusion of assumptions and judgments. For many, the appearance of value is all they require to attach value to something that is relatively worthless. But all in good time."

He halted. "Always best to let all preconceptions go," he added, recreating the sand sketch of the Curve Of Ascension with a single sweep of his cloak.

"But what does that look like? How do I just let preconceptions go? Do I dump them here?" I asked, pointing to the space between the two parallel lines.

"It's more a case of dunking them in your increasing Light and undergoing transmutation. Remember, you are not throwing yourself away nor leaving yourself behind, you are re-expressing yourself with less and less limitation. As you detach from your preconceptions, so they can become flexible and then rejoin you on your curve as support, as fuel and as learning. Oh, and your comments about my attire... I don't take them personally, you know," he grinned.

I felt a bubble of insecurity burst into a deep blush. Was I missing the point or simply being overwhelmed by it?

The tramp leaned forward as if encouraging me back into our tête-à-tête.

"Here's some guidance... Things are very often not what they appear and at some point you will be truly grateful for this."

"Are you paving my way?" I smiled sheepishly.

"Only you can do that. I am helping you sense the lie of the land... and the truth. There! A little joke within our landscape of learning. You don't want to put your valuable energy into building falsehood. Heartfelt truth is the foundation that you seek."

"What did you say? I couldn't quite hear you?" A sudden gust of wind had risen and, like a thief, had stolen his words.

"Just remember this last point." He paused, as if weighing the impact of his words. "Just because your experience is simple doesn't mean it lacks acceleration. All great leaps forward are simple. But if you complicate, if you look too long at the packaging rather than discovering the essence, you will deflect your learning and your guidance. You don't need to make things difficult. Simplicity is a unique style that never ever goes out of fashion."

The tramp winked, his wisdom stored knowingly in

the deep wrinkles of his face. Another gust of wind blew his unkempt hair into his mouth. "Nearly ready to depart," he sputtered as dust and hair swirled around his face.

"What did you say? I can't hear you?"

I was trying to speak louder but my efforts appeared to have no effect. The tramp's words were being swallowed up in the darkening landscape as a dust devil encircled us. I surrendered to trust, knowing in my heart that it was the tool that would guide me to my next beginning.

By Invitation Only

All was calm as I opened my eyes to the dimly lit room. A cool evening breeze was flowing through the half-open kitchen window. Guidance, like my feline guest, seemed to have dissolved as my initiation was completed and I returned to my physical dimension. My attention had moved on to the demanding rumbles of an empty stomach and the wonderful aromas of roasting vegetables and freshly baked delights that were wafting from the third floor through the open window.

"God, that smells good," I muttered as I moved over towards the fridge, hoping that there'd be something equally delicious inside.

There wasn't. But a sudden flash of inspiration suggested a ready made solution. Why don't you knock on 3A's door and say 'That smells really good. Do you mind if I invite myself in?' This idea was appealing for a split second, but then the courage to follow through was extinguished by a shower of ego objections.

"You can't do that," ego said. "You can't just invite yourself to someone's home because you're too lazy to cook. Who do you think you are? They won't want your presumption. It's rude. You're just using them."

"Judgment isn't very nurturing," my Higher Self responded, ignoring the obvious ego interference. "Why not enjoy the smell? Could be tasty! Why not go up and introduce yourself? Make some new friends."

"Because you don't do that sort of thing," I replied out loud, my ego reacting to another attempt to dilute my separateness.

"What sort of thing?" probed my Higher Self, seizing the opportunity to clarify my resistance.

"Ask for food from complete strangers. That sort of thing! Well, not unless you're starving, that is."

"But you are," continued my guidance.

"You've got a point there. But that makes me feel really uncomfortable. I don't like to impose on people. If you're serious—which I think you might be—then that's completely out of the question."

I opened the fridge door again just to see if anything had changed in the last ten seconds. It hadn't.

"What is out of the question? Asking for food or talking to complete strangers?"

Ego was becoming increasingly cornered. "Both, Higher Self! Look, I've only recently graduated from hermitdom to antisocialite so don't rush me."

"Just a spiral of chaos waiting to take you to the next level. We could never push you. It's your ego pushing you around in that limited space called your mind."

I knew my Higher Self was being supportive but my conditioning was still more persuasive.

"The answer is no. I'll go out and get something from the supermarket," I said, preparing to leave. "I've tuned out," I mouthed to My Higher Self, in case there were any more suggestions about 3A.

I couldn't believe how demanding my Higher Self appeared to be. But at the same time, I knew that couldn't be the case. Heart never forced, only ego would demand and force. Perhaps my Higher Self was being fuelled by chaos oxygen boosters or a hidden acceleration I couldn't detect.

By Invitation Only

"You're thinking again... analysing your way out of unity," whispered my Higher Self.

"I thought I turned your frequency off," I grumbled, preparing to lock the door.

"Not mine," replied my Higher Self. "I AM is still loud and clear... If you choose to listen, that is."

I paused with the key in the lock as a downpour of realisation washed away my resistance.

"You sound different," I began.

"In what way?" came the reply.

"Perhaps it's more a combination of sounding different and feeling different. The sense of you is much more present. You are glowing more brightly, as if you've had an upgrade or there's been some kind of shift. You aren't my Higher Self, are you?"

"Not exactly, no. Your Higher Self combines in this frequency, in this unity, but it isn't exclusively Higher Self," added the voice, selecting the words carefully.

"Me and my assumptions. I automatically assumed it was my Higher Self because the communication came from heart and I was back in physicality. Good old assumption! It's obviously still working in this world."

"It started here. It's an ego tool," added the voice.

"You've got me there. But here's a question for you... If you aren't my Higher Self, who are you? Who sent you and what have you done with my Higher Self?" I laughed.

My joke was followed by a long pause, then a sense of anticipation.

"Well?" insisted my curiosity.

"This is the tramp you were just talking to. Your Higher Self is still here and now, just not doing the talking. And you sent for me. Do you remember? The one in the cloak with a flash of purple?"

A tumble of visions spiralled through me, each stopping just long enough to recognise one part. First an expression, then a diagram, then a grand domed building. I pieced the images together and felt an enormous rush of euphoria throughout my body.

"Yes, now I remember you. We were in that huge dome and then we disappeared in that spiralling wind."

I hesitated with my door lock, looking to my side as if talking to a real person.

"But I thought you couldn't come here into this world. Only my Higher Self can come here."

"Says who?" replied the tramp.

I tried to think of the guidelines my Higher Self and I had once discussed—the job description—but I was blank.

"I seem to have misplaced the terms and conditions of my Higher Self's employment at the moment," I replied pompously, "but that doesn't really matter now, does it?"

"Indeed. This Now is very different. Your inner truth has expanded and so have the guidelines. We all share the teaching. It's a joint effort."

"So do you come in unconditional love and wisdom and to shed new Light on my densely populated conditioning?"

"I do," said the tramp, taking his pledge very seriously.

"And can you help me recycle limited beliefs and create wisdom?"

"I can."

"And my Higher Self let you in?"

"You did invite me," replied the tramp, teetering on my doorstep waiting to be let in as I fumbled with my open-heartedness.

"Okay, come on in."

I decided to continue this important breakthrough in my trusted armchair but as I tried to turn the key in the lock it wouldn't budge. I threw my hands up in the air as I realised the ridiculousness of my situation.

"Why am I talking to a tramp that lives in my heart while standing outside my flat trying to get to my armchair?"

I suddenly felt embarrassed and a need to babble my way out of how I was feeling. The tramp, on the other hand, didn't seem the slightest bit phased.

I resumed my conversation with thin air. "It's quite simple; nothing flash, you understand... my... flat, I mean. But it is home," I continued, as if filling time while I tried to get the key to work. "And it has an armchair. It's an armchair of alchemy, actually."

I imagined the tramp sitting down in front of me, just as Mrs Daley had. "We could have some light refreshment. Emphasis on the light," I joked. "Come to think of it, it'd probably be invisible because there isn't much in the fridge. But you're used to that—no form. Doesn't necessarily mean no energy, right?"

"Indeed. Your invitation is greatly appreciated but perhaps another time," replied the tramp. "Your heart space could do with refreshment too. Keeping all your selves in balance is a full time job, you know."

My stomach began to grumble again.

The main door opened and closed behind me but I was too busy talking to thin air to look.

"Okay, point taken. Stick to my original plan. Go and get something to eat. Do you want to come along?"

"Why not?" replied the tramp.

A couple I'd not seen before walked past me to the lift. I felt nervous, standing with the key in my own front door talking to thin air for no apparent reason. I should do something normal, logical, like locking the door. My Higher Self joined the tramp. They were now behaving as though they were rolling around laughing.

"Do something normal?" they laughed. "Instead of talk to us? We can see it all now... the headline: *Middle aged author seen talking to imaginary friends on the doorstep of his creative crisis.*"

"Alright, alright. I'm the one being ridiculous. And

you're the ones who make my life so fulfilling. Dare I say, normal."

They both appeared to be laughing so much that my comment was immediately absorbed in the frivolity.

"What's wrong with us, anyway? Don't you want to be seen with us?"

"Oh, ha, ha! I'm hardly worried about being seen with you two because... well, you're invisible!"

"We are," they howled, still crying with laughter.

"And are you going to keep laughing at my expense?"

"Touchy, touchy!" they replied in unison. "There's no need to get attached. We're laughing at your credit."

"So, I'm actually getting paid to be this?" I threw my hand up in a gesture of frustration as I gave up on my key.

"Put it this way, our relationship certainly helps you get the credit you deserve."

"Good. So, what about this key? How about some creative cooperation? I'll embrace ease and flow and you help me with the key...?"

I stopped mid-sentence. A wave of energy moved through me, fizzing to my finger tips.

"Joy is always the key," I heard the tramp say. "Just need to keep your heart open. Now try the key."

It worked perfectly. I locked the door and began walking towards the main door. Jokingly chastising my Higher Self.

"You just wait til I get hold of you, Higher Self... agreeing to things when I'm asleep, even unconscious," I joked, looking up as if my Higher Self were circling over head.

"Really, if you want to know the truth..."

"Is that you tramp?" I was beginning to distinguish between the two energies.

"Yes it is. The truth is... when you're asleep you're awake and when you're awake you're asleep."

"Thank you so much for clearing that up! It all makes perfect sense now!"

I rolled my eyes back and began to laugh again. The joy was spilling out in all directions. "But perhaps I'm beginning to understand why I often feel like I've been working all night instead of sleeping!"

"Indeed. But all is nourishing. And now it is time to enjoy your meal. You've got the key now. Until our next meeting..."

And with a swish of purple, the tramp was gone.

"Well that was brief." I looked around. "Where did he go, Higher Self? The tramp is never short of words."

"Quite. He is not short of communications. But responding with sensitivity is what is important."

"What? Disappearing like that can be described as sensitive?" I asked, confused.

"Yes." Higher Self became quite serious. "Flow comes because there is space. Such energy needs to make space, as it were, so you will have a period of adaptation."

"So in brief, that means there wasn't enough room for both of you in my heart room?" My conditioning wanted to see how well I was doing.

"Not really," said a quiet voice. "We never leave, just move forward and back. Think of it as into range and then out of it again. All guidance is constant, only we aren't talking to you all the time. Probably just as well."

"And your hints help me de-clutter? Recycle a few attachments and make space within me?"

"Correct. And balance is very important so that the rate of recycling is manageable. The tramp has told you about forcing your process."

"Yep. No going out of my mind."

"No. That would not be of service. Now, what about the task at hand... food?"

"Yes, Higher Self, food."

"There's always 3A, remember!"

"Not that again! I'm not listening!" I said, pretending to put my fingers in my ears.

Armchair Alchemist

"Okay. If you're not curious about upstairs yet," said my Higher Self engagingly, "what do you think about the tramp?"

"He caught me and we by surprise. I didn't know he was allowed here."

"Any guidance that is unconditionally loving and expansive can be in the heart architecture, it just depends on where you are in your process. Your heart room isn't exactly what it used to be. It's expanded to accommodate your growing perspectives. You've built a few extensions; sent out a few invitations. It's all part of your Light grid. I just did as you asked and so now you're going to get more visitors. That'll give you a chance to recycle that antisocialite into a social Light! And quite a potent visitor to start with."

"I dare say his teachings are very stimulating and wise, but how can a tramp be impressive?"

"But that wasn't just any old tramp," replied my Higher Self.

"Well if you mean the tramp I met in the desert, the one who drew all those diagrams, taught me about this ascension I'm on, this process of returning to balance, then... yes, it was. I even saw purple coming out from under his sackcloth. It's definitely him. But what puzzles me is, if the greater Universe is so expansive, why did it send a tramp to speak to me? If I'm a practicing alchemist then surely I deserve more than that?"

Ego was gaining momentum.

My Higher Self went straight for the tool of detachment. "Better guidance than you got this afternoon is impossible."

I was taken aback. "I'm jumping from assumption to conclusion again, aren't I?"

"Yes."

"That wasn't really a tramp, was it? Once a tramp isn't always a tramp?"

"Your new guide was a tramp for a very good reason. But no, that is not his most recognisable form. Guidance is all around and is always available if you are able to see it. There isn't anything better than what is right before you, irrespective of what your ego tells you. Ego always wants more, different, complicated. Ego always wants something separate so it can avoid looking at itself. And yes, you're correct about the tramp—purple is his signature colour."

"Okay, Higher Self. Preparing to feel very, very foolish... can you fill in the blank, please? Once a tramp, always a..."

"Always The Merlin."

"Merlin? You mean THE Merlin? Of King Arthur fame? Knights of The Round Table? Wizardry and alchemy?" Ego was beginning to crush me with my lack of appreciation.

"That's him. There have been many Merlins in the mystery and mastery traditions but this is the great soul that achieved ascension in the lifetime when he was known as The Merlin."

"Well I certainly picked the right master to impress. Why didn't you get out the red carpet?!"

"Listening and opening your heart as wide as you can is all the welcome that is required."

"But why didn't you tell me?" I pleaded, trying to push some of my acute embarrassment onto my Higher Self.

"Not my job. It's all in the discovery. You see, I'm just the introduction service, helping you make room. No point telling you in advance. Where's the surprise in that? And more importantly, where's the learning?"

My Higher Self fell silent.

"But why not? I'm confused. You want to help me but when a great master of alchemy comes to call, you don't announce him. You don't even say 'Pssst! Pay attention! Incoming master with words of wisdom.'"

"If it had been so, then you wouldn't have believed me. Your mind would have taken over again. You would have put one line and one more line together and, before you knew it, you would have boxed yourself in with assumptions from your limited logic, rather than allowing the meeting without judgments, expectations and limitations. It's one of many meetings that comes via chaos so you can process your necessary disturbance. You caught your ego off guard so you could open your heart wider than ever before. Perhaps not the most gracious of realisations but a realisation nonetheless. Remember, guidance never judges; it serves unconditionally, supporting the reclamation of your first nature."

"Whatever it takes?"

"It is always a joy. So, yes... whatever it takes. One choice to trust dismantles the most complicated mazes of self doubt. One joyous response dismantles many attachments to pain."

"So what's important is that I opened my heart when it counted? I've just got to keep that up?"

"Absolutely. When your natural reaction is to repel your world, then... stop, rebalance and choose an alternative."

"And when guidance says something that my mind finds completely idiotic, then listen and give it a chance to soak in?"

"Definitely. Just because you take it to your heart doesn't mean you will necessarily choose it. But to be in allowance is so important in your return to full awareness."

"So what's the purple related to?"

I suddenly saw a flash out of the corner of my eye as if the former tramp that I now knew as The Merlin was keeping in touch with purple light.

"It's the vibration of change; the combination of form, which is red, and flow, which is blue. Red plus blue creates purple. Purple creates change in form," replied my Higher Self.

"So, The Merlin helps with change?"

"Yes. Changing your mind, changing your imbalances, changing your perspectives. You name it, he can help you change it. He is the master of the alchemy of change. For example, through your experiences today you have learnt that love continues whether you are in company or in your own company. Just because one relationship changes does not mean you are lesser because of the change. Just because you are more self loving does not mean you are more selfish. Just because your ego assumes doesn't make it helpful, right or a guarantee of your security. Your experience is up to you; what you choose and what you choose to learn from what you create. The Merlin will always inspire learning and help you find the gems of wisdom along the path of alchemy. That is your path of ascension."

"Fine. Seek and I shall find. But what if I'm being fearful or resistant?" I probed.

"Then The Merlin can help you see ways to change your fear into fuel; to recycle those obstacles that your ego thinks are so valuable and lay them down in front of you as steps on your path of progress."

"So tell me, how can I invite such a wondrous being into my... you know... my inner space—call it my inner architecture—and not recognise him? Seems like I've failed the test." Ego was creeping back into our dialogue.

"The truth of your experience is that you achieved it. It's just that your mind is trying to judge your experience, destabilise your newfound unity. The greatest test was to be with your guest, to allow the experience. Just being in that greatly expanded awareness is an achievement. It takes a lot of allowance. There is cause for celebration, not criticism."

"Thanks. I think there's a compliment in there somewhere!" I was becoming less sensitive.

"You are learning to let the wisdom come into your world, even if you don't know it. Many of your great initiations happen without you being conscious of them. As you are finding out, knowing is not necessarily an advantage. The *direction* or the *form* your experience comes in doesn't really matter, but there will be times when a bit of fancy dress can fool your ego long enough to give you that heart start that you require. No heads up, no preconceptions, no judgments, just discerning how you feel. A bit of chaos tunnelling a way through attachment."

"It's time to move on, Higher Self."

"And so it is."

My stomach's intermittent grumbles had escalated into protesting rumbles.

"So, Higher Self... How about I go shopping and cook up a great night in? What do you say?"

"Sounds fabulous. I'll bring the sparkling conversation and you can do the rest."

"Oh, you're too kind!"

"Not to mention modest!"

As I stepped out into the early evening rush hour, I could sense a thousand emotions being let loose at the end of the working day. People surged into entrances and scattered out of exits. I wondered how many journeyed with inner companions. Did they invite in alternatives that kept them from straying into the scarcities and pressures of so-called civilised living? I hoped there were thousands developing their relationship with guidance and lighting their way from the inside out.

Critical Observations

The next day, I woke before my alarm feeling refreshed and ready to write more. Walking into the kitchen, I heard the newspaper land through my door.

"Gosh, I must be up early," I thought.

I put the kettle on, put two slices of bread in the toaster and collected the newspaper in what appeared to be one fluid movement.

"Well, carpe diem," I smiled as I opened the newspaper. "Never thought I'd remember that old school motto but I do, and I am seizing the day!"

The headlines were grey with the tragedy of conflict. I turned quickly to the arts, entertainment and review pages.

"What's new on the book front?" I pondered, and came

face to face with a review of my recently published book. The opening paragraph read:

"Although a welcome departure from the author's previous style, this novel falls short of arriving anywhere. It is puzzling that such an intellectual zealot could be in touch with the spiritual values of today. Clearly lacking a defined audience, the story meanders in and out of a dreary daydream without demonstrating the alchemical wisdoms for which some have acclaimed it." (A half star)

I was winded.

"Forget about seize the day, that's cease the day! Or has it just been blown to smithereens completely?"

I was both sad and angry. I'd never had much time for critics, much less read their comments, but today was entirely different. I sat back in my chair, aghast. I could sense my Higher Self on the edges of my shock.

"It's only an opinion," began my Higher Self. "Everyone is entitled to an opinion."

"I know that's the standard line, but how do people write such things? What motivates them to rush in and shoot you down? How is innovation going to live if it has nowhere to become understood? Where's the allowance in this?" I shook the paper with frustration.

My Higher Self remained centered as ego tried to compromise my fragile inner balance.

"There is always space for innovation. It flows into the heart, which it is designed for. Some sense it not, others absorb it easily. Nothing more, nothing less. Just like guidance, your work simply IS, irrespective of how others perceive it. They cannot know your heart, nor can they know your truth. Your experience is designed for you, by you, so that you may learn about your unlimited nature.

"You know there isn't one truth but rather an ever-expanding truth that is unique to all. Each soul can look at truth from a completely different perspective, and through the heart or mind. The more love is in it, perhaps the more unified it might appear, the more in common. But, like anything in this Universe, it is always expanding. This is why you can be loved and hated simultaneously, and why those who reject can also learn to allow."

"But why do these types of events come just when you feel you're on a roll? Just when you're getting going?"

"Because they are here to provide acceleration."

"But how can something so damning create acceleration? If I didn't have you to talk to, I'd probably fall head first into a self pity nose dive."

"Head first?" my Higher Self offered a mini pun. "Get it? Head first?"

I didn't respond.

My Higher Self steered our discussion in another direction. "But you know that's not your truth, it's your conditioning talking... ego's excuse for truth."

"I know, I know. But sometimes it's easier to feel like a victim, to feel that these kinds of reviews are unfair. When you put so much of your heart and soul into a brave new direction, how can people dismantle it in just one paragraph?"

"They can't. Only ego can undermine your progress. Only ego can say you have slammed head first into a brick wall of rejection. And you can choose to believe that if you wish."

"This is one of those times when what I know in theory isn't matching up with what I feel," I groaned.

"Rather, the reverse," said my Higher Self. "What ego knows isn't matching up to what you feel in your heart. You are in transmutation. Give yourself space to adapt."

My Higher Self paused as if helping me reorganise my consciousness, then continued.

"Taking the external authority personally is one of the oldest ego devices to deflate your courage and limit your creativity. Ego takes that part of yourself that doesn't believe in you, that wants to beat you up, and cultivates your victimhood with it. As you become more Light, these parts of ego become unstuck and can be dissolved. This is a form of necessary disturbance.

"To complete the transmutation, you are required to remain centred and let these attachments be recycled into Light. If you reattach to them by taking the change personally then your transmutation could be much more difficult. Remember, The Merlin said there would be acceleration, and in acceleration there is always an opportunity for rapid change."

"No, I don't remember that. It must've sped right past me." I hesitated. The hint of a smile flashed across my face, stopping my heart door closing.

"That's a start—a mini joke in the midst of your transmutation," observed my Higher Self.

I was beginning to feel more stable. "Please continue. I want to understand how I can change this state, embrace the alchemy of which my reviewer thinks I'm incapable."

"Alright, hold your horses! There's no need to speed off into imbalance. Just settle in your centre and then we can create the change together."

I relaxed into my chair, let the newspaper drop... and put my cup at my feet. "Okay, I'm all ears."

The energy shifted in the room and my Higher Self adopted the reassuring tone of a benevolent uncle. "Once upon a time there were limited truths that you believed in. Now, many of those have been melted down to fuel your overhaul of truth. What was true yesterday is certainly not true today, and so on. Periods of acceleration such as these are to help you learn that you are required to maintain your centre when you move from one creation phase to the next. These experiences support you in learning just that. They help you balance and, in times of change, reach for balance instead of your old conditioning which is to take refuge in ego and go running back to limitation.

"You are returning to your heart, or remaining within it, so that recycling of these old beliefs and truths can flow smoothly. If the method in your current madness is truly unfulfilling then it will be reflected to you, and you will create an alternative. Nothing is set in stone but you need to be self disciplined so that you can keep expanding your I AM Presence. Self discipline in this case means choosing expansion instead of disappointment."

My gloomy perspective was clearing. "So, what you're saying is, if I'm kidding myself and the reviewer is actually correct about my book then it'd be reflected in my heart and my outside world?"

"Yes. So firstly, what does your heart tell you?"

"My heart says this book is definitely different to what I've done before. It's making a difference, which is what I intended."

"So, is your book getting reviews like this all the time? And, more importantly, do the people you wrote it for find it of service, of inspiration?"

My Higher Self was carefully leading me through my ego's objections.

"I suppose this took me by surprise because it's the first caustic review I've had. And in my outside world, the reflection is that it's selling better than many of my other books. So someone must be buying it!"

"So why believe this review? Why get caught up with your ego?"

"Because I want to doubt myself? I want to beat myself up and I found someone to do it for me?" My reply flowed with surprising ease.

"Exactly. And perhaps, since this is a meeting of alternatives, it's a question of new thought being misunderstood; allowance being temporarily obscured in this acceleration.

"Ego doesn't like surprises unless it has manufactured them itself. Then of course everything is under control and there is no real surprise. Ego thinks it knows it all so, when it encounters something new, it wants to quell a potential rebellion of self enquiry by labelling the new as wrong, unable to fit in, irrelevant or impossible.

"The vibration of innovation, you understand, doesn't come from your world. It can't. Expansion can only come from the unlimited, from the chaos that you are getting to know quite well."

I began to take command of my Higher Self's teaching. "So something new is simply a spiral of chaos. And instead of the ego embracing the change, it tries to repulse it or to refocus onto me what it doesn't like, trying to make me feel it's injustice."

"Yes. Ego can't control heart and heart is your connection to the unlimited Universe. So ego tries to wound you, urge you to dismantle your heart architecture because heart isn't sheltering you, it isn't protecting you from the unknown. But you know anyway that your heart room wasn't built to hide you, it was built to support you and help you expand.

"So you are feeling angry or depressed because your ego's expectations are not being met. Ego is trying to hold onto self doubt, denial and imbalance so it can keep you under control. But if you hold your centre, ego can't hijack that energy. You won't believe the **E**-xternal **G**-overning **O**-rder because you will stay in your heart and believe in yourself."

"Is that what you call ego? External Governing Order?"

"Yes. It reminds you how ego tries to project your power outside of yourself so you cannot use it. It reminds you how it is so easy to believe in form because you are surrounded by it, rather than believe in your inner truth and your heart which is the real architect of the forms that surround you."

"Then the less I believe in ego, the more I'll create from heart and my world will reflect balance, love and abundance?"

"Correct. Ego will get out of your way. It will stop standing between you and what you really want to create. Ego will stop reinforcing what it sees as impossible and you will see the results of your personal change—your personal alchemies of change.

"So do not take ego personally. If you believe your ego rather than your heart then you will see this situation as harming you and destructive. Then you undermine your healing."

"So if I go back through what we've discussed, the most balanced way to look at this critique is to say the reviewer isn't wrong, ego isn't wrong to react, and I'm not wrong to believe in the book. They're all possible perceptions. I am choosing to allow the review but I don't agree with it. Also, I am choosing not to let my ego affect my ability to create nor my internal balance. Then I can recycle the aspects of ego that this situation has stirred up."

"Precisely. There is nothing wrong with your experience and there is always learning to stimulate expansion."

"There's definitely a part of me that'd love to make this relatively simple change into a fight or a drama, but that's just heaping attachment onto attachment and making my ego stronger, isn't it?"

"It is. But you *can* choose to behave differently, and you are. When you are in your heart, CAN becomes **C**-onscious **A**-ction **N**-ow. When you're letting ego take over, CAN becomes **C**-onflicting **A**-ction **N**-ow."

"So," I smiled, "it's no contest then. Conscious Action Now is my chosen path forward. Into my cauldron of transmutation goes, number one, my reaction to ego; number two, the aspect of ego I'm recycling which is 'taking it personally'; and three, a dash of purple for good measure to confirm my commitment to change."

I sat quietly, as if allowing it all to simmer. "Bubble, bubble, no toil nor trouble. Let's pour this recycled energy into the title of my next chapter. What about *Conscious Change*?"

Momentary Learning

I was astonished how easily my next five chapters materialised on the page. My Higher Self seemed to be either standing by or writing with me, I couldn't tell which. The thought of lunch had just appeared when the phone rang.

"Hello?" I said, managing to retrieve my phone before it skipped under my chair.

"It's Andrew, your long-time-no-see friend who only rings you when there's something really right or really wrong. Or, of course, there's always the times when I want something."

"Oooh yes... If I stretch back into the dim and distant past, I think I can just about get a fix on you. So tell me, refound friend... to what do I owe this pleasure? Which polarity are you hanging out in? The good, the bad or the really desperate?"

"Guess. I'll give you a hint. Where do you think I'm standing now?" Andrew was delighting in his trail of hints.

"Now let me see... North face of the Eiger?"

"No, not quite as cold as that."

"What about the Empire State Building?"

"Getting warmer. I do believe your telepathic skills are improving. It's high... and yes, it's man made... A roll on the drums please...! It's the 19th floor, actually."

"Not *the* 19th floor!? That can only mean one thing... And without further ado, I give you Andrew, Editor in Chief! Congratulations!"

"Thanks," replied Andrew, his response obviously lacking enthusiasm.

"Okay... That doesn't sound like the I've-done-it-and-got-the-corner-office-and-I'm-on-cloud-nine kind of thanks. What's the matter?" I was curious that, after all these years climbing the corporate ladder, Andrew didn't seem able to admire the view.

"You know me too well. But I can't really talk now," he replied, suddenly distracted and hurrying down a corridor of urgent priorities. "What about in a couple of hours? Say, a late lunch around three?"

"Fine. Where?"

"Whatever's easiest for you."

"What about that old Italian place down towards Charing Cross?"

"Paulo's?"

"That's the one. It has those old booths and you've got to order by numbers because no one speaks English."

"Right. I know the place. See you there at three," he said hurriedly, and hung up.

I looked at the clock. It was now 1:15 p.m. and I was starving. "Time to make a snack, Higher Self. There's no way my stomach will cope without any food until three o'clock. I wonder what Andrew wants to talk about..."

I stopped in the middle of my own question. "But maybe you know already?"

My Higher Self didn't respond.

"Go on, tell me what Andrew wants."

"That is not part of my job description," came a rather formal response.

"What do you mean?"

"I am here to support you in your journey and processing. I'm not here to snoop."

"I'm not asking you to check up on him, I'm just curious about why he called."

"So you are checking up on him."

"Okay, I suppose you're right. I want to know in advance about something instead of waiting until the Now space that is relevant. But tell me, can you see the future?"

"Since there is no linear time in I AM, how would we be able to see the future?"

"Fair comment. So what exactly do you see while you're guiding me?"

"Guidance is part of a flow. It's your mind that wants

Momentary Learning

to see some guaranteed outcome or right answer. Guidance feels; senses. We sense how you are embracing alternatives, how much of your ego is still controlling your Light nature, and how you are adapting to change. We do not see your form, nor are we spying on you or checking up on you. We sense the flow that is your energy. We help you balance and build energetic structure within which you may learn and expand into your I AM Presence. We encourage you to understand the intention behind your choices and what you are experiencing. So in keeping with the spirit of this flow, what is the intention behind your meeting with the soul known as Andrew?"

"Well, the conversation wasn't that clear... but I suppose it's to help him, if I can."

"So intellectual fascination wouldn't have anything to do with it?"

"You've got me there. You're saying I want to know what's going to happen instead of investing in what's, as I'd see it, going to be created. I'm checking on the destination instead of keeping my eye on my path."

"Well observed. It is not necessary to check on the flow. The flow simply IS. But it is helpful to check on ego from time to time, just to see how expanded you really are. Your experience is just like your guidance—a function of the flow. If you relied on your mind to think that it will turn out well then we would not be having this conversation because you would still be attached to the goings on of your limited world. You understand in your heart, in your true knowingness, that there is a lot more to each moment that you spend in your world and that there are many ways you can spend those moments," replied my Higher Self, appearing to step back a little.

"Okay, I understand your point."

"It's more a question of making a unity," my Higher Self continued. "To explore the expanse of any moment is to find that everything is linked to intention and learning. And, of course, that it all works out. You create your learning, and the better you understand the reflections of your learning, the more complete your world is until your creative intentions are perfectly reflected back to you. When you are in unity with your world, you don't want to control it because it is a part of you. Points are brittle, fixed and inflexible. Unities just keep on expanding. Every phase of learning has a natural beginning and end. It can be experienced within one moment and also spread across many. Enjoy your reflections. Be with them in unity. They will serve you well." And with that, my Higher Self appeared to end transmission.

"Are you still there?" I wondered if I was being tested. But there was no reply, only the hint of a nod.

I looked at the kitchen. It was a chaos of dirty dishes.

"Make toast, tidy up and get to Andrew by three... I'd better hurry up. Let's see how all this works out, Higher Self."

The Creation Code

I arrived at the Italian restaurant after a long wait at the bus stop. It was ten past three but there was no sign of Andrew and the place was preparing to close. It was starting to rain so I huddled under the shop front next door and waited. Quarter past came and went. I was just about to call when I felt a tap on my shoulder.

"Surprise! I'm late!"

"That's no surprise," I smiled, hugging my friend of more years than I cared to remember. "Just like three o'clock, the Italian has also come and gone, so where do you want to go?"

"What about the National?"

"The portrait gallery?" Now I really was surprised. "Don't tell me you've become so famous they've painted your portrait."

"No," he smiled, "but perhaps it's about time I took a look at myself. An honest look. And the one person I could always rely on for that was you."

We hurried across Trafalgar Square and walked through the entrance of grand-and-grey just before the rain began in earnest.

"Perfect timing," said Andrew as we got a snack and drew up our chairs near the window and watched the rain rebound off the pavement.

"So what's up?" I began. "Or should I say, you're up but you're also down?"

"Yep. That's a pretty accurate assessment."

The confident, always-charming Andrew had evaporated. Suddenly he was all washed out. No brave faces or blustering projections.

"I've been Editor in Chief for six months now and I don't think I can take it much more."

I was stunned. Andrew seemed genuinely distressed, almost at the point of breaking down.

"I worked so hard to get to where I am," he continued, "and it just isn't what I expected."

"Does that mean it's not what you thought it would be? Or all of it just isn't any fun any more?"

"Perhaps both," he mused. "I've tried to work it out but nothing adds up. Plus, I don't get time to know what I think because I'm always working or commuting to work or doing something related to work. I've always enjoyed being busy, but not like this."

"Good."

"What do you mean, good?! I'm meant to be working this out and you're meant to be feeling sorry for me."

"Am I? Or is that just what your mind thinks I should be doing?"

Andrew's face went blank.

"You wanted honesty and you can't find answers in your mind so we'll have to go further afield. It's good you've decided to span your honesty gap; the one that opens up between what we really want in our heart of hearts and what we think we should want. Now you're so near to grinding to a halt, hopefully there'll be less resistance."

"But I don't have the energy to resist. I'm just numb, blank. I don't know what I think. How can I get an answer?"

Andrew sounded desperate. "It's no joke!" he insisted. "I really have a hard time dragging myself out of bed in the mornings." His arms slid down the table and he hunched over with his head in his hands.

I silently called upon my Higher Self so that together we could shed some light on Andrew's situation.

"First, tell me how you feel," I suggested.

"I feel knackered and depressed. I've spent so long doing this life and now I've climbed what appeared to be an impossible mountain, I don't even want to stay there. All that surrounds me is fog; no view at all. There doesn't appear to be anything to see. I don't have that sense of achievement that I thought I'd have—king of the castle, ruler of all I survey. I've even lost track of what went into getting there. And there's days when I'm more worried about losing what I've got than whether I'm enjoying it. Have I wasted fifteen years of my life?" He appeared genuinely worried.

"No, I don't believe you've wasted your time at all. But what you have done is pour all your experiences—the wisdom and tools you've gained in the past fifteen years—into one thing, one single target. You've kept yourself so focused that you've lost sight of what you really feel. Strive and drive has replaced balance and joy. I think we can safely say, Andrew, you've got a nasty case of *think-style*." I kept a straight face.

"Of what?" Andrew was completely perplexed, taking me very seriously. "Is this some new disorder I haven't heard of? They're always coming up with new ailments and in my state I could easily have whatever this *think-style* is."

"Andrew, I'm joking! I'm just saying you've got a think-style rather than a lifestyle."

He feigned hitting his head against the table. "Stupidity

alert! Now I get it," he said. "You mean I *think* I'm living but really I'm just forcing myself into oblivion so I can't enjoy anything."

"Yes, something like that. Logic might say you've got the things that make a lifestyle but your problem is that you aren't living it, you just think you are."

"So how am I going to turn this think-style into a somewhere-decent lifestyle?"

"Drive your strive in another direction."

"But there isn't anywhere else left. When you're at the top, there's nowhere else to go apart from down."

"Oh but there is. You've been stuck on your single track for so long, your 'got-to-be-editor, got-to-be-editor' ego babble makes you think that's the only road you've got available. It's one of the roads, but there are lots of alternatives. You don't have to stay where you are, ploughing onwards, and yourself into the ground. This isn't a question of success at any cost versus failure and complete loss. Your ego has managed to polarise your perspective. You can't think of anything else because your vision has been choked by all-or-nothing."

"Okay. So how do I stop swinging from one extreme to another and widen this single track mind?"

"Trust yourself enough to feel, to sense what's deeply meaningful to you. Trust is the bridge between old awareness and new awareness. Get out of your one track mind and rejoin your heart. Just because you've only been working with your mind doesn't mean you can't cooperate with your heart. You don't exactly appear to be ecstatic now, so what have you got to lose?"

"Nothing."

"Great. So that's already widened your one lane into two!"

He hesitated as if trying to put his happy-façade back on but all he achieved was hangdog guilt. "Oh, this is no conversation to have after not seeing you for two years. I feel bad. I shouldn't be burdening you with the meaning of life, the Universe and everything."

"Hey, you aren't. It's your life. I'm just here to listen; make some observations."

"But all I've done is talk about me and what I think I don't have. So now you've told me what you think I really do have, I suppose the polite thing to do would be to ask about you. So, how's your next book going?" Andrew was straddling the fine line between humour and sarcasm.

"Are you really interested or just politely going off on a tangent so you can stop feeling what you're feeling right now? Since when have you ever really done the polite thing? You don't need to tough it out for me."

"I didn't mean to sound cynical, I'm a genuinely interested punter. Really. I read the last one; thought it was you all grown up but with childlike overtones. I really enjoyed it. Got me thinking. You were quite courageous. I realise that now. It caused quite a stir. I saw the review in the Telegraph. Ouch! I think he was trying to stab you with his pen, not write a review."

"Yeah, well he's entitled to his opinion."

"Yeah, and that's the standard line. But you don't really think that, do you? Secretly, you want him to be exposed for the outmoded miserable elitist that he really is, right?"

"Not at all. Secretly and openly, I don't want that. I believe that anyone and everyone can write what they like. That doesn't make it right or wrong, just a perception of their world. It's their angle. As we know only too well, everyone's got an angle. And what I've learnt is to stay in my centre. Then I can see what's really going on."

"With a bit of help from those eyes in the back of your head, right?" replied Andrew, laughing. "This is all a bit too spiritual for me. Come on! Didn't it annoy you? Just a little bit?"

"Yes okay, I admit, in a way it did. I didn't like the review but that doesn't mean I'm going to kill the bloke, it's just that I prefer not to believe in what he wrote. You can't believe everything you read, right? Never let the facts get in the way of a good story!"

"Ha ha! Spoken like a true member of the press. But do you know, this could actually work in your favour. It could set you up as some weird cult writer that *normal* critics despise because secretly they wish they were you. Not to mention the publicity you'd get from not being popular, which of course in turn makes you popular."

"I think you've summed it up well, just like you always did as a journalism student. Good old Andrew, always interested in chain reactions."

"So... you haven't answered my question. How's the book going?" He was determined to get to my answer.

"Well... it's definitely going. I finished a burst of five chapters in the last couple of days. Where it's going is another matter. Still, it's started flowing and that's definitely how I mean to go on."

"Are you travelling again? Like you did in the last novel?"

"Yes and no. You'll have to read it when it's finished."

"Can I reserve a reviewer's copy now, please?" he asked, holding up his hand like a child requesting something during a primary school lesson.

"No. You can go and buy a copy, you cheapskate!"

"Okay, I'll trundle on down to Waterstone's and order a copy like a good boy, along with the cast of thousands eagerly awaiting your next adventure."

"Good. Exactly as I planned," I said with the voice of a comic arch-nemesis.

Andrew's face smiled as he returned to his inner search. "Right. I've had a breather now. It takes time to adjust to all this honesty, you know. So, what about my plans? What am I going to do? Go to India and wait for my new life to download? Go back to where I am and try and make it different?"

"I don't know, Andrew-the-Seeker. How do you feel? Has that kind of inspiration flashed through you lately?"

"Sadly, no. Perhaps more research is required first."

"As long as it's soul researching rather than looking for answers out there," I said, pointing to our surroundings, "so that you can be fixed."

"But I thought we were all part of a big jigsaw and that, if we waited long enough, all the pieces would come together."

"And what are you planning to do while you're waiting?"

"Drink boutique beers and perfect my snooker skills."

"Andrew, you're only two pints away from a lost cause now!"

"I guess so. On a serious note, I thought waiting was helpful, earning me brownie points. No point in changing for the sake of it; making how I feel worse by just storming out."

"No one said anything about walking out on your life, nor waiting for your life to happen, nor polarising your life into some chief-editor-versus-miserable-near-poverty-of-North-London. As a first step, you could do with finding some semblance of balance."

"That being?" Andrew genuinely appeared to be completely mystified about what a state of balance could be.

I opened out my lunch packaging, got a pen and started sketching. I drew three intersecting circles and labelled them emotional, mental and physical. Superimposed over them was a pendulum with arrows showing how the pendulum could swing from side to side.

"If you think of your creative energy like a pendulum, balance is here, in the middle, when the pendulum is hanging straight down. Now, if you can stay around the balance point then you can create relatively easily while keeping your other bodies in balance. For example if the pendulum hangs straight down, all these circles are together making one unified circle. So your emotional, mental and physical states are working well together.

"Now of course, our life is always changing so the pendulum can often swing from side to side. The bigger the swings, the greater the imbalances. So when you reach a life change, it's tempting to swing past the balance point and go to the other extreme. Hence, full on pressure, anger, stress of being Editor in Chief, then swinging back in the other direction feeling depressed, exhausted and a victim of your life because it doesn't feel fulfilling."

Andrew interjected. "So the pressure of being something I'm not... like, not being honest... is making me swing from side to side trying to find something better or something that'll fix me."

"Right. So every time you go to an extreme like working late and pushing yourself to enjoy a lie, you're undermining your core being, your core unity. If the emotional body on the left here gets stretched by your mood swings and then mental body over-extends to the right here trying to keep going, you can easily shock your system."

"So how do I stay in the middle?"

"Firstly, be honest and find out where you are. Are you angry? Pushing? Rushing into the future, hoping it'll be better than the present? Or are you sad, depressed? Feeling a victim of your supposed success?"

"Probably the latter... in underwhelm. I often say to myself, 'After six months at the top, is this it?' I get to work even harder and have more money that I don't have time to spend. All in all, not a very fulfilling package."

"But having found out where in creation you are, you've got a better chance of changing."

"And?"

"Then you follow what I call affectionately in my next book, The Creation Code."

"And that is?"

"First guideline: Be honest about where you are. Then ask yourself if you really want to change. Are you prepared to put your heart into your changes and take responsibility for them?"

"Of course I am. I thought that was obvious."

"Not necessarily. Many people are happier being miserable than they are changing."

"Better the devil you know?"

"Exactly. Being buried under a pile of your own attachments, doing the same thing day in, day out can seem preferable to working your way out. So many have built habits that in truth they really wish they didn't have, but having put so much energy into them they feel stuck, a prisoner of their regimented certitude. But one simple change in intention, one that's backed up in your world with action, can make all the difference. You don't have to be radical, but you are required to do and be differently."

"So," said Andrew, "when, in your heart of hearts, you know you're going against yourself, then be honest and stop doing it? Even if you go through a bit of turmoil while you dismantle those habits that have taken over your life?"

"Absolutely. Now, second guideline: if you don't ask, you don't get. Choice connects you to the unlimited flow of energy—what you might call luck, inspiration, magic. That's the unlimited flow expressed in limited terms. So basically, believe that there are both physical and non-physical ways to fuel your creations. For example, you might have money but you aren't prepared to change your habits in order to have the time to enjoy that resource. You might love something and know what you'd really want to do in life but you might need to go out and get some tangible support before you can make that dream a reality. There's always some part of your creative ability that requires fine tuning but also there are always unlimited alternatives to help you create your dream."

"So just because we don't know there are other ways and

means, that doesn't mean they don't exist?" Andrew's earnest brow illustrated his earnest attempts to understand.

"Exactly. It's up to us to discover them in our research. As we do, we have more and more options of how to approach what we choose to create. Then we have more and more experience of creating alternatives so we don't wait around for the Universe to drop a neatly packaged next-step in your lap. We co-create it with the Universe by doing our bit. It could be that you need to slow down to create a new life. It could be that you need to be willing to change and clarify what you want to change. It could be many things, but what's important is that you see your creative ability as a partnership with the unlimited flow of the Universe that's available to anyone."

"Be go-getting, then. Make it happen. Is that what you mean?"

"It's more a matter of being willing and open. Force less, balance more and create more. There's a whole world of difference between being patient about how, when and where your co-creation is going to come into being, and hanging around waiting for the Universe to create it for you. If you wait around for the Universe to decide for you, your ego will make the decision. And that means more of the same-old same-old because ego doesn't want anything to change. Ego likes isolation, not unity. It wants to be separate from ease and flow. It doesn't want to help you create learning, it wants to keep you in a controllable ignorance where you're dependent and willing to grow into a juicy fat victim."

"There's no hope for me then," laughed Andrew, sticking out his paunch.

"You know what I mean. Jokes aside, let me ask you this. What would happen if you waited around for the paper to be printed? No meetings about the lead, no choices, no intentions of what is going to be featured?"

"It wouldn't happen."

"Precisely. And your life is no different. The Universe can't help you if you don't choose to change. Ego might tell you that you're incredibly busy and you don't have a moment to look into yourself, but that's not really true. You have as many moments to help yourself as you choose. Ego often gets us so busy that we just get more and more wound up in our own self importance when, really, are we creating anything purposeful? Anything that is restoring balance and bringing joy to our lives?"

"I take your point. But I suppose making excuses for what we aren't doing..."

I completed Andrew's sentence. "... Is easier than making changes so we can get a life. Ego relies on us thinking we're stuck and unable to change. But the moment we choose differently, we make a difference. It's that simple."

"So the foundation of change is always up to me and it'd be better if I was relatively balanced when I built that foundation?" Andrew got out of his emotional slump and sat back in his chair.

"Exactly. Change and balance aren't as difficult as ego makes out, they're just unfamiliar. And that brings us to the third guideline: Know thyself."

"That sounds a bit biblical. Are you turning religious on me?" he said, lifting his gaze skyward and waving his hands about as if in a momentary epiphany.

"No, not at all. This is a spiritual discussion, not a religious one. But as always, it's all down to perception. Spirituality is exploring the ways we can be spiritual. There're no set rules because everyone's spiritual nature is unique. For example, I'm not more spiritual than you, and vice versa. We're both spiritual if we choose to explore what, I suppose, we would think of as the greater questions in life. Why am I here? Am I fulfilled? Am I contributing purposefully? Am I living my truth and through love? Those kinds of questions.

"For example, Jesus and Buddha were expanding their spiritual awareness until they came to the point where they were enlightened. Then their example was considered to be one that others could copy. What they'd done had worked for them so why wouldn't it work for someone else? So religions grew up around the wisdoms they learnt through their processes. But they didn't spiritualise their lives in order to create a religion, they simply walked their path, recycling their limitations as they went until there were no more fears and there was no separation. So you could say that *know thyself* could be translated into *understand thy true nature*. Get past your habits and ask yourself simple questions. Those are always the most powerful. Like, are you doing something out of fear? Or love? Is ego running your life or are you supporting your heartfelt truth and listening to that voice inside that is loving? And if you want to find out, then you'll go on a spiritual journey to practice exploring your true nature."

"This is deep. Is that it, or is there a fourth guideline?"

"One more guideline: Magnetism. Creation is a flow, not a force."

"Meaning?"

"You can magnetise anything into your world—a new car, a loving relationship, losing weight..." I looked straight at Andrew. He took a deep breath in, trying to reduce his paunch. "You just need to realise that everything you create is through cooperating with the Universe, not by forcing it. If you want to work with the Universe then be loving, balanced, detached, open-hearted and flexible. When you've chosen what you want to create, be willing to do and be what it takes to create it... given, of course, that your actions and choices are loving. If you try and force your creation, you'll block the support from the Universe. If you think you can get others to do it for you then you won't be experiencing your process, you'll be resisting it, delaying it, or even sending it away!"

"But all this balance and responsibility sounds a bit goodie-goodie, even boring. Don't get me wrong, I do want to change, but all that supposed perfection—the higher spiritual nature—can get a bit wearing after a while."

"That's one way of looking at it. But perhaps it's all the imbalance and pursuit of extremes that's got you into the state you're in now. If you don't believe that, go another ten rounds with your ego and then see how you feel."

"Alright, you've made your point. Balance doesn't have to be boring and just because I could choose to become more self aware doesn't mean I'm going to turn into some know-all puritan!"

"Andrew, you of all people? Turn into a puritan? Now that would really be worth seeing! Dare I say, a miracle! But one thing's for sure, it's your choice. You can be balanced, create easily and enjoy yourself if you want. It's up to you."

"Fine. So just because you're self loving and aware doesn't mean you're going to do all of this by yourself as some test to prove you can do it?"

"Would that be balanced?"

"No."

"So you've got your answer. The Universe is here to help, not hinder. Yes you are required to work out what you feel and the intention behind your actions but that doesn't mean you're alone. You achieve this with the Universe, not without it or in competition with it. But, yes, you still need to choose to do it. No one can get in touch with your heart like you can."

"So no shortcuts, then?"

"The greatest shortcut, if there were such a thing, is unity. Unity means there's no separation and so you get to learn what you need to learn in order to get to where you want to go. The shortcuts you're talking about never take you where you want to go because sooner or later they lead straight back to ego. The ways ego suggests don't give you experience. That means no learning, no wisdom. Ego says you can get something for nothing but really all you get is nothing for something. No discovery, no journey, no progress. And you've spent your energy on that nothing."

"So why can't the Universe just give you what you

need? Why do we have to develop these tools to magnetise our creations? Surely giving us what we need is helping?"

"No, it's not the same. Need comes from the fear of not having. Need fuels the sensation of powerlessness, insisting that there aren't any alternatives, instead of teaching how the person can create what they want. If the Universe were to fix you—do it for you—because of your needs then it would be controlling, not loving. The Universe doesn't really and truly know what you want. Why? Because only you do. The Universe just amplifies what you choose and you find out whether that choice is contributing to love and balance or if it's creating more and more stress and imbalance. This is an unlimited, unconditional flow of love that you're working with. Is it going to keep you in victimhood or support you with alternatives and the opportunity for greater fulfillment?"

"The latter, I suppose."

"Exactly. So I can't create for you, you can't create for me, and the Universe can't create for you or me either. But the Universe wants to co-create with us. And we can all help each other."

"So what happens if ego gets involved in the mix?"

"Ego always wants to control and to reinforce limitation so it tries to force the Universe into the shape it wants, at the time it wants, and in the way it wants. Ego never knowingly cooperates with the greater Universe because it fears it'll be taken over by it. It wants the unlimited to fit into the limited, not the other way around. So, say we avoid change... then we get a more concentrated ego. Everything becomes more limited, we struggle more until perhaps we surrender to change or we carry on regardless until we've reduced our choices down to one. Change or die."

"That sounds a bit dramatic!" replied Andrew, startled by my comment.

"It's not dramatic, it's simply the way the Universe works. If you want to let your ego run your life and go against the unending unlimited Universe, sooner or later you're the one who's going to run out of flow."

"Okay, I get the message. Don't put off change; cooperate with the Universe, it really is my friend. So how do I magnetise a better life?"

"From the top. One: What's the intention behind your change? Are you fed up with the way you're experiencing journalism or are you fed up with journalism?"

"Actually, it's more an issue that I'm managing journalism rather than actually doing any writing any more. Writing was always my passion, what I thought I did best. But then one thing led to another and I went off on a managerial tangent and lost contact with my creativity."

"Well, if your heart's not in it then it's only a matter of time before your current comfort zone turns to stagnation. Then more and more problems are caused by trying to make something that doesn't work, keep working. So... how are you going to get back in touch with writing?"

"I don't know. I'm always so busy I haven't got time because of all the responsibilities at work. Or, to be honest, I'm so stressed that the thought of finding the energy to write depresses me further. The thought of leaving my current job sends tremors all through me. How would I pay my mortgage? You know how it is."

"But Andrew, if you don't mind me observing... and please don't take this personally... but, your first answer didn't have any alternatives in it. You just reinforced what you don't have or you can't do. How about returning to balance and welcoming in some alternatives? No one said you had to leave your job so let's slow down, get out of drama and into balance. Ask your heart this question: What's the simplest way to start writing again?"

"Just... start writing."

"Bingo. Maybe get a journal and write for you. When you get some time at the weekends, just jot down a few lines about anything and everything and see if you're still in love with writing. You don't know until you explore. Give yourself a chance when you're away from the bedlam and pressure of work. Bite size pieces; one step at a time. This isn't patronising, it's balancing! Returning to balance is essential when you get as stressed as you do. If you really don't enjoy writing any more then that'll be a load off your mind. You can let it go and create fulfilment through something else."

"But if I'm honest," he confided, leaning forward, "I think if I started writing again, I wouldn't want to go back to my job. And that's what's so scary."

"Why?"

"Because then I'd have to admit that the last eight years of my life have been for nought. I've been climbing to get into my ivory tower but now I'm a prisoner because I've gone against myself to get the money and the status but I don't enjoy it because I'm not doing what I love." He was winding up again.

"Okay, let's slow down a little. If you've gone against your heart like you said, then you're out of balance."

"Agreed." He stopped rushing to his doomed conclusion and started listening again.

"To get back into balance, you've got to introduce what you love doing back into the mix of your life. You can do that all at once by walking out on your job and returning to writing full time. But perhaps that's rather a lot all at once. Plus, if you don't feel in agreement with that then it would be adding more stress to your already imbalanced state."

Andrew nodded.

"Then there's those eight years your ego is now trying to label as a waste. They aren't a waste, they're the experiences, the path of self that you've walked to get to know yourself. Ego has tried to lead you for some of those years but your heart has never stopped prompting you to listen to what's truly fulfilling. It's just now that voice of the heart is getting louder and louder. You can't stuff your feelings down any longer.

"And that's why you called me and we're having this discussion. You haven't wasted your time, Andrew, but now that you're not in balance with your heart truth, it's about time you got back on the path of heart and started taking steps to rebalance your life. There are lots of ways of doing that."

"Like what?" said Andrew, trying not to sulk.

"Like I told you, by writing a private journal for your own reading; writing from the heart. You don't have to show it to anyone; you don't have to write it in any particular style, just à-la-Andrew. What about promising yourself that you'll look after yourself? How about visiting friends? Get a social life. There are so many ways to get back into heart. You've always been such a social guy."

I could see how his mind was like a ship listing in a heavy storm as the prospect of balance and other ways to live his life started to flow over the decks. Another drama wave was about to break.

"But, say the gentle approach doesn't work? Say, it's not enough? Say, I need to make a leap of faith, more like you... stop doing one thing and move completely into another field? I could do that but how would I know I was making the right choice? What if I was making the biggest mistake of my life?"

"Just allow the alternatives to find their level. Just like when you jump in a swimming pool, you don't rush around measuring where you could, maybe, might, possibly drown! You float around, acclimatise to your new pool of potentiality. See how you feel rather than try and make it fit what your mind thinks is its conclusion. Don't go anywhere with it, just be with it."

"But this is scary stuff. I'm a Taurus, remember. I like everything secure, comfortable. I like to see tangible benefit for my work. Is that too much to ask?"

"Nothing is too much to ask, but the reply is only as good as the question. Although change doesn't have to be difficult, there's always an unknown factor with change because, guess what? It's a change! If you want to get more in balance and more in harmony with your world then you are going to need to do and be differently to make that change. The more balanced you are, the more fulfilled you'll become. You'll stop putting your life off and start living it.

"So let's see..." I mused. "How about asking yourself what you really feel? One: Do I really want to change or do I just want to get wound up in drama? Two: How can I change my life now so that I feel more fulfilled? Three: Am I working for money or being creative and getting paid for it? Four: What practical changes can I make to make it easier to enjoy my life?

Andrew sat up straight as if his posture was going to add sincerity to his answers.

"I'd answer as follows," he said. "One: Yes, I've had enough unhappiness and struggle and I definitely want to change. Two: I can start writing again, maybe a journal. Three: Probably for the money. Four: Work less and get some exercise."

"There you are. That didn't hurt a bit! Your life doesn't have to be forced and difficult. The more you stay in your heart, the less effort your life becomes because you reinstate balance to more and more parts of your reality. You stop trying to find answers in your mind and go into your heart in search of what's going to make that genuine difference. Okay, sometimes people have an epiphany and just know what their heart is telling them. Sometimes it's a path of gradual change that all adds up to a larger shift. But you can actually choose how you change as well as why you want to change. You don't have to pull your whole life up by the roots and, in your case because you're a self-confessed man of security, then that way of changing is probably not the smoothest way at present. So gently and progressively does it. Just because it's gentle doesn't mean it's ineffective. It's just that you're used to your ego telling you that worthwhile change must be a struggle."

I paused as a question began to form.

"So what do you think has been stopping you change until relatively recently?"

"The fear of failure," he admitted. "The fear that I was letting myself down if I admitted I couldn't take the stress any more."

"But if you ask your heart now, who do you think is really being let down?"

"My ego. Ego is the one attached to all the imbalance, drama and stress. Ego that wants a big house and lots of the latest things. But I'm the one that has to slog constantly for a lifestyle that I never get the opportunity to enjoy. So it all becomes so inefficient, even wasteful. As you said, I've got a think-style rather than a genuine lifestyle, living a life with style, grace and ease."

"And so that just shows you, you aren't letting yourself down at all, you're actually starting to support yourself because you're choosing not to waste your energy. Extremes aren't as attractive as they once were. Ego challenges have worn you out so you're now ready to enjoy the balance that has been there all along."

"But I guess I was researching limitation so balance didn't appeal before."

"Balance just wasn't relevant. But now, as far as imbalance goes, you've been there, seen it, done it and bought the T-shirt. You've experienced all the limitation you can and now it's time to sample the unlimited."

We both paused. Our discussion seemed to be coming to a close, as was the café.

"So, one last question," Andrew ventured. "What can you give me for those waves of fear that come over me when I start thinking about the changes required to make a fulfilling life for myself?"

"Oh, you want easy pills?"

"That'd be great!" He was half joking but half hoping.

"What I'd prescribe for your condition is practice! The

more you undergo your changes, the less your ego will frighten you or try to talk you out of taking your life back."

"So the way I'm going to stop fearing change is by doing lots of it?"

"Exactly. Given that it's change from the heart, not change just for the sake of change."

The loud clattering of stacking chairs told us it was time to go.

"Where did two hours go?" said Andrew, astonished at the time that had passed.

"Nowhere that we went, that's for sure! But who needs time when we have now?!" I winked.

"Right! Rebuild, rewire, reconfigure and reprogram. Out of extremes and into balance."

"Now that's a story you can definitely run with, Andrew!"

Servings of Expansion

When I got back from the gallery it was already 7:30 p.m. Daily routine was nudging me to make dinner but I wasn't hungry, I was on some strange service high. Our meeting felt like tangible empowerment. Everything now seemed just that little bit more meaningful, just that bit more possible and purposeful.

Eager to discuss my energy experience, I called for my Higher Self. But instead, a flash of purple came across my vision. The Merlin was back.

"Hello, Merlin how are you?"

"Flowful. And yourself?"

"Eager to ask you a few questions, actually."

"Wonderful. Off we flow then."

"For starters, I'm slightly confused because while I was with Andrew, I had the distinct feeling that you or my Higher

Self, or both of you, were watching me or listening in on our conversation. At one point I even thought it was you talking rather than me... as if you'd borrowed my vocal chords."

"We would characterise it more as a joint effort. You were supporting your higher consciousness which was supporting you in speaking your heart. You were sourcing your help from your first nature, sensing what was significant and not letting any mental bombardments knock you out of your centre. So we were working together.

"Remember, all conscious activity is by invitation only. No genuine guidance can ever take you over against your will. Those who come in unconditional love always give choice, and the opportunity to change. Just because we are hanging around in your neighbourhood of vibration doesn't mean you choose to mix with us. It's up to you. But today, as you are sensing, you gave the commitment to serve your friend and we honour this."

"So you're pouring Light into the less attached bits of us via me?"

"Remember, you are Light, so we encourage you to see that you are reclaiming aspects of yourself that were limited and we are joining with various parts of your Light nature so that you can offer a clearer view. Some illumination, as it were. There's nothing like illumination to expand the choices on offer. Think of it as us joining our Lights together through choice."

"So guidance is for everyone, as and when they ask? Andrew was asking for a fresh perspective and so our discussion provided it."

"Indeed. Everyone has access to guidance but your world can be so full of the busy-ness of doing that individuals never look inside because they are fixed on a certain point outside of themselves. It's normally only in times of stress, difficulty, pain and shock that guidance is sought. But it doesn't have to be like that."

"Is that because we are patterned in struggle, often needing a wake up call to notice how imbalanced we are?"

"Indeed. And the intensity of the wake up call depends on how imbalanced the person has become."

"So now we're working more closely together, what happens next?"

"Are you reaching out of Now into the future of your mind?"

"I suppose you've got me there. I feel such a momentum from today, I suppose I just want to extend that out of now into the *what's next* bit."

"But in your heart you know that what follows is what is flowing now. To make best use of the acceleration and momentum you are feeling, it is to stay in the Now, not project out of it."

"When you put it like that, it's so simple."

"Indeed. So to continue with this simplicity, you will understand that more guidance comes after guidance. Guidance is endless. Sometimes it comes in the reflections from your world, sometimes within a conversation, sometimes it's the visions and pictures that you see in your inner vision, through the eyes of the heart. All are valid modes of guidance."

"I really did feel you. My ears were burning and at one point the whole of my left shoulder was warm as if you were standing right there."

"This is the beginning of understanding that we are not separate. These sensations confirm that your true nature is unending. Your mind may ask what's next because it only has points to focus on. But your heart understands that your true nature is constructed of endless flows.

"As you reclaim more of your unlimited nature," Merlin continued, "you will be able to remain connected more and more. Limitation will become the mirage while the unlimited becomes the tangible reality."

"So if I'd experienced an unconditionally loving action

and my mind asked what's next, it would be more love, not more doing."

"Indeed. We are not changing our story, if that's what you mean. Love is unending and is the foundation of your true nature. And so guidance is endless. Joy is endless. Abundance is endless. It is just that your ego tells you that your experiences of these aspects is static and limited. For ego, love isn't unending because ego fears its loss, or that love will become so overwhelming that ego will be unable to control it."

"Could I say then that I'm becoming more aware of feeling, more sensitive, and my conversation with Andrew showed that?"

"Indeed. The unlimited flow that is love. We weren't talking *about* you," joked Merlin, "but we were talking *with* you, through the consciousness flow that is your higher nature. And you are beginning to feel differently; to unplug your senses from the remote restrictions of the mind. You are rewiring through your heart. You are feeling what it is to actually be connected through your heart. This brings greater meaning and purpose to your experience. You are supporting your greater sentience, not just reacting to the analysis of your mind. You are beginning to truly feel, and it is uplifting. So to keep this feeling going, you are required to stay in your heart, even though it is tempting to switch from your heart to your head when aspects of your expanding world are unusual or unfamiliar."

"And when I'm sentient, I don't shut off from my world or isolate myself in my mind? I choose to keep sensing so as to keep connected to my experience?"

"Indeed. And that is how you can keep rebalancing as you flow through your experiences—keep connected to your I AM and so the experience of your world is flowful, uplifting and enjoyable. Struggle isn't your natural state of being, it's just how you are used to being and doing. When you are in your heart, you are connected to the greater Universe rather than clinging to an existence framed by limitation."

"So I'm channelling higher consciousness? Or should I say, referencing my material from a combination of this world and the greater Universe, from more expanded perceptions?"

"Indeed. You are only too aware that you are still in the physical world but you are not isolated as you were before. You have more and more options as you are undergoing the changes that will allow you to meet more and more guidance. You are developing the capacity to receive on many frequencies... a multi-channel bandwidth."

"I suppose that's why, from time to time, this energy, this Light, can feel addictive... in the sense that you could fear it was going to end?"

"Your Higher Self will always help you adapt to the changing relationship between your limited and Light selves. But there are also steps created by guidance as a whole to ensure that you remain in embodiment and embrace your ascension at a rate that works for you. So you can move into hype from time to time or disappointment or loss at other times. But this is ego trying to destabilise the unifying you.

"Ego sees guidance and the greater Universe in terms of them and us, not a unity that is loving and supportive. But as you are beginning to appreciate the wisdom that is genuinely on offer, you can see between the unity and the conflict; you can allow your outraged ego a few tantrums and remain in your I AM until the resistance subsides. And if ego wasn't there to show you the difference between ease and struggle, you wouldn't realise the progress you were making. Contrast is a great teacher."

"I am so tempted to say you did this just for me... all this ground breaking important stuff. But is that just ego?"

"All the changes and realisations you go through are created by you for you, just as they are for everyone. Ego is simply trying to be important. But you are discerning enough now to see when ego is trying to take credit for something it didn't create. The wisdom of conscious development has been available in your world, to all your world since your research into limitation started. So you could say there is nothing new under your sun and all this wisdom that is throughout your ages has always been here. But the way it is embraced is unique to each individual. So it is especially for you and also specially for everyone else who goes through realisation."

"Infinite guidance for the infinite paths to unity?"

"Yes."

"And where there's a will, there's a way, right?"

"Where there is a choice, there is a way. Will keeps you in command of that choice, loving and creating from the heart rather than letting ego control your creative direction and turn it into an ego detour."

"So will could be mistaken for force?"

"Yes, but it depends on you. With greater awareness you can discern the difference. All phases are as individual as you are. Some can be exhausting, some exhilarating. It all depends on how balanced you are; how willing you are to stay in you heart and keep it open. You cannot force from the heart."

"But let's say I do force. Then I could get resistant, even to you?"

"Indeed. There may be times when you wish guidance is not with you, times when you shut out the wisdoms of the heart. But these will become less and less as your experience of Light and adapting to your true nature deepens. And that's why we are with you.

"And yes, you could react with addiction and say 'I never want this to end' but *I want* is the language of ego, not heart. 'I AM embracing the perfect guidance' gives you the opportunity to keep your connection balanced, also your rate of expansion. When you are in your I AM Centre, ego cannot force you; it cannot bully you into what might be. Its objections and projections are meaningless."

"Wait a minute! Wait a minute! Concept overload!!" My mind was thickening to a standstill as ego tried to stop my inner advance.

"Breathe through your I AM," whispered my Higher Self. "Breathe. There is always room, all ways."

I returned to what seemed to be a strange but new sense of balance.

"I just had a little energetic overload. I'm over it now."

Guidance paused until I'd caught up with my next question. "So, two questions. First, what is healing? I hear it from time to time but frankly I don't think I really understand what it means. And, secondly, are you saying you won't be staying around or that there's more of you and I don't have to stick with only you as a guide?"

"To address your first question... in the processes of ascension, healing is simply dissolving the imbalances that have been created during your research in the physical world. These imbalances can be in your emotional, physical, or mental bodies. Normally the physical imbalances get your attention."

"You mean pain?"

"Indeed. When you've ignored the signs that have come through your other sensory bodies such as the stress of your mentality and the anguish of the emotional body, the resistance has no where to go but to turn physical. To research in limitation, the contrast between love and fear, pain and health, has been essential. But when you choose the path of ascension you are returning to balance and the unlimited flow. So you are feeling the empowerment of unity as you dissolve the pain of separation.

"When you heal a part of yourself, you reclaim it from fear and imbalance. You become aware that it is no longer loving to hold that aspect of yourself in that fear configuration. Your choices have changed. You are no longer limited to the choices that ego tells you are the only choices."

"And what determines the rate of healing and how much healing someone requires?" My mind was trying to butt in with the analysis of how much. Ego wanted to know how much it could control.

Armchair Alchemist

"You do. Healing is a unique process. Every soul in your world has the choice to heal, to choose balance over imbalance, to return to the natural state of ease and flow. But not all choose to take it. The limited part of them says 'This is not possible' and they choose to believe that. If a soul is aware of a self loving choice but doesn't take it then they will not heal. Someone who is willing to make the changes that support the process of rebalancing will gradually heal through the path of rebalancing."

"Okay, so the way I see it, we're back to the pendulum analogy. In our limited world, the pendulum can swing from one extreme to another but when the pendulum is in the middle it might appear to be stationary, not doing anything, although it's actually in a state of balance. This represents harmony with the unlimited flow, balanced and uninterrupted by detours into extremes."

"Indeed. Proceed."

"Through our chosen research in limitation, we haven't necessarily had much time for balance. We don't see energy as endless but as something we've got to grab or try and control in case it runs out. Our fears of loss and lack have created more and more attachments so we've been storing imbalance. The pendulum in our world is always moving from one side to the other. Peace is fleeting because balance doesn't seem to have any value. The more attachments in our world, the more value we attach to ego. If we ignore the opportunities to change, resistance and imbalance can threaten the physical body and we have a tendency, as we grow older here in the physical world, to become more and more resistant until there's no flow and we die.

"So, over to you, Merlin. What happens if we choose to change?"

"Change happens! And as you have observed, change is related to the degree of openness and to the degree of awareness. With allowance and understanding comes a greater willingness to trust and embrace change. Admittedly, the very nature of the physical world means that energy flows more slowly at the beginning of your path of change. Why? Because the flow reflects the limitation and at the beginning of your changes you are putting much energy into recycling attachments. But with practice comes momentum and then, through periods of collaboration with your greater self and guidance, you learn to cope with greater and greater degrees of healing, greater and greater transmutations, greater and greater acceleration in the phases of change until, just like breathing, you don't notice the rate of change that you have mastered. You just see it as normal, natural, and you become perfectly aligned with the rate of change."

"I become the flow."

"Indeed. Your balance enables you to be within the flow. And this creates the feelings of effortlessness. Your ego says your day is going your way or you are lucky but these are..."

"Limited perspectives?" I suggested.

"Precisely. You are learning that, as more and more of yourself is restored to a healed state of balance, you will see that creation is easier and easier. The degree of separation between your inner self and your outer world will also balance until the outer reflects the inner. You will forget what it is to be limited; you will forget what struggle and scarcity is. You will merge with endless love and unlimited energy and you will have completed your alchemy of change."

"So those who complete their healing, who go all the way, as it were... they will master ascension?"

"Indeed. They become Ascended Masters."

"They'd be like you, then?"

"They would be like themselves, in their fully healed state. Ascension is unique to each soul, remember, and every soul that walks the path of the seeker makes a difference, however far they get. Ego, as you know, loves destinations but the path of ascension is all about the journey. One step is to seek, to risk your limitation. The next comes because you recycle your attachment to that fear and your path continues."

"So," I suggested, "the more unlimited I am, the more steps I can take?"

"You are your path. You are your alchemy and your path is a reflection of that alchemy. No path, no ascension. If you have no path, you cannot reach your destination. This is why the destination is never as important as the steps you take to arrive there. So walk your talk and talk as you walk so that you may encourage others in their seeking and in their relationship with guidance."

"Help others help themselves."

"Precisely. Because you are part of the greater unity; you are part of a Light community within form."

"But sometimes I really feel a strong urge to resist people. I avoid them at book signings or don't return their calls. Why should I have such a strong reaction, often to people I don't even know?"

"You will often resist what is of most service to you but with awareness you will learn not to endorse this ego habit. You are a unity so all the new flows of energy that you embrace warm your resistances as well as the parts of you that are open to change. You will not be able to create a relationship with such resistance but you will create learning by asking yourself why you don't want to spend time with that person. Ask yourself what they are doing to provoke your ego."

"So these experiences help me deal with my resistance to openness as well as helping me to embrace my expansion?"

"Indeed. You could be so resistant that all your openness goes into dissolving that resistance. You could also experience accelerating into a new domain, a new environment in which you suddenly meet lots of new people and you find that your resistance has dissolved."

"Makes sense. Cosmic sense, you understand. So my second question... What about other sources of guidance?"

Servings Of Expansion

"You are correct in that you are not stuck with an individual or any single source of guidance. The way you interface—connect—with your guidance is entirely up to you. It is a function of how much you want to learn, how open you are, how well you are transmuting and changing. For example, are you maintaining balance between your physical, emotional, and mental bodies and your Light body? Are you willing and able to incorporate the wisdoms that you invite? Is your energy level at saturation or super-saturation? All of this assimilation process is required to be taken into consideration. Mostly, this is done by your Higher Self but all guidance that comes to work with you is sensitive to your energetic state and to the degree of resistance your ego can exert at any given moment."

"So what's saturation and super-saturation?"

"These describe the state within your own energy field when we observe that you are full... or full to the brim, so to speak; when any more energy would not be of service. If, for example, guidance were to go beyond super-saturation then the energy could be detrimental to your physical embodiment. That would not be loving. So guidance will not go beyond super-saturation."

"So you're keeping me from overheating then? From blowing my limited circuits?"

"In a way, yes. We are also supporting you in building an energetic architecture that is supportive for every cycle of change you undergo. If you knew how many changes you undergo in your energetic architecture, you would simply not believe it. The complication your mind would create trying to understand would literally blow your mind. This is why your ascension takes place through your heart and not your mind. Your heart trusts and can allow the unlimited flow to create what is required for each healing phase."

"So the heart trusts where the mind would wander off trying to find a logical reason to justify what it doesn't understand and end up doing nothing!"

"Quite."

"So don't look to the mind for inspiration? Nor for expansion?"

"Indeed. It would be like looking for an unlimited answer in limitation. You have the capacity to change every-thing, to heal all, to unite all; a complete shift, from one moment to the next, in what you are prepared to allow and integrate. So when you encounter more stubborn aspects of ego, the transmutation effort can require a lot more focus. It may appear that you've hit a wall but really you're simply spending a large proportion of your energetic efforts on transmutation.

"Therefore, your impression of your outer world can be that nothing is going on; or your outside world can even appear that it has forgotten you, or is making your life harder, even working against you. This, of course, is not the case, just ego perception."

"So guidance is a lot more complicated than I thought."

"It is complex, not complicated. Think of guidance as being layers of advice. Your perspective determines how you work with that guidance.

"Remember, the quality of the question determines the quality of the answer. Guidance always provides a different angle of learning. There's no doubling up, just unlimited avenues to expand and embrace more of the love that you are. It's a lot for the blunt gloom of the human mind to work out, so why bother trying?"

"So from my perspective, guidance can see where we're going with the choices that we make, but if we're deviating into fear then you'd encourage us to step back and look at our choices and path again?"

"We do not know it all, as you are beginning to understand, and although we will never save you from your choices, we will always support you in building upon your loving nature rather than your fearful nature. Guidance is a service and it might interest you to know that we learn from you."

"What!?" I was staggered. "You do?"

"Indeed. As you unravel your attachments to your limited nature, we can perceive you more clearly and we can learn more of the general nature of attachment and how we can serve the process of ascension."

"But, wait! I don't want amateurs, you know! I want professional guidance, not fill-ins from Jupiter in their summer holidays!" I burst out laughing.

"I'll send a memo to the guidance task force to remind them," replied Merlin, embracing my joke.

"And if there aren't any more questions, we will conclude our discussion for this now. Remember, all is choice and all are capable of communicating and unifying with higher consciousness, it is simply that not all choose it."

And with a swish of what was now his purple cloak, Merlin was gone.

Making A Meal Of It

All was silence in my inner world. My physical body translated my Light intake into renewed demands for food. I prepared a snack of whatever I could find and it was quickly inhaled.

As I turned the extractor fan off I heard a low beeping sound. I checked my mobile phone. I had four missed calls from Erica. I had a tight feeling in my stomach. Why was she calling? Our next progress meeting wasn't for another two weeks. Oh, it's nothing, I said to myself. She probably just wants to discuss that bad review. And yet the nagging feeling didn't go away. Suddenly I wasn't hungry, I was worried.

My Higher Self hung back in inner space as if smoothing out the right moment to start communicating.

"Any time, Higher Self. When you're ready," I joked nervously.

"Actually, it's a question of when *you* are ready," came the reply. "How do you feel?"

"Worried."

"And why would that be?" My Higher Self appeared to be sensing the level of energy upon which to join our conversation.

"Well, Erica is a very disciplined and efficient editor. She never calls unless there's something important to say, and at this stage there really shouldn't be anything *that* important."

"Important is a relative concept."

"Easy for you to say, you aren't running a business."

"But we are coordinating your ascension into higher consciousness and that is a much greater business than you realise at this stage. So let's put these feelings into context with your ascension rather than with the more 3D mechanics of your world."

"Okay, so what am I learning at the moment? What part of the process am I in? And why have I got the most enormous knot in my stomach which makes me fed up, to say the least?"

"Fed up? That's not very nourishing, is it?"

"No."

"You are digesting your guidance and part of the process you are currently in is recycling scarcity and the limited ways you used to use your energy. You are liberating more areas of yourself that used to be under ego control. Ego doesn't want to lose control so it starts to manufacture these symptoms. In truth, you are going through your fear, recycling it. But your ego is seeking to convince you that worry, which is one of the most common habits in your world, is more useful. Ironically, you feel secure in your worry; it's a comforting place to be where you can go into your mind and go over and over your limitation, convincing yourself you can get or keep control."

"But my answers won't be found in my mind, they can only be found in the heart."

"Of course. Worry is simply the desire to control the unknown, the incoming flow of unlimited energy as it were. Control is an ego habit that can be very difficult to give up

Making A Meal Of It

because it is one of the cornerstones of ego reality. Think of it more as an obstacle in your path, something that stops the unlimited flow rather than supporting you. There is no flow in control, only less and less energy."

"Then what self loving action or way of being can I adopt instead of worrying?"

"Be centred in your inner space, your heart room. Go within and realise that you are expanding, and as you do, so you are experiencing from time to time the difference between the limited and the unlimited. You are expanding out in all directions and that can feel strange so give yourself space to adapt. This is self loving rather than giving yourself time to worry."

"But I was on such a high earlier. I really felt like I'm making progress, making a difference."

"And you are. But what do you believe is one of the uses of the momentum built from increased awareness and consciousness?"

"When I get on a roll, you mean?"

"Yes. This feeling of the expanded moment, the true nature of the Universe; being ten feet tall and having a heart the size of a house... What can this be used for?"

"More transmutation I suppose."

"Yes. And do not underestimate this powerful realisation. Empowerment is an endless flow, an ongoing process; as your consciousness expands, you are capable of more. And that of course, means more transmutation because you require more fuel. And that fuel, as you know, comes from the wonderful changing, rearranging you."

"Well thank's for the enthusiastic overview." I was taken aback at how guidance could always turn the most difficult of situations into the fuel of progress. "So I've hit this wall of worry because I'm really in the middle of more transmutation? That transmutation being the recycling of my attachments to worry, my usual mode of coping with the unexpected that, to be honest, I'm very good at."

"Indeed. And you've spent many of your moments declining your power so that you can focus on worry in your mind. And as you know, each of your moments holds the invitation to infinite expansion. So when you worry, you put that potential into reinforcing worry rather than creating what you want."

"Okay, so worry is just trying to control, and that'll work against my process and progress forward so choose not to do it?"

"Correct. What you are feeling now is all part of the necessary disturbance that creates the energy to fuel progress. And you know in your heart that this requires a dash of the unknown and a pinch of chaos. Such is the recipe of change. So dissolve the grip of the mind and return to your true nature."

I moved my shoulders around and massaged the back of my neck in an attempt to relax.

My Higher Self paused. "How do you feel now?"

"Better, because now I'm aware of a choice between worry and centeredness. You've put it into context. Not exactly an easy pill but it's easier than it was breaking down the habits of a lifetime."

"Make that, many lifetimes."

"Okay, no need to rub it in!" I joked.

"If I may use your words, this was only putting it *in context* with the unlimited Universe of which you are a part."

"Did I say that?" I was completely befuddled.

"Yes, we did say that. But your mind doesn't recognise this. It is muddled as the pathways of assumption and ego habit continue to break down. The mind always thinks it is searching but it is only questioning," replied a cloud of purple.

"I thought you'd gone, Merlin."

"Always within, never without the unity, we are," replied a voice. It continued to echo through my heart as I finally drifted off to sleep.

Healing Acceleration

The next morning, space and energy were at a premium. My mobile phone and I took it in turns as I sneezed violently and it whimpered low battery indications. I looked at my watch; it was nearly 9 o'clock. I felt terrible as my nose ran endlessly and my body ran hot and cold chills. I put the sheets over my head and tried to postpone the day. One giant sneeze blew my cover and I was just about to fumble for a fresh batch of tissues when the phone began to ring.

"D'hello," I managed, sneezing into the phone.

"Is that you?" came the curious and concerned reply.

"Yes, it's be... with, as you cad hear, the head cold from hell. Ad I just woke byself up sdeezing."

"Sorry to hear that but I need to talk to you."

"I was going to call you back yesterday but it god late and I didn' feel too good. So what's news?"

"I'm afraid there's been a bit of..." and the phone ran out of battery and the screen went dark. I fell back into the pillows. The charger was on the kitchen table but I just couldn't summon the strength to go and get it.

So what was so important? I could feel anxiety beginning to build in my mind. Adrenaline kicked in as I bunged my nostrils with tissues and went in search of the charger. It wasn't on the kitchen table nor in my favourite absent-minded haunts. Where could it be? I fell back into bed in a sneezing fit and noticed the cord snaking out from under the bed.

"Aha! Got you!" I muttered, plugging in the phone with a surge of energy and collapsing into a thicket of discarded tissues. "Go od phode, rig! Brig some important relief to by damp day!"

The phone lay placidly for ten long minutes. I was just about to drift off into a feverish fuzz when it rang again.

It was Erica.

"D'hello again. So what's the probleb, Erica? Anythig I cad help wid?"

"Well, to put you in the picture, the publishing house had a meeting of senior staff yesterday. The long and the short of it is that they're going to have to make some cuts and let some people go."

"A'd how does that affegt us? We're in profit; up and coming. Plus, in the d'New Thought section there's only you and d'authors. Dot exactly what I'd call overstaffed."

"You're quite right, but that's not how management sees it. They don't think we're performing as well as we should be. We haven't made the percentage growth up to this point that they wanted, so that means there's been a freeze on advances."

"For 'ow log?"

"It'll be reviewed in two months' time. So basically, at the moment, there isn't any money available until the royalty payments in four months. I've calculated those, given your present sales, and I think they'll increase, particularly after that controversial review. So if sales keep up their current rate, they'll be good but you're going to have to come up with a financial stop gap for the time being."

"Gosh Erica, dis has really cub out of the blue. Seebs so unfair codsidering we're the department that's currently perforbing the best."

"I quite agree. This is just a reaction because of all the conservative dross that they've continued to publish but isn't selling, and those returns have just ambushed this month's figures. It's as if they keep on doing the same thing over and over again yet hoping it'll change. But we wouldn't even be having this conversation if they'd put those efforts and money into creating something new. Anyway, you don't need to hear me remonstrating. Sorry to be the messenger of bad tidings."

"Will dis prompt d'hem to get realistic about d'he drain created by d'he titles dat aren't perforbing?"

"Don't hold your breath. There's a lot of history in these

decisions. I'm working on clarifying the situation but it's going to take some time. I feel this is just a temporary glitch but that's easy for me to say, I don't have to find a wage for the next three months. I'm afraid I'm up to my eyes in mortgage, otherwise I'd give you a personal loan because I really believe in your work."

"Dat's really kind, Erica. B'Means a lot. I'll just have to wave dat magic wand of mine and create the money to get this book finddished."

"Okay, I won't keep you any longer. Get well... and prosperous. Soon. I'll be sending you positive vibes."

"D'thanks."

As I dropped the phone, I didn't know if I felt worse or just terrible. What was obvious was that I couldn't do anything about my situation until I felt better. So I just surrendered, descending into a deep sleep.

I dreamt of a monsoon of rainbows and swirling lights while running through a landscape of moons rising mysteriously over a field of ploughed clouds. All was beauty and harmony. Nothing out of place or in conflict, just the endless sensation of perfection. There were no restrictions or limitations. If I wanted to float somewhere, I could. If I wanted to speak purple, drink words or paint shades of allowance and joy, all was instantaneous. The unending flow morphed into shapes and sensations that created a unity of normal. I wasn't astonished or alarmed, all was just as it should be. Effortless...

I woke up with sweat pouring off me. I found my phone under a pillow and looked at the time. It was 3 p.m. and I had more missed calls, this time from Andrew.

"I haven't much good news this morning," I muttered to the phone, "so Andrew can wait."

My Higher Self replied on behalf of my phone, "Don't assume that each moment is the same, nor that you've received bad news today. It's all in the flow, just like your Cloud Nine," said the voice, bouncing around gently in my cotton wool head.

"When Merlin said I'd have some acceleration, this wasn't what I had in mind."

"It never is," replied my Higher Self, pouring the maximum meaning into the shortest of replies.

"So, good morning, Higher Self. Or should that be, bad morning?! Or even bad afternoon?!"

My disgruntled reaction was half way to sarcasm.

"Here's a recap of all the things I didn't think of." I answered caustically, feeling an artistic tantrum coming on. "First, I've got writer's blank. And now that's become writer's grump because I don't feel supported. Second, the book I was so proud of has been assassinated in the press. Now Erica tells me that I'll have to fend for myself for the next three, or even four months. While trying to finish a manuscript, that's going somewhere I've never been before!!"

I gasped for breath.

"And on top of it all, now I've got this wretched cold and fever. I'm a limited form of dreadful. How then, when I'm supposed to be becoming more unlimited, can things get worse? This just doesn't make any sense."

"You aren't making sense or logic, you are making progress. They are worlds apart," began my Higher Self.

"But things are getting worse, not better!" I interrupted. "Look at me… I can't work and now I've got to pay for the privilege of writing."

"Things are getting neither worse nor better, you are simply flowing through your process, investing in love and expansion."

"Easy for you to say. You don't have bills to pay," I cried, my frustration moving into a head-on collision with ego.

"Energy is spent in many different ways. You are investing in the abundance by recycling scarcity. Just be patient and trust."

But I was too thirsty and too angry to listen. I stamped into the kitchen and hastily filled a glass of water. I'd run out of tissues so I restocked my pockets with toilet paper. My ears popped as I blew my nose and, just as I could hear a little better, the door bell rang.

Who could that be? Curiosity acted as the perfect decoy. I leaned against the door and looked through the spy hole. I saw a stunning version of Mrs Daley, complete with make up and what appeared to be a brand new outfit. The sudden contrast in my world deflated my ballooning conflict. I debated whether to open the door.

"I'm here, Agnes, but I've got a really bad cold. Are you sure you want to talk?" I called through the door.

"Don't worry, I'll cope. Just want to ask you one question."

"Okay," I said, opening the door with most of my face concealed behind tissue.

"Well? What do you think?" she asked, spinning a full circle.

"You look fabulous!"

"Really? Don't go telling fibs, now. Do you think I should change anything?"

"No, Agnes, don't change a thing. After all, the Universe loves you just the way you are. It's up to you to believe it. So what's the occasion? Go on! Tell your sick antisocialite."

"Well, it's a secret, really. But if you're free in the next couple o' days for a chat an' a cuppa, I can tell you the full story then."

"How can you keep me in suspense? My recovery could depend on this information," I replied, managing a joke.

"Sounds like you're in the thick of it with that cold, so curiosity should help you pull through. Always good to 'ave something to take your mind off it. Keep guessing," she smiled. "An' remember to drink plenty o' fluids. I'll see you sooner rather than later."

"Have a wonderful time, whatever it is."

I closed the door just before a bout of sneezing fired out

of my nostrils. "Great timing, Mrs Daley," I muttered, shuffling towards the bedroom.

I suddenly began to feel very weak. I walked unsteadily, tripping over some magazines at the entrance to my bedroom, and tumbled back into bed. The protests of my mind had dissipated and my Higher Self could now reopen our dialogue.

"So you see, life's full of surprises. Everything is changing and it's not what it appears. Your acceleration is supporting you in arriving at a whole new level; a whole new frequency of capability. All you are required to do is surrender, be patient and trust."

"But what exactly does that mean? It sounds wise and helpful but, in the state I'm in at present, I'm hardly in a position to do anything else."

"Then that makes the choice simple."

"Okay, if you put it that way, it's obvious. Stay in bed, get better and think of money another day."

"Excellent suggestion. The true nature of unlimited flow is ease, as you were just experiencing. But sometimes you've got to go through struggle. Your ego doesn't want to let you go or let you see, it just wants to hold you to ransom and tell you that your change is impossible.

"So when you are dissolving the greater extremes, it can appear that you are getting a whole lot of exactly the opposite of what you want. But really you are simply recycling ego polarity. This is all helping you reconnect with ease. Your mind tells you that you should be doing something, you should be reacting, struggling to get things done faster. But as you see, balance is more important at present. You are hardly in a state to react or work and so the Universe, in truth, is making this change easy for you. In this case, surrender is helping you get to your next level; helping you much more than you know. If you try and make yourself work today, you will be ill longer."

"So why did I feel so angry earlier? I'm surprised I had the strength."

Healing Acceleration

"Because the frustration that your ego is feeling in your mind spilled over into your emotions too. Your ego sees surrender as giving up the fight, the conflict. The transmutation that is brought on by acceleration often means that you feel a fieriness in your nature. You feel frustrated or angry because of the situation you appear to be in when in truth it is your ego that is angry because you are dissolving more of the opposition and obstacles between you and unlimited creativity.

"Remember, energetic change is never one fixed equation that has an answer. It is a flow that is complimentary and supportive of the way that you are undergoing your healing. At each moment you could make a million and one choices, so there is no single equation that can ever give you the one answer that fits all. Ego tells you that your experience is easy and it has all the answers but all it has is all the limits."

I was beginning to nod in and out of our conversation. All the talk of acceleration was making me drowsy.

My Higher Self continued honouring my surrender. "Immediately you start moving with acceleration, ego is required to keep up with you. But the only way it can achieve this is by holding you back within its limited terms. This is what causes the friction—the misunderstanding that you've got to try and change your situation, make it better, though actually it is all perfectly in the flow of change.

"If you listen to your ego, you will talk yourself into greater and greater degrees of imbalance so that you end up sabotaging yourself out of change. If you listen to your heart you will realise that you are not required to wriggle out of your situation nor fight it but rather surrender to the rebalancing that will enable you to command your learning and the transmutation you are currently undergoing."

"So there's always a process to my changes?" I replied, feeling more awake again.

"Yes. Always a process and always a purpose, whether you are aware of it or not."

"But the individual choices that I make in order to get from beginning, through middle, and to end are infinite? What counts is choosing balance when I could easily get confused and think my ego is right and my heart is wrong?"

"Precisely. But as long as you initiate into the new, embrace the new, enjoy the new and gain the wisdom of the new, then you can transmute and rebuild your learning architecture. You know that, with each part of your process, you will rebuild your learning architecture to accommodate your progress. Once you've learnt, there is no point in keeping hold of the same structure. So you build something new from the same energy but at a higher energy level. Ego might say 'Oh that's such a waste', but all is recycled perfectly so there can never be any waste. Everything flows back into supporting you, if you choose it."

"So I'm currently recycling the old bricks so I can build something else?"

"You could say that. You are clearing the perceived obstacles in your mind as well as the limits your ego wants you to keep. You are moving from your hermitage to your four bedroom house!"

The image reclaimed some hope that had subsided into ego. "Sounds spacious!"

"Of course. If, however, you do not trust then you disallow your expansion. Your new architecture will take a lot longer to build."

"So I've got this head cold because my mind isn't keen on me changing?"

"Put it this way. You have chosen change and that is what is being supported. But to make the process a little easier, and to calm the opposition of the mind, you have created a cold to dampen the fiery resistance to your changes; you've cotton-woolled your ego."

"I chose this? Well I hope ego is enjoying being bunged up like this!"

Healing Acceleration

"It is of service so that you can undergo the acceleration that is necessary for your progress forward. Everything is right on track."

"Do you mean to tell me the more ill I get, the more progress I'm making?"

"Not necessarily. It's more a question of working with what you've got."

"So if I'd been less hasty about certain parts of my process, I wouldn't have needed to get ill?"

"We do not encourage the analysis of your situation, only its observation. Analysis takes you back to your mind whereas observation helps you stay in your heart. There is no better or worse, just process. What are you learning from your illness?"

"My degree of imbalance?"

"In part. But mostly...?" My Higher Self waited for me to fill in the blanks.

"I suppose it's a function of how I'm coping with my acceleration. I've been through what my mind would easily characterise as more and more negative and illogical situations so my mind is overheating because there's nothing it can do about it. If I trust and surrender as you are suggesting, dedicate to my process and forget about logic, then ego doesn't get a look in to my world, nor can it influence my choices and try to stop me changing."

"Exactly. So you are learning from your experiences, even if they appear to be less than comfortable. It's not what you think."

"That's probably the only aspect of all this that I dare to say is certain!"

"Change is the only constant in your world, and when you are willing to become aware of the nature of your changes, to become conscious and responsible, then they will flow increasingly easily. It is just that you are undergoing a more demanding cycle of change. But nothing, we hasten to add, that you can't handle."

"So, while I'm handling my physical fallout, can you tell me more about trust?"

"Trust is a tool that you use to maintain your processing. Trust bridges from one frequency to another, from one phase of your learning to another. You could think of it as **T**-ake **R**-esponsibility for **U**-nlimited **S**-piritual **T**-ransmutation."

"Okay. If you put it like that, it all appears really worthwhile."

"And that it is."

I could feel myself fading into a candy floss haze of pink and orange. I began to feel cold and gathered the bed clothes tight around me. As my eyes closed I could still hear my Higher Self whispering gently over and over again, "Detach and trust... detach and trust... detach and trust..."

Hark Who's Talking

When I opened my eyes I was surrounded by the smooth feeling of velvet. Dark blue velvet. I looked above me at a canopy of wooden panels and a forest of marble columns. The sun was pouring through a large stained glass window and the warm glow fell as a channel of colour in the centre of my face and forehead. Looking around the wooden borders of my surroundings, I realised I was lying in a coffin in the middle of a cathedral.

"A coffin?!" shouted my mind, sounding a desperate alarm.

But my heart was calm. I was at peace, absorbing the shafts of stained glass blue, taking one breath at a time.

Ego continued to needle my balance sending shards of objection towards my heart. "Is your life about to flash before your eyes!? Is this the end?!" it shouted dramatically.

"No," came the reply of calm inner truth.

"Are you losing everything? Is there nothing left?"

"No, I am clarifying; creating fuel for my new movement forward."

Hark Who's Talking

I felt a sudden wave of claustrophobia accompanied by a feeling of pure peace.

"You'll have to atone for what you've done," continued my mind.

"Ah, finding the at-one-ment," replied my inner truth. "Bringing to unity what is imbalanced."

Part of me was in turmoil, searching for a defence or a conflict. It didn't want to be surrounded by ceremony and religion. Another part welcomed the meaning within this place; welcomed the understanding of why I was here, the purpose within the Now.

I sat up and looked around. My inner communication was silent but I wasn't alone. The inner truth was a new vibration, a new form of guidance.

"Is there anyone here?" I called out as I clambered out of my resting place and addressed the angels poised within blue and gold frames.

"It's only temporary, you understand, until you've completed your tasks; until you are at one with your new level of balance," came the reply.

I looked behind me. The voice was coming from the first row of pews. An impression of a giant youth with golden hair emanated a serene welcome. The vision and the feeling converged into one; a tingle of grief followed by an almost overpowering rush of fulfilment. I looked down at my feet to see if the wave had lifted me above the alter steps, but they were out of focus, distant.

The wave of energy moved back through me like a lunar sea. All was silver and blue.

Sitting down, I grasped what I wanted to believe was solid, ready for the next wave, but the ocean of energy had found it's level and reduced to small ripples moving through me and out in all directions. I sank into deep calm when I realised I'd rebalanced and joined the ocean of energy.

"Who are you?"

"Oh, don't worry about that for now, just rest wherever you are comfortable. This is, after all, why you came to this place. Just because you are accelerating in your ascension doesn't mean that you are rushing around out of balance. You can always have a rest along the path... that is, **P**-eace, **A**-llowance, **T**-rust and **H**-elp."

The first letter of each word was a golden capital.

"So you're saying that my path isn't always moving?"

"How you perceive your path is your choice. The unlimited flow of love, learning and change is always moving but that doesn't mean you have to move all the time. Movement, as you would think of it, doesn't guarantee progress, it's just a vector, an energy flow. It's the intention behind the movement that matters. Is it loving? Is it contributing to balance? These are the questions that support the progress that you seek. Balance is all important because it supports a smooth processing of your spiritual lessons. This is why sometimes you can move ahead by standing still."

"That means if I try to force things, try to get everything over and done with, then I get out of balance, projecting into the future."

"Carry on."

"And so I actually have the impression that I'm making progress but, really, the more out of balance I get, the less I achieve."

"Indeed. The pendulum of life swings back and forth. But you are most efficient when you are fully present. For ego, that is the middle of nowhere. For your true nature it is the middle of Now-Here."

"Because that is the state that supports my I AM Presence?"

"Yes. When you are balanced in your Now, you are in the unlimited flow and able to help yourself, to be helped and to serve others, all of which contributes to smooth and joyous progress. It is ego that tells you your path requires constant *doing*."

I suddenly felt a rush of words flowing into a strong sense of realisation. "So I've tried rushing headlong into my process; I've tried waiting, hoping someone else will do it for me; and a lot of other ways. But if I choose to stay balanced, I can see where I am, which part of my cycle of creation I'm in, and then act, rest, be patient etcetera etcetera and use the spiritual tool that fits where I'm at in that moment."

I paused, as if I hadn't covered everything. "Building balance and maintaining it goes back to the intention behind my choices... Love or fear. Expansion or resistance."

"Quite. And when can you get drawn out of balance?"

"When ego doesn't like me trying to change something. Ego will always try and lead me away from heart so we can both take refuge from change in the mind. After all, it can be easy to think yourself into denial. So then I'm resisting my path. I'm not Peaceful, Allowing or Trusting of the Help from the greater Universe. It always comes back to choice. To feel or not to feel, that is the question!"

"Well observed. So you can make your path without being surrounded by doingness in your world..."

"... and excess doing just brings imbalance," I added, finishing the sentence.

"Excess anything produces imbalance; excess doing or being. If you attempted to stay here longer than is of service, for example, then you would be resisting applying what you have learned here."

"So everything has it's time? And balance is always timely?"

"You are learning."

"And balance makes periods of acceleration smoother?"

"Exactly. You can gain much from appreciating your progress because in turn you are seeing the benefits of balance. When your progress is smooth, you are making progress easily, even effortlessly. You aren't deviating back into your mind or outside your I AM Centre. All is being coordinated from the heart. If you surrender when ego wants to fight change then you will slip back into balance much more smoothly.

"Your ego tells you that progress can only be made by competing, going the fastest, being the best. But these are not balanced wishes, they are imbalancing desires that force you further and further into the imbalance of a future or a past that takes you further and further away from yourself. You are beginning to see that acceleration has many different forms and many different directions. To master acceleration, you are required to master detachment."

I felt a surge of rebellion on the tip of my tongue. "But why here? I've never liked churches. I always feel so... confined, cloistered... judged."

"All the more reason to be here and now—to practice the detachment that is required to be at peace with such irritations and gain the fuel for your path. Do you believe this place can control you? Do you believe this meeting is convened so that you can be judged?"

"No, I don't," I replied indignantly, "but as you've been talking, I've felt a wave of resistance growing towards these walls, as if they're holding me here, stopping me in some way."

"And so how does that link with the practicing of detachment?"

"If I'm going to detach, it's almost certainly going to be something that irritates my ego. But in order to complete the recycling process, I suppose I go through the resistance I'm recycling."

"And?" The youth was encouraging me further so I could complete my new foundation.

"And I feel that means I'm in a place that brings up quite a few attachments. It reminds me of some limited aspect within me that my ego is clinging to; some experiences of when I wasn't able to be as detached as I am learning to be now. So from time to time it's helpful to be surrounded by what I resist so that it stimulates recycling; reminds me of how attached I used to be."

"Well recognised. And it also reminds you of the attachments that you created when you didn't achieve your spiritual target. This place reminds you of what you were so zealously reaching for; a target that you believed was the be-all and end-all of your spiritual development.

"But this was only part of the unfolding truth. You had pieces in the puzzle but not a unity, and your incomplete picture bred misunderstandings that your ego capitalised upon. Ego told you that you had failed; that you weren't good enough, devoted enough, or loving enough. You weren't trying enough. You didn't give up enough. It appeared to control, even stifle, your increasing requirement for detachment when you outgrew these walls and the learning architecture they offered. In truth there was nothing wrong, you had simply moved on. You had progressed. But, without detachment, you couldn't flow your way out of the fixations of ego. Your spiritual target had become your be-all and end-all when your heart was telling you there was something beyond it. Your mind and ego wouldn't let you go beyond what you'd learnt and evolve to the next level."

My physical discomfort was beginning to increase. I felt heavier and heavier until I couldn't sit up straight. I lay down across the knave and surrendered to what felt like an incredible weight.

"And now you are seeing that you do not have to carry this weight any more. You can let go of your misunderstandings and your partial truths. You don't need to cling to the attachments that your ego created in this architecture because you are expanding. You have chosen to reclaim these limited parts of yourself. You are understanding that what was once truth is no longer truth. Truth has expanded. You are now able to learn more, expand your vision."

"So when ego told me I'd failed my cause, or I wasn't good enough, that was just to keep me from detaching and realising that the existing configuration couldn't provide me any more learning?"

"Quite. Ego wanted you to stay within its limited definition of yourself. Ego made it for you and never wanted you to outgrow it. If you did stumble across the empowering nature of detachment, ego was there to redefine it within limited terms. It told you that detachment was loss; that it was when you missed out on something or had to give up everything. Or detachment was when you didn't care and weren't courageous enough to keep trying. But really you just kept on struggling, hoping that what had come to an end, didn't really have to end."

The vision paused just as a wave of tightness moved through my chest and stomach area.

"As you are feeling now, to ignore your heart is to store up resistance and that can cause pain. But with each conscious action to detach, you let the pain and imbalance go. You allow your healing process and you move back into a deeper and deeper state of balance."

"So detachment is like plotting a path back to balance and the fuel for this path comes from dissolving attachments."

"Well put," replied my companion.

I felt a wave of release.

He continued. "And you rise up your curve of ascension by being willing to expand your awareness and keep expanding your truth into greater understandings of what is truly loving. Thus, you enable your path to keep on unfolding because you are unfolding, detaching from the mesh of conditioned beliefs and memories within which you were locked."

"Detachment is elegant, simple and one hundred per cent efficient. You don't lose anything of yourself, you simply enable yourself to re-express at a higher level of consciousness. You reclaim the limited aspect of yourself and re-express it in unlimited nature. When you feel grief, it is merely ego grieving its loss of control. When you feel in suspended animation you are actually allowing, through pure detachment, a whole new Light structure of being. And this will happen over and over again as you rise out of your attachments."

"Is this like initiation?"

"It is a form of initiation. Traditionally, you have regarded initiation as undergoing a test, something you are required to face, to achieve. But initiations can also be the capacity to allow without deviation from balance. Sometimes you are required to demonstrate the willingness and courage to detach, and other times you are demonstrating the surrender, patience and peace that is required to incubate the new you. These are all forms of initiation."

"And so detachment simplifies this complicated mesh of ego attachment?"

"Of course. The less attachment you have, the more flowful and able you are."

"So memories from what I call past lives can also be part of that mesh of attachment?"

"Indeed. All your experiences are held within you. Memories are attachments to those futures and pasts."

"So why don't I want those memories? Don't they describe what it was like to be in physicality?"

"Not quite. Memories are impressions of limited experience so they are attachments."

"But why do they appear so valuable?"

"Because your ego says they are what you came to limitation for."

"But they are what ego wanted me to accumulate?"

"They are the closest ego gets to the wisdom of experience."

"So as my Higher Self has always said, I am in physicality to gain research, to experience what it is to be limited. But that doesn't mean get attached to the memory of that experience."

"All you are required to do is build on the wisdom of your experiences, not the memory of your attachments."

"But I've only become aware of that relatively recently."

"You could say that."

"So while I've been understanding just what it takes to detach, ego has been busy leaving a big impression on me?"

"Yes. But because you have chosen the path of ascension, you are now detaching from those impressions. Attachments are the archive of limitation and memories are part of that archive. Ego wants you to pull out a memory and think of ego. Ego never wants to let you go."

"But now memory lane is closed," I acknowledged, "because I'm choosing to work with my energy in the Now, not scatter it all over the place from the past to the future. That explains why I can't remember my current lifetime any more and I get these really weird periods of déjà vu and sudden affinities with places and people without any logical reason. All my memories are getting stirred up."

"That is so. Stirred up and transmuted so that you can appreciate and cherish the wisdom that remains. The whole structure of attachment is being released step by step as you walk your path."

"And they'll recycle because I choose to let go; to make more use of my Now by letting go of attachment?"

"Exactly."

"I feel like certain parts of me are joining up, coming back together. Like I had a whole sentence strewn, a word here, a word there throughout many lifetimes but now all the words have come together to make a sentence I can really relate to."

"Perhaps it's a sentience you can really relate to," suggested my companion.

"Yes, that's it! A sentience. A new way of feeling about my research in the physical world. Often people have said to me that I'll be lonely in old age because I never put down roots, because I haven't been investing in the memories of a normal life. But, in a way, I won't necessarily have an old age because I haven't built any attachments. I won't be saving my Now for a time when I have less. I won't look back to the good old days because they are always now."

I paused, overwhelmed by the feeling of release.

"So now you are beginning to sense why nostalgia is so powerful in your world. The linear stream of events is not important, what is hankered after is the feeling of love and the feeling of flow. Many want to relive their youth because they think they had more of everything then, when in truth they simply had less attachment. As their attachments grew, their capacity to cooperate with the unlimited reduced and they thought there was less energy with each passing moment. But if you are detached, the flow of energy is always unlimited and always available. As you are finding out, detachment is a forgotten and misunderstood tool, rarely at the top of anyone's list of options."

"Because people think detachment is bad or it automatically means loss or someone just doesn't care," I suggested.

"Quite. But is that actually true?"

"Well, in the light of our discussion now, I'd say no. Detachment in the truest sense means less imbalance, less struggle... less ego. It's ego that's saying 'You don't care' simply because a detached person cares less and less about ego."

"Precisely. Through attention, ego gets to control more and more of you. But if you choose love rather than attention, you keep your options open rather than endorsing ego insecurities. Do you want to worry yourself into old age? Do you want to let ego habits run your life into greater and greater attachment until scarcity is your only option? Or do you want to detach and explore the alternatives that an unlimited perspective offers?"

"I AM embracing detachment."

"Your commitment does you service," replied the vision, becoming momentarily stronger, more radiant.

"So tell me, before I finish my detachment... Was I the Pope? The Archbishop of Canterbury? Or some misunderstood martyr?"

"How can this help complete your detachment process in this place?"

"I thought that if I knew, then I'd be satisfied and that'd help me let go once and for all."

"Do you believe that knowing who you were in a past life can really help you detach?"

The question stopped me in my tracks, just before I could follow my ego down a corridor of intellectual fascination.

"I can see that ego was behind that question. My choice to detach isn't related to who I was but who I am choosing to be right now. I suppose if I go back into that mesh of memories, I risk using this energy to get entangled in the past."

"And...?"

"Then... if the information was on the surface of our discussion, staring me in the face as it were, then it would be relevant to the process. But If I've got to go digging for it then it's quite likely that it's just ego encouraging me to burrow back into attachment."

"Precisely. If you choose detachment, you detach from the need to know. Points of reference in your past are only significant if they can support you in your learning now. If you are tempted to wrap yourself in past glories or future complications then you are still choosing attachment."

"Then we chose to meet in this cathedral because it triggered the recycling of specific attachments that I created during religious lifetimes?"

"Yes. We chose together. Although you may be less aware of that, it was still a choice. The environment was enough of a reminder that all the attachments within this sector of change could be gathered up and used to fuel your rebirth.

"This is a place of newness and peace," he continued, "a place where surrender is appreciated and peace cherished. This is somewhere you can choose to detach from both your past and your future simultaneously. This is the place of rebirth, a rebirth that is born of your commitment to detachment and your surrender to change; a rebirth in the Now. By being here you are going beyond the understandings you previously achieved in this area of your spiritual nature. You are expanding beyond the futures that your ego was investing in. You are initiating into the energies that bring you endless rebirth. You are beginning to truly believe that the greater flow is unlimited, effortless and endless. You are beginning to understand that true evolution comes from love, simplicity and balance, not from hardship, force and scarcity."

"But how come getting here felt like wading through treacle? Like a series of increasingly demanding obstacles? Surely that means there's an element of trying, struggle and suffering in there somewhere?"

"For your ego, that is so. But it is becoming less of you as you become more of your real self. And if you do not take on increasing degrees and depths of transmutation, how will you create the acceleration that you require for your greater leaps forward?"

"So these individual hurdles helped me get a run up so I could leap here, as it were; undergo a more comprehensive detachment process that lead to a major rebirth?"

"In essence, yes. During this period of acceleration, ego struggled to keep you within your limited nature. It was upset as you released your ignorance. It became aggressive as you dissolved your conflict. It felt undermined as you cut a path of clarity and simplicity through what was once an endless jungle of attachments."

"So which part, or parts, of me have changed?"

"Your awareness and your capability have changed. You are no longer confining yourself to an individual stream of guidance. You now know there is an infinite collection of guidance ready to support you in your path of empowerment. You step forward, they step forward to greet you. You choose to change, they support you in that change. You are now beginning to feel what it is to believe that anything and everything is possible and not to be frightened as a result. And your willingness to believe has brought you here."

"When you say *here*, you mean this frequency, this state of awareness and rebirth?"

"Yes. The energetic architecture is appropriate. It is formed from what is familiar in your experience. You believed in your childhood, and in previous lifetimes, that angels could do anything. They create without fear and their creations are perfect and effortless. Thus these figures embraced the unlimited nature you were seeking to reconnect with. They were, and are, the form of hope and unending flow."

"So angelic energy helps me break up my attachments to the impossible; all those ego habits that tell me *You can't do this* and *You can't believe that*."

"Yes. Angelic energy inspires hope—the feeling that there is a flow within which anything is possible. No form can contain the unlimited but impressions of the unlimited can be felt in the flutter of angels' wings for it is the flow of detachment."

"So the more I detach, the more I can work with this unlimited flow?"

"Indeed. Make the detachments and leaps of faith that honour your heart and you will release your attachments to limitation."

The giant blond youth paused as if checking all sides of my Light architecture.

"And it is done. We thank you for your trust. We embrace you. And so it is."

And as the angel stood to leave, his waist appeared to go through the floor and his head through the vaulted ceiling.

"Wooooooooow!" My gasp echoed around the pillars. "You really don't know how to fit into form," I chuckled. "You are truly endless."

With a hint of a smile, the majestic being dissolved and a single tear rolled down my face. I'd always felt uncomfortable when people spoke of tears of joy and the feeling of serenity. Now I was feeling it for the first time. I stood up so I could look and embrace the unity of my space.

Hark Who's Talking

Almost simultaneously, the building shuddered with the sound of the ancient west door closing. I turned to look. It was a not-so-shabby-looking tramp who I now recognised as The Merlin. He took grand steps that dwarfed the gothic distance between us and was arrived in no time.

"Ready to play?" he asked, producing two footballs.

"What? Play football in a church?"

"Where's your sense of detachment? All those memories of solemnity and misery... aren't you over those yet? Seeing them from a different angle, a detached one? Could be fun, dribbling through the past; passing through those lingering inner obstacles. You don't know if you don't practice."

"Okay, I surrender. As ridiculous as this might seem, I've got the feeling it could be a lot of fun. Here goes."

As I turned to face an empty congregation, my heart began to fill with the change of pace. I placed the ball on the ground ready to start dribbling down the first row of pews. Merlin did the same. I kicked the ball tentatively as if warming up. Merlin did the same. And then I felt an enormous rush from behind me and a commentary ignited in my head.

'And it's the beginning of the run as the players surge forward through the narrowest of gaps. A tussle... and a rebound there... But the acceleration continues as they skillfully weave past man made obstacles. And with another leap of faith... Yes! They're in the other half! The crowd are hushed as they pause to refocus and enter the final build up. The whole team is converging, sensing it's Now... and what has seemed to be a one man effort receives a torrent of support from all sides. It's a quick one, two. And it's a...'

The commentary had risen to an excited garble. *'And it's a...'*

"It's an achievement that brings the scores back to even, back to balance," said Merlin, turning the commentary from inside out. "Everyone's a winner!"

We had both arrived at the other end of the pews, facing the west door.

"Congratulations. You've won back a part of self and all you've got to show for it is joy!"

"What? You mean I've given up all that scarcity and struggle?" I joked, catching my breath.

"You tell me."

"Yes, I have. I AM arrived at a new level of self, a new balance between Higher and lower Self," I acknowledged, pretending to give an acceptance speech. "And of course, I'd like to thank my manager, The Merlin, for his endless support. Oh, and let's not forget an expanded sense of humour and detachment! And all the other members of the team that I can't really mention now because I don't have a memory and it could get really boring... because, of course, they're endless..."

I turned to Merlin.

"Thank you," acknowledged Merlin. "You are most welcome to your new sense of self and your renewed sense of joy. On behalf of all, as one voice, the voice of many, we thank you for your efforts for you are much easier to see with a spring in your step and that glow in your heart."

"What do you mean?"

"Put it this way. Your commitment to detachment has enabled us to see you more clearly. Your command of detachment has cut a path of clarity through the gloom of limitation. Before, our service was like tailoring a suit while you were wearing a sack but now that you're more aware and more detached, we can see and serve your dimensions much more easily."

"Great, Merlin. So now I've got my glad rags on I'm ready to pour that unlimited flow into a book."

"Wonderful," he smiled.

And as we raised our imaginary winners' cup I felt my feet lift off the ground.

"The power of enlightenment," smiled Merlin. "Shall we fly?"

"Yes we shall," I replied.

And with that, the west door opened into a flood of light and we dissolved within its endless streams of gold.

Stepping Back Through Lack

When I awoke, it was as if I'd been asleep for centuries, like a pre-Raphaelite effigy. My body felt like a lump of stone.

"There's no rush, you know," began my Higher Self.

"I don't expect I'll be rushing anywhere feeling like this!"

"Surrender is your best tool at present. You are chipping away at your density so that you can break down your ego resistance. So it isn't so much of a surprise to be resting, is it?"

"If you mean that everything happens for a reason and I'm transmuting some deep stuff, hence this prolonged period in bed, then yes, I sort of understand. But if I'm getting lighter, why do I feel so heavy? I feel completely zapped."

"That is the weight of contrast, the relativity that you still have in your world. It will pass through your Now soon enough. You are feeling how dense you are as you consolidate and assimilate your new Light. As you know, change takes some adaptation in your world; not necessarily time-based but more dependent on your abilities and capacities."

"So my capacity to change isn't as flexible as I think? And part of this is leaking out of Now and flowing into the moments that I see as coming afterwards?"

"Think of it this way. As your I AM grows in its capacity, your ability to adapt and assimilate will increase. And since there is no time apart from that which is in your mind, what's the hurry? If now is all you require, why push beyond it?"

"Alright, alright. That makes me the struggler, not the seeker. No more hints necessary."

I surrendered to rest, sinking into the bed while imagining

my alchemy of change flowing throughout my slab of physicality. My need to know was dissolving. My need to measure and compare was dissolving. I'd only been in suspended animation for a day and a night. It was my mind that thought it was a hard night of wasted struggle.

As I stopped forcing, I felt better. The change was so apparent. I tried to move but couldn't. As I wriggled back and forth I realised that I was lying in a straight jacket of blankets. Unravelling myself, I laughed at the part of me that had expected struggle and was used to it.

"Good job I listened to you, Higher Self, or I'd have really wound myself up."

"The mind can certainly appear powerful. But as always, it has all the appearance and none of the experience; all the thoughts and none of the intentions. But that is why you have chosen ascension—to experience the difference; to understand your infinite nature through unravelling your limitations."

My Higher Self paused. "It appears that you have a visitor."

The urban priestess had returned and was rubbing her face against the window. She paced delicately back and forth punctuating her caresses with goldfish-mouthed meows. I was now feeling light enough to let her in.

"Hello, travelling one," I said, as if greeting a long lost friend. She jumped from the bedroom window sill straight onto my bed and settled in the centre of a nest of discarded bedclothes. She winked proudly.

"That's a nice spot you've found yourself. Looks like you've taken over."

She blinked her confirmation.

"So, my little High Priestess... if you don't mind, I'll take my leave and get a cup of tea." Another blink acknowledged her consent as she stretched out into total relaxation, except for the odd pulse from her tail.

While I boiled the kettle my mind wandered back to

Stepping Back Through Lack

my financial shortfall. I analysed my options with a list of expenses.

"No more flash cash for a while," I announced to the cat. But she didn't seem the least bit concerned about my half hearted attention seeking. I returned to my financial doodle.

So where was I? Oh yes... With bills, overdraft, credit card payments, mortgage and food I'd need at least 1,500 a month to survive. If I was budgeting on the safe side then this would mean no funds for up to four months. At the end of the column, 6,000 stood out in bold.

"So high and yet so far," I shrugged.

Returning to my bed, I negotiated around the cat, lay flat on my back and let out a huge sigh.

"Well, my Urban Isis, where am I going to get 6,000 from?"

She blinked with her all-knowing yellow saucers as if to say, "It's simple; don't you get it yet?"

Reluctantly, I picked up my phone and dialled the bank. I detested asking for an overdraft at the best of times but my current financial position only added to my sense of humiliation. A helpful and efficient voice told me I wasn't eligible for an increase in my overdraft but they'd happily review my situation in four months' time.

It appeared that the same person worked for my credit card company as a similarly helpful and efficient voice told me that I was also not eligible for an increase in my credit limit... though it could be reviewed in four-to-six months. I'd never been in this position before. Ego didn't like how it felt.

I heard an echo of a rhetorical question. "How are you going to change if everything stays the same? It's the unfamiliar you are feeling, not failure. Believe, believe."

"But I am believing," I replied out loud, "and I'm adapting as best I can... I think. I've put everything, even my savings, into this big shift while things were getting off the ground. I am believing, but I'm also required to believe in thin air at the moment and that's less than comfortable. What am I going to do, Higher Self? Do I have to get a job and try and write at night?" The thought of giving up the writing that I really loved made me feel sick.

"You're giving up ego," came the reply, "not writing."

"But how do I do that?" I was caught between frustration and disillusionment.

"You are thinking again instead of focusing on your intention."

"I don't know what you mean."

"Your mental conditioning is strong. Your first reaction was to work it out, to analyse your options, be logical and rational."

"So this isn't the way to go about it?"

"It's one way, but by no means the only way. Ego is used to telling you that analysis is the only way because it can keep you out of your heart and in your head. Analysis will pick your centre apart. It'll keep you from your I AM Centre, not help you co-create with it. Discover the unlimited nature within your circumstances rather than going by what your ego tells you is possible. Analysis is more like a creative afterthought, a kind of *p.s.* that your ego wants you to exist by."

"Obviously I need to approach this differently."

"Do you believe in the detachment process?"

"Yes I do."

"Detachment doesn't mean you are to focus more closely on your existing assets then work back from there. Detachment is stepping back, taking in the greater view, daring to dream. It is all and more.

"There is nothing wrong. You are recycling your limited perspective, not embellishing it. So when you undergo transmutation, you widen your options, not reduce them. Ego always encourages you to think of what you already have rather than what you can create. Ego has no resources because

Stepping Back Through Lack

it disallows flow. Heart has all of the resources but you are required to stay in your heart to benefit from them."

"Okay. So what would you suggest as a starting point? Obviously not logic and repeating the same with more and more struggle."

"Quite. It's time to get creative and that starts with intention. Clarify what your intention is and then you can cooperate with the Universe. When you clarify your intention, you can't panic or let your ego make assumptions or demands on your behalf. But what you can do is feel the centre of your creative power."

"So return to I AM Centre and sense what I want to create?"

"Exactly. Forget about the physical requirements for the time being. Ego is tempting you into focusing on what you think you don't have, the scarce nature that it thinks is creation. But you are no longer ordered around by ego, you are independent and becoming responsible for your natural ability to choose. It just takes a little practice. But you are getting the hang of it. So work with the flow, don't panic yourself into less and less flow."

"Alright, I AM detaching from worry. Worry is only my ego's desire to keep control of my world and keep me limited."

"Excellent."

"And I AM clarifying my creative intention."

"Very good. And...?"

"I AM creating the perfect resources so that I can complete my current novel."

"Wonderful. Now that you've sent out your intention, the greater Universe can help you. When you worry or believe you are a victim of your situation, you choke your creative connection with your unlimited aspects. Worry is trying to control what your mind doesn't know. Do you believe that is helpful?"

"No. Control is limiting and the mind is limited. Mind is designed for this place," I said, gesturing around the room, "the form of the physical world."

"So worrying just clogs up your connection between your limited self and your unlimited self."

"My what? I'm afraid you've lost me there, Higher Self."

"Picture this simple analogy. Imagine a drainpipe going through your head to the centre of your heart, and that pipe connects you to the flow of unlimited energy. Then if you leave your I AM Centre and go back into your mind, you are no longer in the flow of the Universe, you are taking yourself away from the unlimited flow that can support you. It's as if you are clogging the drainpipe with fear and complication and making it more difficult to work with unlimited alternatives. You understand that unlimited energy is not polarised into good or bad, it just is. It's a flow of neutral that expands the choices you make. Choose with love, you get love. Choose with fear, you get fear. This is a neutral, unlimited, creative cooperative."

"So the more I worry, the more I expand my fears and reduce my belief in alternatives. It's as if worry makes me willing to hold on to my ignorance and my resistance to believing there's another way. But as I understand deep in my heart, I'm never a victim of this flow, right?"

"Correct. Unless, that is, you choose to support your ego and your fearful nature. If you support yourself with loving consciousness then you will create a world that reflects that love. Your creative power always works best when you are in your I AM because you are balanced, working with guidance and connected best to the unlimited flow."

"And so it's up to me to keep my connection open; to see beyond ego objections and to remember where I start my creations."

"Yes. And the place to start?"

"In the heart," I rhymed, completing my Higher Self's

hint. "When I start a creative process in my mind, I'm not using intention, I'm using the limitations of logic and analysis."

"Yes. And until very recently you were not able to discern the difference. But through the detachments that you are now making, you are beginning to see how you create and when you use your heart and when you use your head." My Higher Self appeared to hint at an image just outside of my vision, an image of wings.

"Being with the angels, I began to realise what it was like to work with unlimited energy."

"Indeed. And you are beginning to see the self disciplines, responsibilities and benefits of working with the unlimited flow instead of the conditioned limitations of your mind and ego. If ego meets something it doesn't know, it simply says it is impossible because it doesn't know how to control it. When you step into what appears to be impossible, then you begin the possible; you open up to the unlimited."

"Is this some sort of test? An initiation I'm undergoing?"

"You could say that. A test of your ability to embrace the expansion that you seek. Do you want to play with your expansion or do you want to be your expansion? Embrace it at your very core?"

"I want to expand but I just don't see or feel how to do it at the moment. I'm a blurred visionary, if that makes any sense."

"That is the starting point of your expansion—the acknowledgement of what you don't know. You are turning away from your ego's attempts to control everything. You are saying that if this isn't working, what else is there? But that doesn't make it wrong, it is simply an invitation to the infinite. Remember, conditioning isn't wisdom, it's just the repetitive routines of the mind. Do the routines of the mind embrace the unlimited?"

"No, they don't want to let the unlimited in because

ego and the mind would say that it'll cause chaos, instead of admitting it'll assist change."

"Exactly. So no detachment, no change, no new. Same ego, same mind, same habit, same result. But embrace intention, embrace the unlimited, create change and expansion..."

"Okay, I see what you're saying. But why don't I feel the buzz, the enlightening? Of late, everything appears to be going downhill. There's a sense of sadness."

"That's just ego. Your commitment to your path means that with the processing of fear into love, ego sees everything getting just that bit steeper. It is ego that is slipping downhill and you who are adjusting to the increased processing and the increased gradient. You are continuing to climb, to explore your unlimited nature. And as you adjust, you become more comfortable with your new level of awareness and your path will appear to flatten out. In truth you will simply have adjusted to the new and deeper level of processing.

"You are feeling ego's depression since, yet again, you have done something loving. You've chosen the expansion of chaos rather than the security of logic. Your ego is slipping away from you as you move upward and outward on your return to your expanded unlimited nature."

"So It's all downhill from now on for ego because I'm choosing less struggle. I'm not listening to ego and taking the easy way out, I'm feeling my way through the uncomfortable so I can reunite with that piece of me that was lost to ego."

"Yes. And you are feeling ego's sadness as it loses yet another part of you to love; as it sees that control has let ego down."

"So this will all pass?"

"Always. Because your experience is a flow. When you take back responsibility for your choices, there is always that unfamiliar state, the possibility of being wrong, out of control and uncomfortable. But it's simply different and only temporary. When you choose empowerment over limitation—choice and

Stepping Back Through Lack

change over fear and resistance—then you go back through ego to return to your centre; you allow the unlimited to return to that aspect of yourself. Ego grieves the loss of the limited you because that is another part of your greater self it can no longer occupy. And you know only too well how much ego loves to be occupied."

"I suppose self discipline is the tool I need to use to keep looking at my creation in an unlimited way rather than a rational way?"

"That is one tool, but there are others. It just depends on your experience. Your experience isn't an equation, it's a flow. It's not ego with *one-fits-all* but rather a sort of mix-and-match. Sense where you are and then choose from the heart in that moment which tool is of service. You now have many tools such as discernment, patience, surrender, allowance. In truth, an infinite portfolio. This phase of your development is showing you just how many tools you have to practice your mastery; to keep on discovering the real you."

My Higher Self appeared greatly enthused. I moved closer to the cat as she purred into sleep.

"Think of these periods of gloom or relentlessness as the gathering of endless fuel, the fuel that will take you where you want to go and magnetise all that you require to get there. Ego says that it's easy to be limited, and that may appear to be true from within your world only because struggle is normal. But when you detach, you see how effortless creation really is. You have experienced this and you will continue to experience it when you are at one with your world. Don't you prefer that kind of ease?"

"Of course I do. It's just that detachment can be challenging. If you told me that at this time tomorrow I will have 6,000 and all will be well in my world, of course I'd detach right now."

"But where would be the detachment lesson in that?"

"Yes, exactly. I recognise that I'd be asking you to take

responsibility for me, to do it for me and I know you can only advise and encourage. It's me who undergoes the detachment so I can feel and appreciate the change."

My Higher Self suddenly softened. "When you feel fear, you feel the fear of ego as it knows you are about to embrace change and discover yourself by risking your ignorance; risking your insecurity; risking your attachment to what is. Do not mistake consolidation for safety. Consolidation doesn't mean you can excuse yourself and wait for the Universe to fix your situation. What you are going through now will all change soon enough.

"These are not moments to slide into denial or self pity. When you consolidate, you are taking a breather on your path but your intention is still magnetising what you want. And after you have assimilated your progress, you will continue. Being safe is creating a **S**-ecure **A**-rea **F**-or **E**-go. Do you want to be secure and watch your unlimited nature flow past?"

"No, of course not."

"Then go with the flow. Your intention has been acknowledged."

"It's a no-brainer, then!"

"It's all a no-brainer. You can only be detached and honour your expansion if you come from your heart. No brain or mind required!"

"Okay, so I'm in assimilation, allowing all the cosmic nature of myself to rearrange. I'm not waiting for something outside of myself to fix me, I'm allowing the inside unlimited to help me build my capacity for change."

"Bravo! You have arrived at an awareness well worth assimilating."

There was a deep silence. Tears welled up in my eyes. "I do believe," I said to my Higher Self out loud. "Somewhere in here," I gestured to my heart, "is a place where I believe that everything, every moment I spend in this experience, is making a difference; that it's always contributing to my learning without justification or rationalisation. It's just that that sense gets misplaced, obscured sometimes. I jump to the old patterning of *What's the worst that can happen?* instead of *How can I flow with the unlimited?* But it is changing."

"Yes. Always. It is changing in all ways."

We paused in unison, as if checking if there was anything left to add.

"So it's time to rest, Higher Self?"

"It is. There is a misunderstanding in your world that when you aren't doing anything, creation stops flowing. But that is ego talking. Creation is endless. Picture it as a constant coming and going that just keeps on flowing. What you require in each moment is always flowing to you, from you and through you.

"That sounds awfully familiar," I said, feeling a warm glow of reinforcement. "You told me that before. It seems so far away now, so long ago, and yet it was only a matter of weeks."

"And so you are recognising how energy flows, how awareness is united. It isn't a matter of time it's a matter of feeling and being in your now. From the moment you embrace your intention in your I AM, you are in creative cooperation with the unlimited flow. The more you practice, the more faithful your creation is to your original intention. When you force creation, you constrict that drainpipe of unlimited energy. When you try and *make* it happen instead of understanding what is happening and *allowing* it to happen, guess what?"

"It doesn't happen."

"Exactly. And that's where the detachment comes in— the place of balance between doing and being. Detachment helps you balance if you are doing too much and, for that matter, if you aren't doing enough. But that sacred place of balance can only be restored by your belief in detachment."

"And that's what I was doing in the church. I was standing back; seeing the layers in something that had appeared so flat. When I detached, my experience could show me. The structure, the conditioning dissolved into the background and what really mattered became more obvious."

"Yes. You arrived at a place where you hadn't believed before. You had toyed with limited definitions but when you felt the energy of Archangel Michael, you understood what it was to believe; to believe in yourself, in your process and in the detachments that you are making."

"So it's to continue believing that everything is contributing to the expansions I seek, even if I don't know, can't understand or don't see how they fit?"

"Correct. You will believe until it becomes first nature; until doubt becomes a relic in the museum of ego, something you used to burden yourself with long, long ago in the very dim and limited past."

My Higher Self appeared to take a long, satisfied breath. "And our unity is almost complete. One last question. When you are capable of being completely detached, what will you gain?"

"Is that a riddle?" I was suddenly confused by such a question.

"Of sorts. But all riddles have a path to and from their answer."

I filled in the pause. "Alright. I believe that if I detach, I'll find the answer."

My Higher Self beamed broadly.

"Let's walk this path," I ventured. "If I'm detaching then I'm unburdening myself from ego and limitation. So when I'm fully detached then I'll not fear lack or loss, I'll be in complete cooperation with the unlimited Universe. From a heart perspective, I'll gain everything but I'll no longer have the desire to control it. I'll just flow with it."

"And so we have arrived at our unity."

"Am I in saturation?"

"Of sorts. Time to assimilate the nature of your creation. Rest well."

I felt my Higher Self step back. I looked down at the cat, stretched out from my hip to my knee. I stroked her gently. She purred, acknowledging me with a flick of her tail. I decided to take her lead, gently moving down the bed until I was fully horizontal.

"Well cat, it's a good job I got this cold," I whispered, "because where else would I get all this material for my book? Effortless creativity. I think I'm finally getting the plot."

I Am Heart

Isis—which I'd now decided to crown her—woke me with a flick of her tail and a touch of a paw. It was completely dark apart from the glow of street lights.

"Sorry, oh wise one, I didn't leave a window open. Allow me, your Royal High Priestess."

I lifted the sash window to let a cool evening breeze in and a cat out. She stood on the bed watching me return as if to say, 'You didn't receive my telepathic pulse. That isn't what I want at all.'

"What do you want?" I asked, blowing my nose to relieve the pressure in my ears.

She sat and purred her reply. I moved toward the kitchen and she sprung off the bed, quickly entangling her body and tail around my legs as I walked.

"Watch out! If you trip me up, I'll never understand your secret mission."

I turned on a glare of kitchen lights. "Ouch!" The intensity caught me by surprise.

The cat continued in her attempt to merge with me as she purred in time to my movements.

"Oh, Isis, you've made a believer out of me. I'm getting a strong third eye message... you want... now, let me see... Food?!" She sat immediately to give her dimly lit human servant a confirmation.

"I don't know if it's wise to feed you. What's your owner going to say? I kidnapped you for literary company?"

She blinked and purred irresistibly.

"Alright. You picked me for a soft touch the minute you jumped through my window, eh? But don't go making this a habit or I'll get in trouble with your owner, whoever they are."

I opened the cupboard. There was a variety of tasty options just waiting to be cooked but I still didn't feel hungry enough. I opted for quick and surprisingly healthy.

"So, Isis, on the menu tonight... for starters we have sardines on toast, followed by a main course of sardines on toast, followed by... yes, you guessed it... sardines on toast. What do you say?"

As I opened the tin, she purred and meowed her approval.

"Okay. Two orders of sardines on toast coming up."

The toast vaulted athletically out of the toaster, narrowly missing Isis, sending her behind the washing machine to seek refuge.

"Don't worry, all's well," I assured my mistress gently, smoothing her down and enticing her out with an abundant serving of sardines. We sat alongside each other like a well worn pair of carpet slippers.

"How is it down there?" I enquired.

Isis looked up and purred.

"Compliments to the chef, then?"

Collecting up our dishes, I noticed an envelope had been slid under my door. I was curious as all mail was delivered to the mailboxes at the main entrance. It was addressed to me with my flat number and *Delivered by Hand* written in the top left hand corner.

As I opened it I got that strange sinking feeling I'd had before I became ill.

The letter was from the Residents Association.

This is to inform all our members that there will be a meeting regarding emergency maintenance to the façade of the building on

I Am Heart

October 20th. Due to deterioration of structural portions of the masonry, all owners are required to pay £1,500 to the maintenance fund immediately so that work can start next week to ensure no further deterioration. The budget for the forthcoming work will be reviewed in October to see if any further contributions are necessary. Look forward to seeing you all in October. Yours Sincerely, Judith Wilson.

I crumpled. "Not another bill," I muttered.

The cash register in my mind rang out loud and clear. "And that comes to a total of 7,500!"

I felt a mixture of anger and despair. Just when I thought things were looking up. I'd begun to believe a way out of my financial downturn; I expected to see the debt stay the same, maybe even reduce, but I never thought it would get bigger.

My efforts to detach didn't appear to be working. What was I doing wrong? I demanded an urgent meeting with my Higher Self but there seemed to be no answer.

I sank back into bed, discarding the Residents Association's missive on the floor. I felt my ego wrapping my head in a damp blanket with 'Victim' written all over it.

Isis sat down by my side as if she was in for the long haul, gently tucking in her front paws and settling into a quiet meditation. I wondered if she was trying to tell me something.

I could feel my ego embellishing my difficulties with new layers of dissatisfaction, resentment and apathy. What was the point of all this spiritual development and expansion if I was going to feel like this?

On top of that, my Higher Self had abandoned me.

The minute I thought that, I knew I didn't really believe it but my reaction and attachment to something that certainly hadn't met my expectations was all my ego needed to start burying me under layers of depression like falling autumn leaves. Everything seemed to be falling apart.

Isis remained motionless, giving off only the odd purr. I stroked her head gently. "You don't have these problems, do you Isis? Why?"

It suddenly occurred to me that Isis was free because she had mastered detachment. She could visit, live and eat in a variety of places and be fulfilled.

I decided to follow her example and meditate. I sat up in bed and put my hands on my lap, palms upward. I began to feel a sense of caring and understanding lifting me out of form.

Moving beyond the nagging disillusionment of my ego, I began to practice what my initiation was all about—detachment. The more I allowed the protesting inner victim its say, the less it spoke. The more I allowed my situation instead of hoping it was something different, the more I could feel the balance that had temporarily deserted me. I felt strangely refreshed with a renewed determination to maintain my balance.

"And so you have arrived," said my Higher Self. "Mental distress is transmuted."

"I AM creating the perfect help," I echoed my intention throughout my heart room and settled into my inner space.

Everything was literally up in the air; the furniture, the books, the crystals were all floating in slow motion, including me. There was no gravity and nothing was fixed. I tried to do what would pass for walking, had there been any gravity, but I ended up tumbling in circles, around and around and around. I began to laugh at the ridiculousness of my situation. I had no control.

"And which part of that surprises you?" I heard my Higher Self chuckle.

"Okay, it's abundantly obvious that I'm out of control and in the greater flow of the Universe. I'm just assimilating, that's all."

I felt like I was adrift and yet there was a gentle current flowing through my heart room. All I had to do was surrender to join it.

I relaxed as my heart vision floated out of the main room, down a corridor of pearlescent peach and pink. It was like looking into the perfection of a pearl—an endless merging of natural beauty. Nothing was too much or too little; the balance was perfection.

"Wonderful. You've arrived at last. Quite a journey," said a voice from behind me.

As I was about to turn, I heard, "You are arrived. And, beloved one, you are most welcome. Please take your place."

I felt my feet touch what appeared now to be a floor, and I was seated at a great banqueting table filled with brightly coloured food and exquisite decorations. Everything was glowing; all a flow of beauty untainted by disbelief or comparison. Everything was made from a pure sense of Love.

"Now that you are flowing through the last of the turbulence, you can begin to regain your centre. Your expanded centre, of course. As you've seen, nothing will stabilise when you are in turbulence so surrender is a much more useful tool during changes such as these."

I was unable to reply. I felt choked with the Love that was coming from everything and everywhere in the room, even from the room itself.

"You feel the Love that is your world."

I nodded as tears rolled down my face, followed by gulps of laughter. "So much joy," I garbled. "So much, I don't know what to do with it all."

"Just allow the flow. Be and absorb what is truly you. Although this is natural, it is far from your normal; far from what you think you are. So be calm, adapt."

I sat back in my chair, relaxing into the flow.

The words of love continued. "Your heart is reconnecting with this flow. All you are required to do is be with it, saturate yourself with this balance. Everything is loving, you will come to understand this. The Cosmos is a unity and Love is the constant. As your truth expands, so the way you can give Love and receive Love also expands. You are in the process. There is no need and there is no worry. When you radiate Love then you will attract Love. When you give Love, you will receive Love. When you open your heart wider, not close it to the unknown, then you allow more Love to flow through your heart to assist the changes you want to make."

"I don't want to stop loving," I insisted. "It's just that sometimes in my world, it appears that I'm boxed in and I have to keep dissolving more and more obstacles instead of feeling freer and freer. Sometimes it seems like the world's against me when all I want to do is make a difference."

"Beloved one, keep your heart open so that the difference can take form within the flow that is love. Love magnetises, and balance builds your ability to magnetise. When you feel the benefits of rebirth, the struggles of detachment are quickly forgotten. They dissolve in your expanding capacity to love."

"I understand that, but believing it and being it can be far from each other at times. I want to keep my heart open... Let me rephrase that... I AM keeping my heart open. It just feels so confusing when I apply guidance and things seem to get worse instead of better."

"Do you believe the unlimited would deliberately destroy your loving foundation?"

"No, it's my ego that's trying to tell me it isn't working. And it's ego trying to tell me that I'm failing and should return to what I know rather than allow what I sense to unfold. But it can be difficult."

"Not so much difficult as unfamiliar. You are being asked to trust what you don't know, and you don't know how to do that."

"I suppose you're right."

"But you don't need to know how to do it for it to become a reality. You aren't trying to lock your reality into place here, you are allowing your reality to flow. So belief enables you to flow with your turbulence until it is changed, rearranged into more of what is fulfilling and loving and less of what is fearful and stagnant."

"When you say it like that, it makes perfect sense. But

ego is currently telling me that what I want is getting further and further away and I'm compounding my mistakes because none of this is worth it since I'm creating more uncertainty and insecurity than I am support."

"But do you believe that?"

"No. A growing part of me wants this," I said, gesturing around the room. "It wants to feel this flow. It wants to believe that this is natural and that all can be changed through connecting to a greater sense of self."

"And so it is. You have come here to assimilate your allowance so that you may authenticate it in your world. And your fragile balance can grow strong because there is no worse or better here. There is no excess or loss, there is a simple balance of Love. Not the love that is defined, scattered and separated in your external world but a Love that is constant, unified, balanced and rich in its unending support."

My companion paused, anticipating my question.

"When you say love, it's hard not to ask what kind of love you mean. From the limited conditioned perspective, it's difficult not to divide love into definitions rather than seeing it as endless, flowing through different situations."

"But ego seeks to drip feed the true meaning of Love to you. Love being limited to certain circumstances and not to others is an invention of your ego which has isolated itself from the real nature of the Cosmos. It tells you that some are lucky in love and others are not. But you have moved beyond this limited understanding of Love. You are now expanding your perspective and allowing all those limited definitions to be part of your growing understanding of Love. You are beginning to realise that the Cosmos is made from Love and all your ego can do is alter your experience of this cosmic truth; block it out with fear and resistance. But you are choosing heart more readily and it is your heart that has brought you here."

"So when you talk about Love, why do I feel awkward?"

"Because it is a relatively unfamiliar and little-explored state of being, in truth."

I felt a rush of energy from the top of my head to the tips of my fingers and toes. "Another expression of Love?" I asked as I recovered from the euphoric sensation.

"Yes."

"This is all wonderful, really, but from my relatively limited perspective I still require a bit of definition."

"Very well. Let us start with self love. This is perhaps the aspect of the loving unity that is most in question currently in your process. The disturbance that you've been undergoing appears to be more and more intense, to the point where you have questioned if you are doing something wrong. Are the choices you are making supporting your world or undermining it?"

"Well, as I understand it, if I'm being self loving then they will be supporting it. But that's the reason for questioning myself—my situation at present isn't that supportive."

"Supportive of what?"

I paused to consider. "Oh, I get it. It's unsupportive of my ego, not my heart. My ego wants to be safe so it's actually the one that's causing me to doubt myself, reflecting its fears back on me. This is why my worries are related to my physical structures of home and money."

"But you have chosen to continue with your process and not to be waylaid by your ego."

"I certainly have. And that's why I'm here—to get the whole picture, not just ego's side of the story."

"Is it not wondrous?"

My host paused.

"Yes, it feels great. It just takes some getting used to. This flow has such a feeling of enrichment it's easy to get lost in it. The sensation is so massive it's difficult to understand just what it is. I know what I'm saying sounds like I'm tiptoeing back into analysis but that's not my intention. It's more a relative observation. When expansion goes beyond anything I've experienced within limitation, it can sometimes be so different that there appears to be no difference at all."

"In some ways your observation is accurate," said my companion who was following my words with great care. "But it is always tempting to look from within your limited world rather than see how your limited world fits into your greater world. You are a drop in the ocean that is Love. Sometimes you feel the waves of progress, sometimes you do not. What is important is that you always feel and you understand that you are always surrounded by Love and you are Love.

"Mental distress," he continued, "is a very strong diversion that ego loves to use when you are in the middle of change. But the more you believe that everything happens for a reason, the more you can appreciate in your heart centre why you undergo what you undergo; why you choose to change; and why, with every change, you are learning to rebalance yourself and to allow more and more Love and, as a result, experience more and more Love."

"And so it flows on!" I enthused.

"Yes. And on and on and on... without end," he added.

"Self love, then, can help me be disciplined so I keep my balance while I undergo change?"

"Certainly. Self love literally regulates the flow of Love. It regulates the allowance and assimilation and the authentication of Love in your world. Self love does not mean holding on to the vanities of ego such as self interest and physical appearance, self love is the loving discipline that enables your awareness of your heart and the truth of your heart in each moment."

My guide paused then prompted me to eat. "Please take whatever you wish from this table. Be with what you love. Recycle the fear of losing what you see before you. Lack is an illusion."

I rubbed my eyes and stared at an almost overwhelming choice. I was as though I were seven years old all over again with the best birthday party in the world. Everything was overflowing with joy, freshness and fulfilment. As soon as I spooned food onto my plate, the serving dishes seemed to refill almost instantaneously.

"Everyone is welcome," said my host. "There is always an abundance here, as you can see."

And I knew deep in my heart that anyone could sit at this table and they would find exactly what they wanted. For the first time since I arrived, I wanted to be in that belief. I wanted to allow the flow of magic that surrounded me completely.

"How do you do this? How do you make such an incredible choice for anyone and everyone?"

"Choice is what you make it. Guidance helps you understand this unending flow but if you are unwilling to explore then it remains hidden, undiscovered. That is what makes your process unique. When you devote to your inner sense as you do now, you begin to understand how empowering choice can be. Your ego once told you that you could only be devoted to something outside of yourself; that you could only gain love if you gave yourself away in search of the approval of others; you could only have power if you had control. Slowly these misunderstandings became normal. Self love became a vain reflection of ego. Devotion came to mean giving up responsibility to a power beyond your own. Selflessness meant you forgot your true nature and put yourself at the mercy of your ego.

"But now this has changed. You realise that there isn't one single way to love or to be loved. Ego is not the only way. I AM is the way; a gateway of choice that reconnects you with endless Love. It is the way of the heart that embraces the way of all seekers.

"The heart understands your intentions, your attachments and your joys," my guide continued, "and as you coordinate a more expanded view of yourself, you see that Love can flow through all your avenues of change and be reflected in all your creations. The more ways you explore, the closer you become to your true nature. And thus you are rebuilding, expanding beyond the limited definitions of ego. Devotion becomes a self loving balance that enables you to give unconditionally and receive unconditionally. Balance will enable you to serve without controlling your environment or depleting yourself.

"So when ego questions if it's really worth it, you will see beyond that superficial evaluation from the mind. You will sense the new level of Love and you will feel the difference. When you are in ascension you are returning to the wisdoms of your heart. And as you return to be Love and create from Love, you find those wisdoms right where you left them before you went on your research trip into limitation."

"So as I rise out of limiting conditioning, I'll see how my ego had a tendency to separate love into limited definitions that suited its own agenda."

"Correct. Ego simply can't cope with love because it is too overwhelming. Ego simply seeks separation. It accentuates one aspect of love over another, depending on what will maintain control. Ego keeps many under control by the fear of the loss of love when, in truth, that is the greatest illusion in your world. But it is only when you discover the freedom and joy that comes from cooperating with the Cosmos that you start to believe that love never ends."

"So when one aspect of love ends in our life—say, a romance ends—then ego seeks to convince us that love has ended?"

"Indeed. When in truth it is simply a completed experience of the learning of Love. Love as a whole always keeps on flowing."

"So it's to believe that we're always loved? We're always capable of love and every loving choice we make is contributing to expanding our experience of Love and ability to love?"

"Absolutely. Choice is love; Love is choice. When you offer choice to yourself or another, you are giving the opportunity to learn and to practice unconditional love; to practice unlimited creation."

I was beginning to feel more in the flow of our conversation. Love didn't seem to be as massive nor as trivial as before. It was valuable and yet everyday. If I was detached enough then I could recycle the fear of losing love; I could see endings as beginnings or simply one big endless loop that was always expanding. I could see my world as a unity that supported me, not just a place where there were lots of things missing with a long list of disappointments.

I felt more inspired to ask questions. "I'd like to take some examples of the flow of love. What happens to people who get their heart broken when a romantic relationship ends?"

"Ego defines this experience as heartbreak. Higher Self and I AM offer an alternative perception. The heart has expanded and the process of the expansion has met with such internal resistance that the person experiences pain as a result."

"Pain being resistance to feeling?"

"Yes. The soul has chosen to increase its capacity to love but they do not see that this expansion may be spread over many experiences. In other words, more than one relationship. Ego fuels the fear of the loss of love and security and the person believes their heart has been broken, rather than their heart has become expanded. Ego continues to convince the person that they can't love after this experience because love could only exist within this one relationship or that their heart is now unable to love again. Such are the limitations of ego."

"So just like any creation, the way Love arrives, or the form it comes in, can be very unpredictable?" I really felt I was beginning to understand.

"For the mind that is so, but not for the heart. The flow of love is unlimited and natural. Its arrival can appear ill-timed or daunting to ego, and yet it always supports the most efficient expansion. Whether the awareness is present to match the flow is another matter. But the flow continues because Love is unending."

"And that's why people often say that you find love when you're not looking?"

"Yes. For most, *looking* implies having fixed ego targets or expectations about the person they want in their life. This creates attachments to what love *should* look like. But in truth, looking is looking into self and going on the journey of Love that will magnetise a loving relationship. One half is the self that is radiating Love and the other half is the reflection of that Love in your environment."

"So when Mr Right or Mrs Right turns out all wrong, it's really that the person doesn't know themselves very well so the relationship they create isn't a very accurate reflection?"

"You might say that but, as you know, there is no wrong, only learning. But there are many ways to learn and one way is struggle.

"Beloved one, limitation is ingrained in you. Part of that conditioning means you expect things to be strugglesome, even though it is only one possible way. If you are unaware of alternatives then struggle is the principle path of learning. And if a person doesn't have a deep awareness of themselves, they will require many experiences to build self awareness and a relationship that is profound and lasting.

"At many stages of self discovery and learning, ego is only too willing to convince seekers that they have made a mistake rather than seeing they have achieved vital learning. So it is more a case of reflection. For the type of love that those in your world call soul mates to become a reality, a deep understanding of self is required. The more experience a soul has of Love, the more opportunity the soul has to create a deep and lasting reflection of Love; what you would call the genuine article— the soul mate that loves you for you, unconditionally. And that stands out from a crowd of conditionality and compromise."

"So it all comes back to building self awareness. And if I

listen to what ego thinks it *likes* in a person then I'm unlikely to deepen my understanding of Love."

My companion nodded knowingly. "The heart always has the answers you seek. Ego just detours away from the meaning."

Feeling more in harmony with my learning, I decided to try another angle of love and relationship. "What about people who don't show love because they think it's a sign of weakness?"

"Be with the Love that surrounds you and perhaps you can answer your own question."

"Okay..." I breathed through my heart. "If Love is the unlimited fuel of everything then ego would fear how empowered the person will become if they show love."

"Correct. Please continue."

"Then ego feels weak and incapable and the mind convinces the person they would also be weak and incapable if they are loving. And as long as the person chooses to believe this then it follows that it is their experience of Love."

"Yes. It can change as soon as the person changes what they believe. But as long as they limit their choices, they limit the Love that can flow through their lives."

"So if, let's say, I become unconditionally loving, does that mean nothing will bother me and I will be able to accept anything in my world?"

"You are edging towards the logic of your mind. Rest within your heart, beloved, and your Now. This is a complex question that embraces many understandings of Love. That is why you are thinking about trying to work it out. But as you begin to discover the many layers of Love, you are required to stay in your heart because it is there that you can sense what this means. As in all the explorations we have discussed, there is no single answer, there is simply guidance related to the angle at which you observe this question in any moment.

"Love is not an equation, it is an ever expanding flow. In

simple terms, the state of unconditionality is one of detachment. There are no conditions attached, there is no fear of the loss of Love nor the lack of Love. There is no fear of the loss of energy nor the lack of energy."

My companion stopped for a moment. I was now becoming familiar with their *assimilation pause*.

The space around me bulged into a droplet of pearlescent brilliance. I felt a rush of unparalleled euphoria as my heart united with my surroundings. I'd run out of superlatives many moments before as the desire to measure my experience dissolved. Instead, I was learning to accept; to be with this space; to be in Love and without limitation. The feeling began to dissipate just as my companion continued.

"Allowance and acceptance may appear the same but there is a subtle and powerful difference between them. What is acceptable for one soul is not acceptable for another. Acceptance is related to the individual experience of each soul and to the degree to which their ego can influence and control them. But allowance is a state of being that unifies the external and the internal.

"When you are truly unconditional, you are capable of being in allowance of all your experiences because you realise they are an unending flow of Love and learning. However, this does not mean that you agree with them, nor that you will support or reject what they represent or offer. But you will not attempt to control them or to project judgments or create attachments between their flow and yourself.

"When you are in allowance you can be in dynamic harmony with your environment, even though it may not reflect your personal truth. If you are in allowance of it then you will not attempt to conflict with it, you will simply see it as a flow that is giving you the opportunity to allow."

"So allowance doesn't mean being a doormat, putting up with just anything?"

"No it doesn't. It is a delicate and powerful state of

being that is always built on a foundation of balance. So allow yourself the flow. Let your creativity flow, synchronised in the phases of your ascension. Never berate or criticise yourself, just allow yourself to listen to your heart. There is nothing wrong, even if your ego tells you there is.

"When you are trying to figure out your world, you are setting yourself aside from the flow of your heart. Instead, flow with the truth of your heart, then you will be in the unending flow and you will work with the Cosmos to unravel your attachments. That way, you can be free and joyous in your creativity.

"You know we always support you but you are also aware that we cannot support that which is the victim within you. So understand that we are always with you and, as long as you are within your heart, you are unravelling your attachments so that you can feel and be the real you. You are Love and Love is you.

"The Universe can never be against you. It is your ego that is against the unity because it was born from separation and a lack of Love. It knows nothing else. But sooner or later, even ego knows you will find what you are seeking because it is only a matter of detachment, discernment and discovery."

"Not a matter of time?"

"Oh no. Linear time is a figment of your ego's imagination. The infinite unity has no time for linearity."

"So if I look at my current situation as being part of the loving unity, which bit am I blind to? Which angle of the unity can't I see?"

I paused as my question echoed around and around in my heart. Sitting back in my chair, I was finally willing to surrender; to allow the answer rather than keep forcing it out from my heart.

I was beginning to realise how far attachment went. I was surrounded by abundance and love and yet I was still tempted to find my answers from limited conditioning rather than cooperate with my surroundings. I sensed an answer forming from deep within me.

"I'm learning how to make ends meet. I AM learning to allow the flow and then the ends will meet." I felt a sudden burst of joy that lit up the whole of me like the brightest smile possible.

"A brilliant connection! You detached and look what it brought you... an infinite flow of understanding. Ego tells you that if you detach, you won't have anything. But in truth, one single detachment unleashes an endless flow. So keep on releasing. Detach from your assumptions about Love. Detach from the limitations you currently place on flow. Believe you are an infinite giver and receiver. Believe that giving and receiving happens simultaneously and in balance.

"You don't need to keep score, just balance," he continued. "To open your heart is not to believe in just anything nor to give yourself away. To open your heart is to unite with the unlimited more and more. It is to detach and rise above the limitations that your ego imposes.

"What you are undergoing now is simply growing pains, that is all. The unlimited flow is there for the choosing."

"So closing my heart is a choice. Opening my heart is a choice. And staying where I am is a choice. I can allow all of those but I'm choosing to remain open. I AM willing to open my heart to the next level. I AM open to help and guidance in this next phase."

"And so it is. You are arrived at your expansion. You are beloved... coming into the awareness of your true nature. Flow well."

My companion was wavering as if preparing to leave.

"Just before you go... Can I ask who you are? Or what you represent?"

"This is the consciousness of Love, the flow of emotional bliss that is Sananda. Bathe in the peace that is unlimited creation."

I felt a wave of Love rush through me with the delicate balance of a humming bird and the inundation of a Moon tide. I had never undergone such expansion. I had never felt so understood, so loved. Tears of joy rolled down my cheeks as I dissolved into a swirl of pearlescence and our loving unity was completed.

Overturning Assumption

As my eyes opened, Isis was fast asleep on my lap. I lay back in a feeling of lightness that lingered from my meditation. I felt like I was full of holes. Or was I just creating space?

Isis continued to snooze while I hoped that the love I'd felt with Sananda would radiate and continue to expand in this Now. After all, if I believed in my unified nature then all that loving connection would never cease. There was no on-off switch, just the choice switch.

Isis looked like she was able to be in her greater consciousness while remaining in her physical form. I marvelled at her detachment. Oh to be a cat. How they seemed to be naturals when it came to allowance. There was never too little time to relax, to explore or to heal.

As my moment of pure connection dissolved into the sounds of rain on the window, I felt strangely inspired in what would seem to others a depressingly gloomy bedroom. It was eleven o'clock and I was wide awake, ready to start a day's work at the beginning of the evening.

"I'm going to run with it, Isis, even if my day is now completely topsy-turvy." I scooped her tightly curled body off my lap and placed her gently on the bed. She looked drowsily indignant at my moving her but recurled her sleek limbs and returned to her circle of contentment.

I moved to my makeshift workstation and began to type whatever came into my head. The first few lines seemed blurred, until I allowed the flow but as I read it back, it was a subject I'd never seen before and it didn't fit in with anything I'd previously written. I wanted to stop and complain to my Higher Self that this wasn't a chapter that would fit now, that it should come later when there was space. But I knew better than to listen to the analyses of my mind.

I could sense my Higher Self was smiling at my apparent attempt to conceal my rummagings into logic.

I wrote and wrote. When I glanced at the clock again it was nearly 4 a.m. "It'll be time to finish my hard days night soon," I chuckled, yawning and stretching.

The bedroom door suddenly closed, startling me. "As one door closes, another door opens. It's the way of the Cosmos; a unified way into which all truths flow," a familiar voice said.

"Making a point, Merlin?"

"Let's call it, making a unity. Too much attachment in a point, and far too limited for where we are going."

"And where would that be?"

"Let's meet in your inner space so that we can go on our next journey."

"Okay, but before we do that, please can you answer me one question?"

"Just one?" teased Merlin.

"Why am I writing like this? Why is my day all mixed up? Am I suffering from book lag?"

"You are absorbing chaos. No wonder your mind is mixed up! You are not the soul you were. Quite some achievement—a creative expansion your mind can't control. Now that is definitely a path worth travelling... **P**-urpose, **A**-ction, **T**-ruth and **H**-ope."

"But that's a different path than last time."

"It always is. Another angle, another moment... all leading to change."

I was beginning to feel sleepy as I closed my eyes in preparation for meditation. I was just about to fall into a deep sleep when Merlin appeared right on cue, drawing me back into conversation.

"All is as it is; all part of the perfect flow. You are an unlimited creator stepping into the knowingness of it; into the willingness and the belief of it. This is a Cosmic Truth. Your experience of it might cause you to think differently, but that does not alter the truth of it."

"Then how am I going to change my experience of it? For example, how am I going to create a life in which I feel like an unlimited creator, one that's reflected to me right down into this part of me in this material world?"

"To feel and see your unlimited creative nature in your material world on a regular basis, you are required to allow the unfolding of your ability to believe. This is a process, not a series of results. If you do not have the unfolding, you don't have the becoming. If you don't have the becoming, you will never truly detach because you will always be chasing results and will remain attached. Are your results more precious than your process?"

My mind came to a standstill. I felt unable to reply.

"An interesting answer," said Merlin, testing my underlying intention.

"But I didn't answer," I replied, attempting a defence.

"Your silence is your answer. This is an observation, not a criticism. The mind and ego have long fixated on the results of your world rather than how you arrive at them. How do you think you have become so attached?! Why do you think that your history repeats itself?"

"Because nobody learns how to change, they just chase ego expectations?"

"Indeed. The result takes over from the learning and the wisdom is lost. Do it longer, with increasing struggle, even misery if you will. Such are the repetitions of ego. But do not change and do not learn the reason that it does not work. Do not stop and step back so that you can look below the surface and find the buried treasure of realisation. Oh no, stay in the darkness, then you won't be able to see what you are missing!"

"Alright, alright. On behalf of the human-ish race, we aren't really that bad, are we?"

"Who said anything about bad? Just attached is all."

"Okay, attached. But detaching?"

"Indeed you are. And to undergo detachment is to regain the ability to value your path. And that is to value yourself, the precious unlimited being that you are."

"So I'm judging my unlimited capability by the results in this limited world, not by my overall progress?"

"In a way, you are. Your current chaos is supporting you in moving from valuing the quantity of your life to valuing the quality of your life. Detachment is a very important part of this process because it helps you stand back from the results of limitation to see the real progress you are making. Then you can see what is genuinely valuable."

"So a lot of what ego values isn't actually important?"

"It will become less and less important as your process evolves. Call that your *becoming*. You are becoming the unlimited nature that you truly are. And as you shift from ego to heart, and from attachment to detachment, you create a complete value-shift."

"It's time I believed that this process is working, even though the way it's working is a bit of a mystery. If I keep detaching and opening my heart wider then sooner, hopefully, rather than later, I'll create what I require to finish my book?"

"Indeed. And so it is... an endless process of exploring. Shall we become a little more?"

"Why not?"

"Can you assume your connection?"

"You mean meditation?"

"Indeed. Meet me in your heart room in a couple of your moments."

"Oh, Merlin, that could take an age," I joked.

"It did until very recently," he chuckled. "But if it is to be an age, make it a golden one. You'll require it where you are going."

"Okay, one connection coming up."

I dimmed the lights and settled into the armchair. I began to let the seeming contradictions of my physical world float away like passing clouds.

Something had changed. I felt strangely optimistic as I began to grow into the reality of everything happening for a reason rather than for a result. There was much more flow.

I heard another door close in the building and felt a now-familiar arrival of energy and heat in my right side. I asked the warmth to fill the whole of my body and began to feel heavy.

Merlin brushed past me theatrically. He stood in front of the familiar oak doors of my heart room.

"Ready?" he asked.

"What's the hurry? I thought you couldn't be rushed? You don't have the time for rushing; too linear for you."

"This isn't rushing around in space, this is gaining acceleration so you can support more transmutation. There is a vast difference between the speeding vectors of your world and the accelerations of realisation. Time to gamble with your life a little; expose yourself to the risks that your ego thinks are so threatening and help you see that they are really enriching."

"And how are we supposed to do that?" I asked, feeling my head in a spin and my world dissolving within it.

"Come this way and I'll show you." And with that, Merlin pushed the great oak doors open with both hands.

"Let the games begin!" he announced dramatically.

Your Money Or Your Life

"Time to get off the merry-go-round. Open your eyes," continued Merlin.

I did as I was asked and with a swish of cloak and a flash

of purple we were standing in the middle of a casino. "Let's go and play the tables!" he enthused.

"Merlin, what on Earth are we doing here?" I felt a bizarre sense of outrage. "I don't have the money to gamble, much less lose it trying!"

"Who says you need money to gamble?"

"Okay, you've got me fair and square. The Merlin:1, Assumption:nil. But how do you expect me to carry on gambling? You can see what a poor loser I am," I grimaced. "Emphasis on the poor," I added apologetically.

"Oh I think that makes it 2:nil because, you see, I can't see the poor loser. However, I do choose to see the unlimited creator in the making. But I am glad you raised the subject of poverty—that is exactly why we are here!"

"Now I'm at a complete loss!"

"Let's walk and talk; get this flow on the road."

"Okay," I replied, recycling yet more ego protests. I listened intently as we wove in and out a collection of blackjack tables.

Merlin was definitely on a roll. "One of the cornerstones of ego is loss. Another, as you know, is lack or scarcity. The other two are fear and control."

"So what of it?" I replied with a hint of anxiety, as if an important question had unfolded and I'd missed the meaning.

Merlin paused, emphasising his next teaching. "It is quite an irony then that, without these cornerstones, you, the unlimited creator, could not have experienced what it is to be in form. Fear, control, lack and loss have enabled you to live inside the cube, slowing down your unlimited nature so that you can become attached and know what it is to be in a body, an individualised aspect of consciousness."

"You mean, the experience of physical form is all thanks to slow-travelling energy? And to density, fear and control? And, I suppose, ego?"

"Indeed it is! Well put! In this way, the state of form is all thanks to ego. But the experience of it... well, that's a different matter. As you change, the experience changes. Ego is still encouraging you to fix energy within those familiar corners; to box up your world to bring less and less flow. But now your world has gone upside down. No longer is form, fear and falsehood normal. Flow, flexibility and Love are becoming normal. And you are beginning to see just how fragile inflexibility is."

"What I understand from what you're saying is that the four corners of ego were useful when I wanted to be limited, but now they're coming unstuck with every conscious choice I make. At least, some of them are. But how unstuck they become depends on my choices. Correct?"

"Indeed! And so each time you make a creative choice, there is still the ego echo—the recurring temptation to make immediate reference to fear, control, lack or loss. And that is what you do if you start your choices from your mind and not from your heart."

"So, when I started protesting at the beginning of this meeting, I was assuming that I couldn't gamble because I don't have any money and I just let ego draw in those four corners of limitation. I feared loss. I thought in terms of scarcity and I wanted to control my world."

"Indeed. But you can change that by examining your intentions and your assumptions."

"So, for example, I could suspend my material reality when I return to it and say, What if I had no money problems? What would I create?"

"Exactly. Believe that you are one hundred per cent in the unlimited world, even if your experience of it leaves a little to be desired," Merlin smiled wryly.

I began to embrace our conversation more fully. "So I could work on an assumption that I wasn't in my box of limitation. What if I could one hundred per cent believe my unlimited capability; take it as normal? Then what would I choose?"

"Now you're getting in the flow of this! With these fresh eyes, how would you behave? What would you observe? What would you see as your flow of creation? Take this casino, for example... What would you see here in amongst all of what your mind has labelled *gambling*?"

"If I'm honest," I leapt straight in, feeling sure I knew how I felt, "I assume it's throwing money away because I don't believe I can win. And also, casinos make huge money so most people must lose."

As the words bolted together in my locked-tight logic, I realised I'd fitted myself back in the box, forming all of my answers from conditioning. I thought I knew but I hadn't really understood my feelings and intentions.

"The thing is, I can't afford to gamble," I added apologetically, feeling cornered and disturbed by the sound of paying out slot machines and cheering from winning tables.

"Or," countered Merlin, "perhaps you can't afford not to! When you run out of flow because you don't let yourself have any, ego tells you that you don't have any money, therefore you can't afford anything! Does that mean you don't have any alternatives? Does that mean something so magical and wonderful as your own creative abilities don't count? Do you want to trade in your unlimited creator ability for something as mundane as money?"

We'd arrived at the one-arm bandits. Rows and rows of them were flashing their electronic hypnotism.

How fitting, I thought—I'd just held myself to ransom and not thought anything of it until the words had fallen clanging into my Now.

"Not much of an alchemist," I muttered.

"Be your Light and you will continue on the path of alchemy. That was a slight stumble, nothing that you can't recover from in a moment," said Merlin, sitting down beside me.

"But what are you doing sitting at one of these machines? You probably already know what combination is going to come up. Or at any rate, you don't require this to create what you want, so why bother?"

"Because we are here to learn and teach, one to another, and all the way around again. And if alchemy is a unity, an endless loop of creation, then at any point of observation, nothing is excluded, it is all part of the picture. That is why you are learning in this place. This is all part of your creation."

"But you told me to move beyond money. You said I was to embrace having endless unlimited ways."

"The guidance was to embrace the unity that you are and to realise that you are embracing much more while excluding nothing. Money is still an option amongst your unlimited selection. This is why you are currently up to your neck in detachment. Quite fitting, don't you think?"

"What is that supposed to mean?" I felt completely overwhelmed.

"Let us look into your attachments; the transmutation cycle that is your current alchemy. What are you detaching from?"

"Scarcity?"

"And so that is why you are surrounded by...?" Merlin waited for me to fill in the blanks.

"A casino that I judge is unsupportive? And a belief that I can't win, even though I just walked past people winning and the machines were just paying out."

"Well done! These are enriching observations. So why not go with the flow? Detach and allow your scarcity to dissolve rather than resist the flow and end up making your process more difficult. Be open to winning because you've got nothing to lose. Why? Because if you've got nothing to lose, you are detached. If you are detached then you are allowing your unlimited nature instead of worrying about what you don't have. How can worry help your creative capability?"

The air appeared to thicken with awareness. I was wondering how I could merge with it. "Okay, it can't. And the more I worry, the more controlling I get and the less flow I experience. And, more importantly, I start questioning my creative ability. And that just leads me full circle back to my ego justifying me existing in scarcity. So I surrender. No more worrying and trying to control the unlimited flow."

I felt a wave of energy go through me. I swayed gently as if the Universe had just nudged me into recognition. "I just realised something. Some bizarre part of me finds it comforting to worry about what I don't have. Absolutely ridiculous really."

"Abundantly absurd," smiled Merlin.

"Perhaps that keeps my ego entertained… thinking that somehow, if I worry more, then my creation will be worth just that little bit extra in the end because of all the stress."

"How quaint."

"That's a polite word for it, Merlin. Perhaps *without value* is more accurate."

"Let's just say, without flow. Worry is a concentrated point of attachment—yes, that word again—beyond which your ego wishes you not to venture. Ego will string it out until you believe that worry is a never ending barrier stretching far into the foreseeable future. That is, if you worry enough. Ego will then prove to you that reinforcing what you can't do and limiting yourself is, of course, just as productive as actually understanding how your creations are unfolding and contributing to the rewards you seek."

"That's ridiculous!"

"Limited. And you don't have to listen to the scarcities of your ego saying 'It's this way or nothing' or 'It's always been like this so it's always going to remain like this.' So we are back to flow. From your perspective, what is stopping your flow?"

The penny dropped.

"Oh, I get it. I'm actually disallowing money as a form of creation. I'm not dealing with what's right in front of me."

"Exactly!" smiled Merlin. "Just because you embrace what is right in front of you, such as creation through money, it doesn't mean you are stuck with it. Call it a familiar starting place; a form of creation that you are used to," he hinted.

"But it's just not the only one?" I responded.

"Indeed. It is, however, the one way that your ego has seized to distort the creation stream, telling all that will listen that money is the only way of creating, the only way to fulfilment."

"So because of a limited perspective, money has become the only way of creating anything?"

"Indeed. And if you're financially challenged that means you are useless, even worthless. But your heart never views your endless potential like that. It tells you there are lots of ways to create something. Ego is there just waiting to reinforce what it thinks you are lacking... if you are tempted to listen."

"So that's why I disallowed this place... because I'm attached to not having any money. I thought that to be surrounded by what I currently don't have was the last reflection I needed to see, but these surroundings are exactly what I required in order to dissolve the polarity within me."

"Precisely. You are naturally abundant, it's just a matter of tapping into your abundance ability. You can always create in life whether you have money or not. So there is flow in every situation but, to stay in the flow, you are required to remain open, allowing. This place has already given you valuable learning so you could say you are already a winner. You just haven't won what your ego expected. Your winnings are immaterial but, as you are finding out, wisdom is priceless and it is to demonstrate willingness and openness so that you will receive the abundance of learning that is on offer, irrespective of your ego's assumptions."

I felt a sense of purpose ignite within me. "Can we talk more about giving and receiving?"

"Certainly."

"Giving and receiving is all part of creation, right?"

"Indeed. You could say that, in a way, the cycles of giving and receiving sketch the flow of the infinite."

"So how, in my case, does this get so out of balance? I've been giving in my work in the sense that I've been working with the flow of ideas and suchlike. So why has the receiving appeared to dry up now?"

"It is always to realise that giving and receiving are chaotic like the unlimited flow. Sometimes there is more giving, as ego would perceive it, and sometimes more receiving. Sometimes it is to address the balance so that the two may flow into one, into unity."

"So it's important to keep in balance so that the chaos is not too extreme?"

"Indeed. Balance is always supportive."

"And I suppose I must be really out of balance to have no money?"

"In a sense. But balance is a relativity and it depends on what you are achieving in your overall unity."

"What do you mean?"

"There are times in your experience when there are many factors influencing what you see as your giving and receiving. As you move along your path of ascension, you will be flowing with a greater sense of abundance rather than ego's subtotals and isolated tallies that try to convince you there is no value in your experience and that there is only value in form."

"Sorry, you've lost me."

"You are not lost. It is ego that is falling behind. But we understand what you mean. So with greater awareness and reunification with the greater you, when you experience lack, you are detaching from a collection of moments in all your experiences of lack in limitation, not just from the situation you are currently in. Think of yourself as healing a certain band of energy, a certain frequency within you and, to achieve this, you are recycling a selection of attachments from many different experiences. But they all have a frequency, a band of energy in common."

"If I understand this, it's like saying that I'm detaching

from attachment frequencies, say, 70 to 80, for example. Within that band of energy there are lots of attachments to scarcity which have been stored at different times and within different experiences, even different lifetimes. They're all of the same level and they're all linked by being examples of scarcity."

"Life is never an equation, always a flow. But we understand your simple analogy. Continue."

"So as I learn to recognise the nature of scarcity, then I can recycle frequencies 70 to 80 and return that part of my energy to an abundant state rather than letting my mind continue to occupy me with the scarce conditionings of ego."

"Yes. You are choosing to recycle a part of one of the greatest misunderstandings in limitation—that there is a limited flow of energy and a limited way to enjoy that limited flow."

"Is that why I've gone from financial flow to no flow in the space of a few days?"

"Indeed. It is an opportunity to recycle a larger chunk of the attachment to scarcity that you have. Coupled with your increasing capacity, the contrast appears on the surface to be going from flow to nothing when it is actually going from flow into transmutation. These cycles will always come and go. Understand that these discussions support you in developing the awareness of your changes so that you don't reject your path forward but embrace it. Awareness helps you transmute smoothly because you are more open and embracing of alternatives during your changes."

"So in the long term, it'll all come flooding back."

"Indeed. But you know what I am going to say."

"Don't measure giving and receiving? Be unconditional and trust in the unlimited flow?"

"Precisely. If you start to measure how much you are receiving or giving at any point in your process, you will be letting your ego take over your creativity."

"So what's happening in our creativity when we feel drained? When we feel like we've given too much and there's nothing left? It can be when we've tried to give and then people have demanded more and more until we just feel exhausted."

"Ego control and imbalance is making its presence felt. There are many perceptions and interpretations of your example as it is dependent on the intention behind the action. Here is one understanding. Ego has encouraged you to give and give and give and then you have become out of balance. If you project beyond what is required to maintain balance, you feel that there is nothing left when in truth there is just no balance left. You are feeling the weight of the burden of ego. It's ego that says to move further and further out of balance and not be in your heart. It's ego that says you can't stop giving and that you have to carry on, even if you are in pain because of your lack of balance."

"Okay, let's take another angle. What if I'm mean and ego has conditioned me to be resistant to giving? How would I get back into balance then?"

"You would get the opportunity to give... to help you return to balance. If this opportunity was ignored then you would reach a degree of imbalance in which you felt you were being forced to give. Or that you lost everything so that you had to ask for help and thereby recognise that there is no separation from the inner and outer world."

"Would that be like giving everything at once to make up for a long term resistance to giving?"

"In a way, yes. But for those who are unaware of their giving and receiving imbalance and they just let it become more and more out of balance, such extreme experiences can appear to come from an uncaring Universe that is working against them. Or it can seem to them that they are unlucky victims of life, that everything has been taken away from them, or that they have made a huge mistake. How many in your world ask 'What have I done to deserve this?' In truth, they could ask of themselves 'What have I not been aware of to create such extreme imbalance?'"

"So really," I began, fuelled by a growing understanding, "both situations are as extreme as each other; they are both as scarce as each other. One person is letting their ego exhaust them by giving too much and the other is exhausting themselves through their resistance to giving because they want to hoard what they have. In the end, because the imbalance is so extreme, one will have to give up giving to restore balance and the other will need to learn to give if they are to dissolve their resistance and fear of loss."

Merlin smiled. "Such are the burdens of ego. Is it not strange how the fear of not being enough can be so exhausting and the fear of losing what we have can become so costly?"

He paused as if right on cue. Shouts of joy came from the roulette wheel as a big winner was born.

"Comedy... It's all in the timing, he pondered. "And it would appear that congratulations are in order."

I was just about to ask what for. The winner over there? But my reply came from the heart. "Okay, I'm beginning to see the reflections in this world. So that means it's congratulations all round."

"You are beginning to realise that you may receive when you least expect and from the least likely source. This is why allowance creates flow and your allowance does you credit."

We stopped at a one-arm bandit machine.

"Shall we play?" asked Merlin.

I still felt reluctant and sensed the conditionality creeping back, my ego saying 'What's in it for me? Can Merlin fix your problem? Go on, ask him to fix it for you.' I tried to silence my ego's escalating demands.

"Talk, talk, talk. That's all there seems to be until we return to the peace of our hearts," grinned Merlin. "The process is so much smoother there, so much more enjoyable. Joy never leaves there you know, you are always in joy!"

I couldn't help myself. "But will it pay my earthly mortgage that's due in two days?"

Merlin immediately rephrased my question into a lighter and loftier intention. "I AM creating the perfect resources in each moment," he said, and pulled the handle on the nearest one-arm bandit.

The machine erupted into a crescendo of light and sound promising financial miracles. My heart began to race as I eagerly watched the outcome. But three different symbols clunked their way to the finishing line.

Nothing.

I felt my expectations deflate. "And what's that supposed to teach me?"

"That you can not live through the path of another. You are required to recycle your own attachments," replied Merlin nimbly. "All is abundance here. There is no need of anything. Well, perhaps some wisdom would come in handy."

"Ha, ha, ha. Well, since you're all cashed up with your abundant awareness, you could spare some sympathy for the limited me still chasing instant gratification!"

I was feeling more than a little disgruntled.

"Moreover, I really believed you could come up with the jackpot. I even felt it when you pulled the handle. Why didn't it happen?"

"Who said it didn't happen?" challenged Merlin. "Are you back in the pay of your ego?"

"Of course not. That's far too costly."

"And so remember, money is only one way of creating. Creation can come through the tangible form as well as the intangible. If what you require doesn't flow into materiality one way, are you going to disallow the other possible rewards and the other possible avenues?"

"No," I replied indignantly. "I just got caught up with my ego there, hoping you'd save me. I was well and truly attached and I can feel it now as disappointment."

"Alright. Now let's play another game and see if you can create what you really want, not what your ego wants. Nothing like practice to dissolve the doubts within you and master your creation skills. Did you realise there are three players here?"

I paused and looked around there was no one else in our row.

"Oh, I get you. You, me and my ego trying to play against me?"

"There you are! A winner again! Realisation—a treasure worth discovering. Pieces of eight, pieces of eight," he sang, drifting off into the crowd like a parrot guiding his captain.

"Wait for me. I'm all at sea," I joked, hurrying to catch up.

"It's all hands on deck, you know. Sails to be set," called Merlin. "Time to start steering your course, me 'earty."

The Root Of All Evil

Merlin cut a purposeful figure as he navigated through what appeared to be an unending wave of people. Instead of trying to catch up, I balanced and practiced going with the flow, sailing as best I could through openings as they became available. Soon we were shoulder to shoulder in the crowd.

"You're getting the hang of that detachment," he smiled.

"Thank you. So what's our next game?"

"Oh, I thought we'd take it up a notch; go a little deeper; increase the intensity. More layers and more players but the principles remain the same. Here are your chips. There are lots of different types; makes it more interesting, eh? Don't want to go to one particular well too often; could get a little dry."

I was a puzzled by his comment. "What do you mean by *a little dry*, Merlin?"

"Sometimes, when transmutation is working on a deeper level, it can seem to be relentless. So it's always good to keep your heart open with humour and variety. That way, you keep the flow going and you keep going with the flow. You aren't tempted to get fixated and try and do all your changing through one angle of self."

The Root Of All Evil

"And that would have me slipping back to ego?"

"Indeed, that is possible. But you could also become a little harsh upon yourself, even zealous. That would never do."

Merlin fell silent and I knew I was being asked to step up my play; start applying the guidance I'd already received rather than be a passive bystander. It was time to be active, not encourage my ego's desire to be spoon fed. Just because I didn't know did not mean I couldn't experience. Whether I made my learning with wisdom and guidance or without, I was still learning.

I arranged my different colour chips on the raised cushion. They had writing on them. I felt sure it was a denomination but the words were too long for that. I looked closer. The pink chips said *Ignorance*; the gold ones, *Attachment*; the blue, *Judgment* and the ruby red ones, *Resistance*.

"Those are parts of my life I certainly don't mind gambling away," I muttered. Merlin gave me a broad smile.

The crowd went hush, waiting for the game to begin.

"What are we betting for?" I asked in a lowered voice.

"You tell me," Merlin replied. "The choice is yours. It's all learning—the mysterious, the obvious and the hilarious; all learning."

"Are we betting for a combination to come up or are we betting against something?"

"It's up to you how you use your creation stream. A little hint though: to create, you are required to be in your creation stream. Just a little hint."

"All bets please! Place your bets, ladies and gentlemen," called the croupier.

"What do I do? I don't know the rules. What should I be focusing on?" I had no idea. I felt I was in quick-drying indecision.

"No more bets, dice rolling."

"Damn," I whispered, as the dice rolled near me. "I'm not even in the game."

Merlin leaned forward. "If you are choosing to be in the game and are going to practice the game, it's best to be in it. Remember, being attached keeps you out of the flow of experience, not to mention the flow of abundance. The fear of loss creates loss!"

"I thought I knew that!"

"Your mind thinks it does but what of the practical? Get in the flow and you'll pick it up as you go along. What are you willing to bet? A bit of Ignorance? Maybe some Resistance? Pick a chip, any chip. Everyone's a winner," smiled Merlin. "Everyone's a winner."

The plays had been completed and the bets were being called once more. I took a couple of chips from my pile of Ignorance and put them in the centre of the playing field. Quite apt, I observed as I was still no closer to finding out the rules. I began to feel a rush of energy, but not like before. I was becoming less and less attached to the outcome and more and more interested in being in the game.

"Wonderful. You are beginning to play. Very important. The result is only a line in the story, you know. It's the *The end* or the *Once upon a time*. But what counts is the bit in the middle. It's how you play, how well you are connected to your Now, how present you are. That's what matters in matter. How can you create the material rewards that you want if you aren't present, holding that mould of intention still in your Now so that you and the flow can pour in your happy ending?"

Merlin began singing, "*It's not what you do, it's the way that you do it... It's the way your heart teaches you that counts,*" he reinforced. "It all adds up you know. It's all a form of learning."

"Given that you know what you want, right?"

"It is all learning. Win or lose, you still get to go home with some learning. The trick is not to make a habit of learning through struggle. The middle bit is worth studying because it's in the middle bit that you find out if you know what you thought you knew!"

The Root Of All Evil

"You mean, whether I'm actually honest about what I want?"

"That, too."

The dice throw was completed in a flurry of disappointment and a shift of gaze in my direction.

"Oh, well done," said Merlin clapping. "It appears you've become a winner by risking your ignorance. But your ego didn't know that, did it?"

"Fortunately for me, ego didn't have a clue."

Merlin handed me two new chips. They were purple but had no inscription.

"What are these?"

"Oh, where's your spirit of adventure? Want to know everything? All in good time. It's for me to know and for you to realise."

"Okay, I only..."

And then I realised the joke. I'd won by risking my ignorance but now I wanted to know everything all over again.

"The scarcities of the mind," observed Merlin.

"I AM remaining open," I replied quickly, placing more chips on the table, this time three blue ones. I felt a shudder of self judgment pass through me. There was a sudden hush at the table as the biggest bet won and all were swept before it.

"Total clear out. How can he win and everyone lose? That doesn't seem fair," I remarked.

"Masterful magnetism," came the unexpected reply. "The player is aligned with the unlimited. They understand what they are creating and they are detached. Do not judge. Judgment stops the flow. But you can always discern from your heart; allow understanding to find its place in your world. Judgment creates stubborn attachments and points between which your ego can string you out. Never enough; too much. Do you want to keep rebounding between judgments?"

"Do you mean don't jump to conclusions or go to extremes?"

"Indeed. They aren't of value. Only the flow will help you create what you want. Simple abundant flow. It doesn't need points, it is endless and flows in all ways."

Merlin paused.

"Do you believe you lost because the other player won?" he probed.

"No, I didn't mean that. It was just such a dramatic win, it took me by surprise. My ego reacted so it could play the victim. If I'm maintaining an abundant perspective then there's always an abundance for everyone. There's no point in feeling a victim of the supposed flow of abundance in our world. The same unlimited flow is available to us all, it's just that not everyone sees it like that. Most people see their world in terms of scarcity; what's running away, running out, running past; not what's right here and right now."

"An abundance of awareness, indeed," added Merlin.

I was completely quiet. I whispered my intention before the dice roll, "I AM creating the perfect resources to finish my novel." I took three of the gold Detachment chips and placed them on a narrow band towards the outside.

The croupier halted momentarily. "Table maximum. Please be advised we have a single bet at the table maximum."

For a brief moment, I wondered what I'd done, but I stood still as the doubt blew through me. In a moment, the dice roll was over. Merlin handed me my winnings—five purple chips. I let out a loud cheer.

"It's my lucky night!"

"It certainly is not," he replied firmly. "It's your Conscious Creation night! These are the moments when you begin to believe; when you see that luck is but a fancy name for being in balance and in the flow, not a cosmic payout for being good or something random that happens once in a blue moon.

"Remember, your ability to create lies in your heart, a balanced intention and a detached nature. When all of these come together, it's a wonderful feeling. But it is also a natural feeling. The euphoria, the 'luck' you are feeling, is really that connection to the unlimited. It feels so intense and so wondrous because you've been creating with ego for so long that you've forgotten what it feels like to create consciously through love, not fear."

"So when those people win the jackpot, it's because all those aspects have come into harmony?"

"Precisely. For whatever reason in their process of learning, that is so. Whether or not they are aware of that is another story."

"But it doesn't happen all the time. Why?"

"Because your limited nature is more familiar and also because big winnings come with big learning and spiritual responsibility. Your capacity for such flow comes and goes."

"So what happens to those people who win really large lotteries and have incredible amounts of money one minute and then a year later they have nothing?"

"They are learning abundance. And they are cultivating the awareness to deal with abundance. For many, sudden wealth does not mean that they suddenly have the awareness to cope with the healing issues that wealth brings. Many create such influxes to help them value other aspects of their life; to get money into perspective, as it were."

"So you're saying they find out that money can't buy love and that if suddenly they have so much money, that doesn't necessarily mean they'll be able to cope with the change, or that it will fix what they feel they lack or what's missing in their lives."

"All is learning. And as we have said, money is one form of abundance but it is not the only one. All can learn from what they receive in life but sometimes the learning comes more suddenly and sometimes the opportunity to learn appears overwhelming, or is rejected."

"So if—or should I say when—I win the lottery, I'll get the opportunity to put money into perspective?" I joked.

Merlin scowled at me comically.

"But Merlin, seriously, why is our world becoming so obsessed with money? Why are we tearing up the beauty of our home just so we can hoard more things?"

"Because it is a strong creative habit within the humanity. The familiar is chosen over the expansive. It appears to be easier to believe what seems secure and guaranteed. Money has become so valued because it appears safe, not because there is any actual value in it."

"And that's just perpetuating an ignorance that ensures scarcity continues," I suggested.

"The poverties of the mind and the attachments to imbalance run deep within the physical world. But when the true nature of abundance is embraced, then the value of money is understood."

"So there are always creative alternatives?"

"Yes, all ways. Look at you. Your mind told you that you could never win anything in this place but you have gained much. Not necessarily what you expected, but you have become enriched and the night is young and there is so much to play for!" he said, diverting his eye towards the table.

I took the lead this time. "Okay, Merlin, it's time to detach and recycle what this last chip represents. I play it with an open heart and with all the completeness of detachment that I can manage."

As the dice came to rest, everything moved in slow motion as the players' faces dropped and Merlin and I appeared to stand back in a bubble of detachment. In a moment the crowd began to thin and all the chips were taken. Merlin gave me one purple chip. I was surprised but accepted the chip willingly.

"Why are you surprised?" he asked.

"Probably because I'm conditioned that you either win or you lose. If you lose, how can there be a reward? But if I'm as unlimited as I choose to be then I can never lose, I'm just required to change my perspective so I can see what my detachment has brought me."

"And so the big gamble has been taken!" said Merlin, smiling broadly and tipping his head in recognition. He turned and headed off in search of new learning.

"Wait for me!" I called.

"Waiting is for those who have time," he called back. "Creation is for those who are in the flow and in the Now."

Assimilating Abundance

"What gamble, Merlin?" I asked eagerly as I caught up.

"Balance, of course. Would you like a rest? Maybe have a drink?"

"I wouldn't mind, but why now? I'm getting on a roll. I might even be in danger of actually enjoying myself!"

"Good. Then you won't mind enjoying yourself in a different way; soak up some of that achievement. Appreciate your own creativity. Be with the abundant soul that you are."

"You mean, smell the roses?"

"Indeed. Connect with the joy of your path."

"Okay, those roses are growing on me. I mean, the idea is growing on me. Oh, you know what I mean. All this detachment training has been thirsty work. Look at me; I can barely form a sentence!"

Merlin found a quiet bar tucked away in a corner of the casino. It had large comfortable chairs that were easy to fall into.

The waiter set two blue smoking drinks down on our table. "Just give me a nod at the bar if you'd like another order," he smiled.

We acknowledged his hospitality and sat in a unified company of silence until words began to bubble over into the peaceful ambience.

"Guidance, you're amazing. This would probably have been the last place I would've chosen to understand and practice abundance. But that's what makes it so perfect."

"True. But what you might judge to be the root of all evil always has flow, it just depends on your perspective and your intention. You can look at this place as part of the unlimited creation flow, and money and gambling as part of that flow. Or you can look through the eyes of ego and say that money isn't everything, it's the only thing! Then money becomes the root of all attachment."

"So by judging this place, I was actually resisting a form of abundance."

"Indeed. But you were also struggling with the feeling that money could easily become an attachment, and that was part of the reason you didn't want to come here. You knew you were risking attachment."

"But now I understand that attachment to money is a choice, just like any other form in limitation, there's no need to resist the unlimited flow. I can be abundant and detached and this place can support me. It all depends on my perspective."

"Your awareness does you credit. The unlimited flow is always supportive, it's just a matter of understanding how, why and what it is supporting in each moment. Money has simply become convenient in the limited world—creation in isolation; at arms length. Ego tells you that if you have money, you can create; if you don't have money, you can't. But with awareness you can experience differently."

I suddenly became excited, sitting up in my chair, launched into a deeper understanding.

"This means that in limitation we get attached to money being the shortcut creativity. We can rush from 'I want, I want' to 'I've got it, I've got it' in one easy step through money. But the bit in the middle, the bit where we learn how to value and appreciate our creative journey, understand its purpose—that gets missed out."

Assimilating Abundance

Merlin interjected. "And does the limited world value the infinite learning in each moment?"

"Of course not. There's no time for that," I joked. "We're all too busy chasing money and the promise of more, more, more. That's why the true nature of creation appears to be a mystery. Unlimited creativity is just waiting to be discovered but everyone is too busy dashing around to actually appreciate that quantity and convenience have taken over from quality and abundance."

Merlin smiled broadly, acknowledging my realisation.

He continued. "And so money is fast becoming the form that can embody the four corners of attachment. You can fear losing it; you can try to control experience by using it; you can even think you have no value if you don't have any of it. Ego has used the form known as money to tell you that there is no other way of creating. And for some of your experience, you've agreed with ego. Money has appeared to guarantee certainty. It's been seen to bring instant satisfaction; it's protected you from the losses of the unknown, the unsupportive world that ego tells you lies beyond the mind. Getting attached to money as the only way of creating ensures your greatest scarcity—relying on ego."

"So getting attached to money limits your creation stream. For example, if I was coming here every night, desperately attached to creating a big win, then I'd be creating from scarcity?"

"Exactly. And in so doing, you'd be pushing that big win away. And you know what they say?"

I said the first thing that came into my heart. "Don't gamble what you can't afford to lose?"

"Indeed. And what does that mean in energetic terms?"

"Don't gamble past your balance point and into attachment? Don't chase the Universe or try to force it to flow into a particular form just to please ego?"

"Well explained. Creation is a flow that you magnetise

through yourself, through loving intention. The moment ego fixates on money as being the only way to create, the flow becomes a single form and the infinite ways to expand are limited to just one."

"Okay, so one side of the creation coin is the belief that money solves everything. What about the other side? Is it the idea that the only way to enlightenment is to give up everything? How can both of these exist?"

"Because of the extremes and polarised views in your world. If ego cannot convince you to believe that money is your only form of creation then it will try the other extreme where it is believed that unlimited creation doesn't include money at all. Heads, ego wins; tails, you lose."

"Then both of those extreme perceptions mean I end up attached?"

"You could, but hopefully you would realise that it was just ego attempting to control you."

"So attachment is the root of all evil, not money?"

"That is a much more supportive and accurate perspective. If you look at the word *evil*, it is really *live* backwards. Evil is simply the desire to encourage something that is already in imbalance, into greater and greater degrees of imbalance and so greater and greater attachment. All those in materiality have had experiences in which the little devil inside encourages them to become more and more attached. This can be tempting in your world because attachment appears to be the known quantity that offers security."

Merlin paused, moving slightly forward in his chair as if inviting me deeper into our conversation. "But, as you know, the Universe is always changing, unfolding and so the security that ego seeks is really the desire to run away from the unlimited and hide from change."

"But that's the little devil inside talking again."

"Indeed. But no matter how real this devil may appear to be, it is not a person. Nor does it have form, it's just concentrated fear giving you the impression that it has influence. Fear can nudge you into doing anything but that doesn't mean you choose to do it."

I nodded in agreement.

"The opposite of evil is live," he continued. "So if you want to live, you require greater and greater degrees of balance and openness to change. That will bring greater and greater flows, creations and detachment."

"So that means I don't have to deprive myself or be in a state of struggle to be detached. I can continue on my path and recycle my attachments when it's obvious in the flow of experience that they're ready to be transmuted."

"It is always supportive to embrace a self loving balance. You are not required to force your changes so you can get to the *detached winning post* first. That is just ego talking. If you rush yourself, you force yourself and actually slow yourself down by reinforcing the very attachments you are trying to dissolve. If you try and *make* yourself detached then you will become the opposite."

"Attached?"

"Yes. Force is not flow and forced intention is simply control. This is why play, joy and humour are so important in the detachment process."

"So enjoy the path, don't make it into a struggle by trying to do too much or to rush the process. If you're endlessly abundant then there's no point worrying about running out of fuel, right?"

"Well done! You just won the lottery of abundance! I think that calls for a celebration."

He gestured for the waiter to bring us what I assumed would be more drinks. The waiter arrived in a blur of movement and put three glasses on the table in a row in front of Merlin.

"Okay. Don't try to learn through assumption, right?"

"Hmmm," replied Merlin.

"Time to play Find the Lady?" I suggested, but I was

confused by the glasses being transparent and upward-facing, concealing nothing.

"Perhaps it should be renamed Find the Goddess," replied Merlin, "if infinite creation is indeed what you seek."

He paused, honing in on the row of glasses and dropping a single olive into the glass nearest his right hand.

"Think of yourself as having invested heavily in form, so much so that you went the whole hog and got into embodiment. Glass one represents form; density; the attached state of being. While you were exploring form, you became aware of the tangible," explained Merlin, flipping the olive into the middle glass. "The tangible offered a greater degree of choice and awareness within your world of form. During your experiences in the tangible you realised that it wasn't just a case of ego's way or no way, there are lots of ways of experiencing in form. As you moved from dense to tangible through choice, you let in more Light."

"So my experience of myself became less dim in the tangible. Is that what you mean?"

"You could say that. More light on the subject. As your awareness became more tangible, you created more room for expansion and realisation."

He tossed the olive out of the second glass and over his shoulder.

"What was that?" I asked, laughing at his spontaneous olive missile.

"Look into the third glass. What do you see?"

"Nothing, of course. You threw the olive away."

"Look again. Tell me what you see."

"Okay, I get it—space; the intangible; the absence of form but not the absence of flow."

"Bingo! So that last area you are discovering is the intangible—what is called invisible, magical, even miraculous. The invisible and the unlimited; the Goddess nature that is the flow of unlimited creation. It's just like the air—just because

Assimilating Abundance

you can't see it doesn't mean you can't be with it. Go with that flow and create with it. That is what you do when you breathe, is it not?"

"So all these flows make up the whole of my experience. They aren't better or worse, they're just different expressions that I've been exploring. During ascension, it's a cocktail of all three—dense, tangible, intangible. And through detachment we're reconnecting with the Goddess? Hence we're finding the lady?"

"Indeed. Finding the flow and remaining aligned with it. So it is to rejoice in the abundance of the unlimited. The fact that you can't see it is such a minor detail; truly irrelevant."

"And just because we can't see it doesn't mean we can't experience it."

"Exactly! All is a loving unity just waiting to be embraced. You are never without it and you are always supported by it, whether it is tangible, intangible or dense. It's all a choice."

Tears welled up in my eyes as if I'd stumbled across the most precious feeling in all of my worlds. Something so immaterial was bursting with everything. It was completely now; a fulfilment that included all I'd experienced and the expansion of the heart I was yet to discover.

I looked deeply into Merlin's eyes. "And the ego says it isn't worth it," I said, my voice trembling with emotion.

"And ego cannot sense the knowingness of the heart. It doesn't know what joy is. All ego has for comfort are distance and its transient long-lost cousins such as instant gratification and infatuation."

I burst out laughing at Merlin's dry tone.

"But it is never to beat up ego for its inadequacies, nor to pity ego. It is simply to detach. For ego was never designed for unlimited creativity. It has all its chips in limitation; all its energy in the first glass. It needs you to keep playing, keep amusing it because it is the loneliest part of the Universe. Although ego will never admit the darkness of separation, it really is trying to keep you attached to your materiality for company's sake so that it doesn't have to truly feel what it is to be isolated and alone.

"And now you can see why it's been a game of such high stakes and why ego doesn't want you to create without money because that would mean you are creating outside one of its greatest attachments. For the longest time, ego told you that material challenge meant greater deprivation and suffering. Ego's world of creation may consist of *to have or not to have*, but this is no longer your world. You now realise that you create from love, from joy and balance, and from a growing understanding of abundance. You progressively risk your attachments so that you can experience what an unlimited soul you truly are. Now *that* is the game of your life, one that is always worth playing."

"Flow on Merlin. There's always an abundance and we can never run out, right?" I replied as his words merged with the blue of our surroundings and mine began to slur.

"And flow on, we will," he agreed enthusiastically. "To your tasks, brave magician! It's time you discovered the jackpot you've deposited in your heart."

A Fan Of Creation

It was 8:30 and I awoke to the sound of a nearby builder's radio Beatling its way through *Can't buy me love*.

"Can't buy me love, eh Merlin? You've certainly got a sense of humour. Checking if I'm paying attention to my guidance, are you?"

I yawned a long, luxurious yawn worthy of Isis. My nose stretched with a flaking protest, suggesting I could actually be flu-free.

Talking to Isis, I walked into the bedroom. "Move over, cat. Crusty nose coming your way."

A Fan Of Creation

But I couldn't find her and, as a cold draft wafted in through the window, I realised she'd gone. I felt a pang of attachment. But just like any other aspect of my world, she was part of the unlimited flow. She'd always arrived with detachment, and now left with it.

As I lay in bed, I had no desire to sleep. "More logic out the window," I muttered. "Awake all night and now I'm not tired! Conference with my colleague..."

I launched a discussion request in what appeared to be a very quiet heart room. "Is there any one there?"

"Of course. Are you feeling better?" replied my Higher Self, as if caught by surprise.

"Were you off somewhere else? Gone on some all-expenses-paid trip?"

"More a progress report, actually. Things seem to be full steam ahead."

"Great. But I require some more tuition on how I'm going to fit this unlimited creator into life here."

"All questions welcome. Proceed."

"Abundant flows need to be refined since my mortgage must be paid tomorrow. So after my night on the tiles, I now know that I can create the income I require to finish this book, and that means being more open... open to an unlimited way that this can flow to me."

"Correct. And of course you remember that too much planning works with the opposite effect of the spontaneity of the greater Universe?"

"I guess that was a hint not to analyse this to death? But if I can fill you in on some of my realisations... Before, I had a tendency to clog my creation stream by betting against myself. I didn't believe that I could cooperate with the unlimited flow so I preferred to live in the past; to live with conditioning, self doubt... basically, what I'd known."

"And that's why you've spent energy until now dissolving those attachments to lack and scarcity. But now your investment in Light can pay off. So how are you going to magnetise what you require?"

"I AM expanding my horizons. From the casino experience, I know I could win my 7,500. Alternatively, I could get a job, I could ask for another type of loan or get an advance on royalties. Being open to anything and everything is the key."

"Ahh... Now you are becoming a fan of creation. You are opening up and out to all the possibilities. You CAN: **C**-onscious **A**-ction **N**-ow!"

Just as I was about to ask another question, my Higher Self fell silent and the doorbell rang simultaneously. "Homework on the doorstep," said my Higher Self, and stepped back.

I walked back into the living room. Opening the door, I was happy to be met by Mrs Daley.

"Just thought I'd invite m'self in. You were in my inner thoughts. I didn't think it was wise to leave it too much longer."

"Come on in, Agnes, it's lovely to see you. Don't worry, I'm not at death's door, I'm actually feeling much better."

"You look like you've been dragged through a hedge backwards! That cold certainly took it out o' you. Or is it somethin' more?"

My mind proudly presented my mortgage statement, waving it in front of my eyes.

"I'll put the kettle on, Agnes. Take a seat and don't look in the bedroom," I said, closing the door quickly. "It's a picture of chaos!"

"A pretty view, then. Chaos is, after all, the order of the heart. But you look like you've been restructuring right to your very core."

"Yep. This certainly wasn't just any common cold. I think it was a viral showcase. But all things happen for a reason and it's certainly given me plenty of time to think things over."

Mrs Daley looked at me long and hard. "But that wasn't

A Fan Of Creation

what you were meanin', was it? You're not short of ideas for your book?"

"No, not really."

"But you've got another problem, a more pressing one that requires an immediate solution."

"Okay, Agnes, you've got me," I admitted, passing her a steaming fresh brew.

"Well, I'm all ears. An' I'm a great problem solver. So, tell me the whole story." She stirred her tea with extra vigour.

I felt a flush of embarrassment. Surely Agnes didn't want to hear about my financial problems. More's the point, I didn't want to hear my financial problems out loud. That would be like a blast of cold air waking me out of my denial to see what I'd much rather forget.

"Well, here goes... I've got financial problems."

"Now, that wasn't so difficult, was it?" whispered my Higher Self.

"Well, look no further," replied Mrs Daley. "If you're not 'appy with your investments, I can put you right there. That's what I do best—make money."

"It's more a question of negative wealth, Mrs Daley. Work is going well but, due to politics and certain other reasons, I'm not getting my usual advances. They're restructuring the company, you see..."

"Oh, so it's money you want?" She sat back in her chair as if commanding the whole room.

"Oh, Mrs Daley, I really wasn't hinting, just explaining the situation."

My Higher Self chipped in, "Now you can release all that pressure you've been putting yourself under."

Mrs Daley was deep in thought. I was tempted to recoil from honesty and change the subject.

Again my Higher Self was there. "Oi! What do you think you are doing? Shying away from the truth that can only support you?"

In my heart I replied, "I know. It's just that this kind of truth feels so uncomfortable."

"Any truth that is worthy often feels uncomfortable because it's putting your ego under pressure," continued my Higher Self. "Still, it's out now. The worst, as ego sees it, is over. You've admitted that you are connected to everything and that you can receive."

"Alright, alright. I'll take that as an observation rather than a criticism. Now butt out of the conversation, please," and I turned my attention to Mrs Daley.

She began to speak just as we both reached for words. "You've got such invaluable intangibles and you're worried about money. Amusing really. Although I think the Universe is laughing with you, not at you."

She picked up some of my sample chapters that were on the floor next to the armchair. "I love to weigh things with my 'eart," she smiled. "Hmmm... these are precious. You've been busy with your downloading... and there's more than one character in 'ere; multiple gems. They require a little more explaining, more pictures to paint. But it's a lovely view; quieter than your first tale. But still waters run deep, eh?"

I was silent, consumed with emotion and trying not to show it.

"So 'ow much do you want for them?" she gestured with the unfinished pages. "To finish them, that is?"

"Oh, Mrs Daley. I can't sell them. I'm contracted to the publisher."

"But I don't want to buy them, just help them make that delicate walk from the immaterial to the material."

"Agnes, I wasn't..." I stopped mid sentence, as if my Higher Self had dropped a heavy burden on my left shoulder.

"Well, you really are quite 'ard to 'elp, but... I'll ask you again. 'ow much money do you need to get your manuscript completed?"

"Seven thousand," I mumbled.

A Fan Of Creation

I felt the figure looming large, as if on a billboard.

"But I don't expect you to pay, Mrs Daley. You don't really know me. Yes, you've looked after the flat but we've only just become friends."

"Well, if we thought that true friendship was founded on 'ow many years or 'ow many words then where would us antisocialites be? Consistency doesn't give us a window into another's 'eart, it's connection and an open-'eartedness that puts us on the same wavelength. That's what makes the difference. That certain something, that resonance that means it all makes sense in the 'eart. So perhaps it's time we put linear time aside and be in the Now. After all, if we spent all our lives relying on our expectations and assumptions, where would we be, eh?"

"Stuck."

"Exactly! An' after our conversation the other day, you know me better than anyone in the last ten years. An', in fact, that was what I called in to talk about. I wanted to thank you."

"Thank me for what?" I was surprised.

"Our chat. Our mutual exchange of Light and opportunity. You got me thinkin' about where I'd got stuck. Can't live in the past, y'know, it's old hat before you know it. Familiar, I'll grant you, but old hat. And I'm far too old for that already." She faded into a dream-like state as if she was drifting off.

"Mrs Daley?"

"Agnes, please. Like I said, please call me Agnes. So... back to our business. I was just checking."

"Checking?"

"Well, I'm gettin' a feeling that the figure you quoted me is..."

I cut in. "It's high, I know, Agnes. Please don't worry..."

"Let me finish," she said firmly. "I'll give you... eleven... just to tide you over."

My jaw dropped, unable to form a sentence. "Eleven thousand, Agnes?" I stammered.

"Yes. I like that number. An' the way the residents

committee is going, you could need it. So, eleven thousand it is, then. Agreed?"

"Yes," I replied shakily, daring to believe my delivery from the unlimited flow.

We shook hands on our cosmic deal as we exchanged the promise of the material for a promise of the immaterial.

"Done! Paid to the soul with a fabulous book in the making," she exclaimed.

"Do you want interest?"

"No, you daft idjeutt, I just want you to stay interested in your book... an' a few cups of tea along the way. What goes around comes around, that's what I always say. An' that's the true infinity of the Cosmos. We're all 'elp, courage and purpose to one another. Today, my purpose is to serve and yours is to receive, but our last meeting was the complete reverse. Think of our courage as investing in all the other aspects of ourselves, the unlimited parts of ourselves.

"Purpose," she continued, "is a cosmic investment that truly pays off in the end, not because you're worth it but because you become worthy of it. An' that makes it all worthwhile. The trick is being current, managing to link all of these in the same lifetime. Now, that's a trick worth stayin' around to conjure. Anyway, enough o' this babble, I'd better be going. An' your mortgage is due."

"But how do you know that, Agnes? Are you really psychic?"

"I pay attention," she said, pointing towards my statement, somehow mixed in with the sample chapters I'd taken to Erica.

And with that, we both laughed and cried, shedding tears of joy and relief.

"Thank you so much, Agnes, you've made my year! Shall I write you into the pages?"

"Well, why not? Now I'm a paid up member o' the order o' chaos, seeking my true nature, why not indeed?"

A Fan Of Creation

"Okay. Look out for yourself in the next chapter... magic where you least expect it! Simple but one hundred per cent efficient. And you know I'll pay you back just as soon as the publishing politics are resolved?"

"Of course you will. But remember, I know where you live!"

"Yep, there's no denying that! But now, Agnes, it's your turn. You might have rushed me off my feet with your generosity but I still remember you saying you had something to tell me. The curiosity helped me get through my flu so you can't leave without telling me! What's it all about?"

"Backgammon."

"Play on," I smiled.

"Well, after our chat, I thought about 'ow I keep pretty much to myself... an' when Albert was alive, 'ow we liked to play games—bridge, and other games such as backgammon. So I thought to myself, 'Why not start playing again now?' But I want a real game, not just sitting in and playing against myself. So I googled backgammon and started playing on line."

"Who'd have thought it! So are you playing professionally now?"

"Well, I am on the advanced level but, like a lot of things in this world, you go in one direction just to turn and face another, right?"

"And?"

"Well... I met someone."

"Ahhh... So that was why you were looking so gorgeous the other day?"

"Yes. An' after twenty-five games over one week, we decided to meet."

"And? Is he as handsome as his picture?"

"Handsome isn't an adjective I'd apply in his case but he's beautiful in lots of different ways. An' intelligent," Agnes added quickly, clearly smitten. "An' he's got a background in finance, and he's so modern, but still a gentleman. An' he's..."

She paused, as if about to reveal an indiscretion. "... he's younger than me."

"Agnes has got a younger ma-a-an! Agnes has got a younger ma-a-an!" I pretended to taunt her.

"Well, not that much younger. Only five years."

"Good for you! So when's your next date?"

"I don't know but we're going to meet online tonight an' I think we're going to go ballroom dancing tomorrow. We signed up for some classes. I can't remember, so I thought I could learn all over again. But differently, with a different man, that is."

"Wonderful. Good for you, Agnes. You had the courage to go for what felt right."

"An' so did you!" she promptly added.

"So... partners in courage. We're just undergoing different initiations, eh? Would you like another tea?"

"No, I'll pass 'cause I have to do my shopping, and then I said I'd meet Ronald online at 3 p.m. And I've got to do my online banking before that... transfer your money. Can you give me your details?"

"Certainly." I gave Agnes one of my yet-to-be-filed bank statements. "Thanks again, Agnes. You're such a godsend. Please, just one question before you go. There's been a black cat hanging around a bit; very friendly and sweet. Do you know if she belongs to anyone in the building? You are, after all, the Queen Of Surveillance here. I thought if anyone would know, it'd be you."

"Oh the black cat. Yes she does belong to someone but you've seen what's she's like. She really doesn't belong to anyone but herself. She's a free spirit."

"I know curiosity killed the cat, but I was just wondering about the owner... in case anyone is missing her. She was here a lot when I was ill in bed."

"Well, I can't tell a lie. She belongs to me. But I've 'ad her ever since she turned up as a kitten. In my book that means she's part of everything an' she's welcome to stay as long as she wants. I've let her come and go as she pleases from day one. She's a free spirit an' a good friend, an' we both love it that way."

"So you don't mind if I feed her? Or if she stays here from time to time?"

"Not at all. It's perfect, really... that we both chose you as a friend. An' after all, what goes around comes around! Don't forget to send me an email to tell me you've got the money."

"I'll check tomorrow morning, first thing. I promise."

"Thanks for letting me 'elp you." And with that she was disappearing downstairs, almost jet propelled.

A single tear rolled down my face as I closed the door. I was astounded that she was thanking me.

"That's the power of balance," whispered my Higher Self, "and the joy of giving at it's best... right under you nose."

"Just like you said... flowful," I acknowledged.

"Yes, the unlimited is always flowful. The magic is recognising that flow."

Inner Vision

My sudden creation breakthrough spurred me on into a clarifying clean up. The flat smelt of old and a past clinging to the forgotten me. Out with the old and in with the new, I thought, opening the windows to let in some much needed fresh air and, some moments later, Isis.

"How are you?" I enquired. "I missed you this morning when I woke up."

She blinked at me as if to say, "It takes skill to live without attachment."

"At least I know who your owner is. A good friend of mine, actually. She says you can stay as long as you like, which, I might add, is normally what you do anyway, right? All in the flick of a tail and the power of the moment, eh, Isis?"

I walked into the bedroom as Isis curled up neatly in the unmade sheets.

"I'm going to have to move you, sorry," I apologised.

She buried her head as if to say, "You don't really mean that, do you? Besides it isn't convenient just at the moment."

But as she purred to the sound of the birch tree touching the window, I couldn't move her from a peace that she seemed to be soaking in from all directions.

"Okay, I'll leave the bed till later," I said. "As if there was ever a deadline for that... But I will pick up all those discarded handkerchiefs before they stick permanently."

Isis kindly allowed me to work around her, deep in purring continuum.

I looked across the living room and was startled to see Erica sitting in the armchair.

I looked again and there was no one there.

I looked again just to check.

"Higher Self, are you teasing me?"

"No, you've just got incoming through your inner-net. Can be a little unpredictable when you translate it with your limited senses."

"Thanks!"

"You see, your interface isn't standard in the rest of the Universe."

"I'll take that as a compliment. So what you're trying to say is that someone is thinking of me? On my wavelength, as it were? Connecting in?"

"That's it."

"I see what you mean. Normally my ears burn... Only teasing! So, is that a prompt to call Erica?"

"Are you asking or are you telling?"

"Asking."

"What do you feel? Are you in the mood to share your good fortune? Not perhaps the one you think, but it's of value anyway."

"I'm sure I have no idea what you're talking about. But yes, I will ring Erica. And you're right, it would be helpful to tell her that one of her starving authors has conjured up a solution. Team effort, you understand."

"It always is."

I made a new cup of tea and sat in the armchair. The space seemed to be radiating a whole new beginning.

I dialled Erica.

"Good morning, Erica. How are you?"

"All the better for hearing you in that tone of voice! You've vanished your cold away, then?"

"Yep. And operation Rabbit-out-of-Hat is completed. I've created what's needed to get the book finished and I won't be needing to find a job."

"The invisible becomes tangible? Quite a performance!"

"Absolutely! You always understand, Erica, even if you don't know or it doesn't make sense. And now you're going to say that you wouldn't be much of an editor if you didn't, right?"

"Exactly. We're behaving like an old couple anticipating each other's words! But I'm very glad that what you've been going around has come back around to support you. Can you send some my way?"

"Sure. What's up?"

"Actually, your little shower of inspiration couldn't have come at a better time. But curiosity first... How did you get the money?"

"Do you know what? You wouldn't believe me if I told you. It's so magical! Let's just say, it comes from one magician to another; a joint foundation."

"Can you tell your magician friend to find an angel to teach me how I'm going to make these numbties here understand quality and the changing world of publishing?"

"Erica, if anyone can do it, you can."

"Thanks. A much-needed vote of confidence. I just can't

see how. The board appears to be getting stuck further back in the past every time we meet. What part of 'It doesn't sell any more' don't they understand?"

"Sounds like they can't see for fixation. Perhaps you can paint a whole new perspective around them and then be patient. They might look up and out of their stagnation zone and get a different view. You never know."

"And pigs might fly, too!"

She hesitated. "Oh, I'm sorry. I just keep meeting endless resistance. It begins to wear me down after a while."

"Why not ask for help? Maybe it's time to hang up your viking spirit and charm them into change rather than trying to drag them through a baptism of fire. You never know, you might have some support in there somewhere."

"I doubt it." It seemed like Erica was trying to carry all the resistance that surrounded her.

"Look, just unburden yourself. Look at your world as if it's wanting to help you, even though at the moment that might seem ridiculous. All I'm saying is, don't expect them to be against you. It sounds like they don't know if they're coming or going. And yes, they don't appear to be ready for innovation yet but there's always an opportunity, and you only need one."

"Okay, maybe I've been too harsh on them. Frustration getting the better of me. I always feel that this evolution is so obvious, but it just isn't in their reality. The end of the era has been and gone, yet they still don't know it's happened! It's so irritating. Not even a hint of overlap, rush of realisation, or gasp of urgency. Nothing. Absolutely nothing."

"But just because they don't know doesn't mean they're automatically against you. What you represent, if you can introduce it gently and in bite-sized pieces, is just what they require. It's just that if you give it to them all at once they'll feel overwhelmed, completely out of their depth and that'll just cause more resistance. You are your answer, Erica, just keep

Inner Vision

inviting them to join you. Keep your heart and mind open to alternatives. I've learnt that what we most require is often right under our nose. The Universe isn't against you, it's just your ego doesn't want you to progress to this next stage. It just wants you to struggle with 'same-old same-old' until you're exhausted and give up. But it doesn't have to be like that, truly."

"Go on," encouraged Erica. I could sense her rekindling her enthusiasm.

"Ego's always telling us what's logical, not what's magical. Perhaps you've got more help than you know. All you require is one of the board members to see a mixture of cosmic sense and common sense and they'll stop doing 'same-old same-old' and start producing something people actually want to buy. When things get intense then we can all shut down and refuse to move into the unknown. So the trick is not to force but to create; not to shut down but to take a rest; rebalance. Then we can do all over again what we were trying to do, but differently. Open the door by turning the key differently. You know in your heart what needs to change, so give them the opportunity to reach for that solution. Give them an opportunity to shine in their finest hour as cosmic timing ignites practical solutions so innovation can be born."

"Okay. So invite them to see the obvious?"

"Yes! Because, unfortunately, the obvious isn't quite obvious enough yet."

"So you're suggesting to be more open and don't assume that all of the board members are in the same boat?"

"Absolutely. Detach. Stand back from all that help you aren't getting and let the help flow in from somewhere you haven't thought of. Anything could happen but there can't be vision if you're standing in your own way! Vision requires space and you need to invite them into the space that is vision, not just assume that they understand the path of their own changes. Many can see others' changes but they can't take one step to change themselves. What about that new-ish guy? The one who inherited his stake from his father? Is he new school or old school?"

"Who? Nigel? Oh, he's so new in the business and seems totally disinterested. He rarely even turns up to meetings; always pursuing whatever you pursue when you're a man of leisure."

"But you never know. He could also be the bridge you're looking for. He could be close enough to that old school world to influence the board and bridge the gap between them and now. Maybe he could feed them change, the change that you've been trying to get across but do it in a way that's more palatable for them. I'm just saying, Erica, that these are the times to remain open... to the most probable, the last resort and anything in between. They're all options. And just because someone doesn't spend much time on something doesn't mean it isn't a quality job or a wise perspective. It's not what you do, it's the way that you do it."

"Okay, okay, my free-flowing, full-flowing magus. What about getting some of this down on paper?"

"Your wish is my command."

"Off you go then and leave me in pieces so that I can rethink this jigsaw! You might have something there... just understanding how it all fits together..."

And the line went dead. Erica the Red was already busy finding an answer in her problem.

"Hmmm, that was a call worth making," said my Higher Self. "Seems that you're beginning to embrace service."

"Well, Higher Self, I wouldn't be a magician in the making if I didn't. Besides, who said inspiration was a one way street?"

"Indeed. And there's plenty more where that came from."

"What do you mean?"

My phone began to ring, shimmying across the table towards me. "Oh, I get it."

I could see it was Andrew calling. "Hi, Andrew. How are you?"

"Been better. Do you have a minute?"

"If I'm honest, Andrew, I've got a chapter buzzing in my head so I can't give you my full attention at present. Can you call back later?"

"What about we meet up tomorrow? For lunch?"

"Of course. But won't that be difficult for you with your deadlines?"

"Actually, I've got a few days off. That's what I was calling you about."

"Is everything alright?"

"I think so. Or perhaps I should say, I hope so."

"Now you've got my attention. What's the matter?"

"It's nothing really, just a few dizzy spells. Oh, and then I collapsed at the office two days ago. That's why I was sent home... to recover and get some tests done."

"That doesn't sound like nothing. Are you really okay?

"Of course! You know me... strong as an ox."

"Yes, and as stubborn as an ox too. Not to mention eating like one!"

"Okay, that's enough of your bedside manner! I wanted sympathy, not honesty!"

"Hey, at least your sense of humour is intact."

"So, shall we say 11 o'clock at the George and Dragon?"

"The one in that village you claim to live in but no one has ever seen you there?"

"That's the one. I'll bring the George and it sounds like you can bring the Dragon!"

Crossing Over The Line

As I settled back into my chair, words flowed freely into a precarious jumble I called chapters seven to nine. I began to warm to this new flow. The less I tried to work out what to say, the easier it became to type what wanted to be said.

"Who says we write books?" I muttered, smiling. "They guide us so that they can be heard; a joint effort from that big unity of which we are a part. The cosmic co-creation, eh Higher Self?"

My Higher Self nodded and smiled simultaneously.

"And it appears there's quite a crowd gathering," I smiled as I felt the brush of Isis' tail.

"Hello, friend. How are you?"

But Isis wasn't interested in giving me a reply. Instead, she checked my new environment with her chin and tail, searching for the magic button that would, with one push, rearrange the place into the mess she'd known.

"You can keep on looking, Isis, but the past has gone."

She stopped and looked through me and out the other side, still unconvinced.

"See, Isis, I've turned over a new reality. But don't worry, there're still sardines in the new one."

The word sardine had her leaping into the kitchen before I had time to say dinner. I followed my hungry charge.

"There you go Isis... new house," I whispered, opening the cupboard. "And... da-daaaah!... I've even got you a cat bowl. How about that for service?!"

I cut up a portion of sardines and suddenly Isis was very interested in her new bowl and my service.

"There you go, hungry goddess," I said, placing her bowl in what was becoming her familiar place, next to the stool.

She purred in between mouthfuls and looked at me as if to say "What's wrong? Aren't you eating too?" But I wasn't hungry.

I returned to my desk and continued to write what was flowing through me.

"Effortless creation, eh?" said a familiar voice. "Allowance... such a magnificent tool. So simple and yet so efficient. I wonder what your productivity experts would say of such things in your world?"

"Merlin? That is you?"

"Indeed."

"Y'know, Merlin, they'd probably say it's a lot of rubbish. And then they'd correct you, saying that allowance is a state that means being allowed to do what's within the rules, not cooperating with the chaos of the unlimited. Chaosity and spontaneity are for the immature; those people who don't want to surrender to the inevitable grow-up-and-get-seriously-old scenario. Us creative types either don't know what to do or we're just dreaming about things we'll never achieve."

"So you are glad of an alternative perception?"

"You bet! We certainly wouldn't be having this conversation if there wasn't one to be had!"

Merlin seemed to be monitoring the flow of my answers, listening to the sound rather than the sense.

"Are you checking on me?"

"More a case of sensing the flow of energy through your more limited structures. Hold still... this won't hurt a bit."

A sudden sensation had me shaking my head as if trying to dodge a wasp. "I don't know if I like your investigations, prodding into the depths of my limited mind," I joked with a serious edge.

"Is that a protest?"

"No, not at all. It's just that I feel like I'm a lab rat in an experiment!"

"You are your own experiment and we are just here to help you dislodge a bit more of that limitation, in your mind and your emotionality. It's a choice."

"It's alright, I believe you. Carry on with the help. It's just a curious sensation, that's all. I know you can't tell me what you're doing because it'd disturb an already fragile mind and motivate my ego to resist you, but..." I paused, searching for a question rather than an answer. "How exactly is this helping?"

"It's teaching you allowance," replied Merlin, as if he was in a cupboard somewhere at the back of my mind, or searching through my discarded memories.

"Seen enough cobwebs yet?"

"Not exactly," came a discerning reply.

I found myself becoming impatient, as if I was waiting for an exam grade or the results of my annual physical.

"And your conclusion is?"

"No conclusions. We aren't results-oriented, remember? It's not what you be, it's the way that you are being; the flow of you. You are always shifting so there aren't any finishing posts or targets. The quality of your experience is what's important. It teaches you how well you know yourself; how deeply connected you are with your heart. So we are seeing your why's, how's and where's—the intention behind your research—not the how-muches, is-it-worth-its, or how-long-is-it-going-to-lasts."

"So not a lot of use measuring progress, then?"

"Indeed. Parameters just limit flow. Where is the space in limits? If the humanity spent all the time it thinks it has understanding its intentions instead of measuring its perceived results, where would the experience of your world be now?"

"Where, indeed? No point in going with the flow if I'm going to junk it up with the expectation of results."

"Precisely," said Merlin, continuing to spin around as if checking every angle.

"Can you stop now, please? You're making me dizzy," I protested.

"How can change manifest if there isn't any space?"

"Okay, I bow to your wisdom, Merlin, as always. Is this some necessary disturbance? Space making? Or fuel efficiency? Whatever it is I think I'm reaching my limit. I'm feeling a bit land-sick now. I'm all spun out!" I felt the need to hold onto the desk.

"It's just your mind. It's only used to working in one direction."

"That being projection, I suppose?"

"Sometimes. But enough of that." Merlin's investigations ceased. "Fancy a little excursion?"

"Alright, just let me find my centre first."

I closed my eyes and sent the intention of balance throughout my being.

"All present and correct now. So where are we going?"

"Visiting," said Merlin hurriedly. "But let me introduce you first," he said, his words appearing to flow in slow motion, emphasising each one.

"Okay, as you wish. You do all the 'How d'you do's.'"

We met outside my heart room. The big oak doors were closed tight.

"Shall we go in?" asked Merlin.

"Certainly." And with that, I pushed the solid doors of centeredness open and walked into a room I'd never seen before. All was interconnecting dark wooden panels. I could make out a large wooden table with eight chairs arranged around it. There were a few candles burning dimly as they prepared to go out. This wasn't the Light I was used to.

"What's this?" I asked, turning to Merlin. But the doors had closed and he was nowhere to be seen.

"Embrace Love and listen to your heart. All is not what it seems," came an echo through the keyhole.

The room began to rock with a series of tremors. I caught a glimpse of a form at the end of the table as I lunged forward to grab something to hold on to. The tremors continued as the candles went out one by one.

As my eyes adjusted to each decrease in light, I began to make out a shadowy form at the end of the room. It paced in an agitated way and turned its gaze towards me.

"I don't know why you're here but it's time to leave," it said in low but forceful tones.

I had no idea how to reply. I'd never had an experience in my heart room like it. Everyone and every experience I'd known had always been so supportive and enlightening.

The form was growing in hostility. "Did you hear what I said? You must leave. There is no place for you here," insisted the form, punctuating the end of each sentence with a frustrated pound on the table.

With eyes and senses now adjusted to my situation, I balanced before answering the growing threats. I searched in my inner sense for a reply.

"I AM choosing to stay," I stated.

"You can't survive here," said the voice threateningly. "You've got no practice in this kind of frequency. Go back to your spoon feeding. Your adviser's leading you everywhere by the nose. Where are they now? Deserted you, have they? Leave now. You don't have the skills to survive here."

But the courage was growing within me and I could sense Merlin observing my responses. "What you think is for you and you alone. I AM learning from this place and I AM choosing to remain!"

I felt a surge of energy rush through every part of me and the candles reignited as the aggressive shadow slammed the door at the other end of the room.

I breathed a big sigh of relief and sat in one of the chairs as the light within the room continued to grow. Soon I could see the whole room clearly.

Merlin stepped through the door through which my dark agitator had left.

He stood and clapped enthusiastically.

"Well done, well done!" he cheered. "Your first transmutation of extreme polarity!"

I was surprised by Merlin's entrance. Also at his enthusiastic compliment.

I felt a huge shiver through the whole of my body.

"A few after shocks I see," he said, "but nothing you can't handle."

"I'll be the judge of that... once I work out what that was."

"Perhaps you'll be the observer—much less attachment and much more benefit."

It was a few moments before I could reply. "Who was that? And what were they doing in my heart room?"

"That was ego. Ego wasn't exactly here, that was more a very strong projection giving you the impression that ego was here."

"And so what's the point of a very strong projection?"

"It gives you an understanding of the type of distortions and shocks that can go through your energy field, particularly when you meet the more stubborn aspects of ego."

"So this was a face-off with ego?" I asked, still astonished that the presence had felt so real.

"Let's call it a shadow-off. You are correct in that ego cannot stay in your heart room, such is your natural Light. But it can, from time to time, project itself anywhere, even give you the impression it can threaten you. But as you know, all is choice and if you are balanced then such intensities can be recycled with little or no disturbance."

"It certainly was intense. Ego was giving me the impression that I could go no further and that it controlled me."

"Indeed. Ego wanted you to believe that you couldn't remain balanced when presented with such a contrast. But as you demonstrated—without reattaching to conflict, drama or complication—you are quite capable of choosing your natural lightness over the conditioned darkness and limitation of ego.

"Polarities are simply extremes taken to extremes. Remember when you were gambling with your attachments? This is no different. It is still the pendulum of self. It can be balanced. It can swing from force to suppression, from victim to zealot. And if these minor swings become fuelled by ego, they gain greater and greater amplitude. You could have fought what you faced in your heart room, but then you would have become attached and made ego your experience; you would have chosen to endorse ego into greater and greater extremes."

"But I didn't?"

"Indeed, you did not. We are delighted to say you chose Light; you chose RealLife. These periods of alternate realities are just as potent as what you think of as your real world. These are Light achievements that support you in your material life too. You are seeing that your essence is Light; that the essential you is Light, not the darkness that ego says is real."

"So a Light perspective helps me unite all my Lightness, in form or out of it?"

"Aha! And thus you acknowledge the genuine nature of self."

"Then how did ego seem so real? And how did Light nature become so dim?"

"In the material world ego can easily persuade you to forget yourself, your true self. There are so many amusements, distractions and sensations. They are all attachments that can impress on you the importance of form and sooner or later obscure the significance of Light. Your sensory makeup is designed to reinforce limitation. You are surrounded by form and unless you choose consciously, you only sense form. If you were surrounded by space then your perceptions would be different. Through detachment, you find the space within the form. And you begin to see the Light. Sometimes the contrast can be shocking and have you heading straight back to the attachment of what you know."

"Or I can choose differently and not listen to ego."

"Indeed. All is choice and you are demonstrating your commitment to Light. But never underestimate ego desires. Ego uses its creativity to get you more and more attached. It creates more and more opportunities for greater and greater degrees of imbalance and tries to hook you in. Ego can be very, very persuasive, so choice can quickly become ego choice. Then the mind takes over and imbalance stabilises through attachment until imbalance is the normal state of being."

"So it's easy to underestimate the impact of ego and that's why it's easy to forget why we come into form?"

"Yes. Many descend into limitation with big agendas of change and transmutation but, once surrounded by form, they forget learning through heartfelt choice and instead learn through ego. Such is the draw of ego. Then they simply learn to maintain form."

"But if heartfelt learning is maintained then the Light can shine and keep on growing. Is that what ascension is all about?"

"Yes. The return to purpose and the return to Light. But balancing Light and purpose is one of the greatest challenges in your ascension."

"What do you mean?"

"Some honour their steps along the path of purpose but are not able to balance that with the changes required within their embodiment."

"They don't achieve ascension then?"

"They don't in that lifetime."

"So to go the whole way, you've got to keep embodiment in balance and purpose intact?"

"Ascension isn't an equation, as you are finding out, but these are simple guidelines that are useful to follow. It is to realise that every choice you make adds to expansion and an expanded relationship with all the parts of yourself that are not in form. Think of yourself as a lattice of loving consciousness with a few lumps of ego trapped within that lattice. These more stubborn ego impressions have come from lives spent in extreme imbalance."

"Is that why, in ascension, you undergo necessary disturbance? To shake these ego imbalances out so that they can be transmuted?"

"Indeed. Necessary disturbance is all part of the transmutation process. As you know, light and dark cannot co-exist. At some point, fear nature, or density, must either turn in on itself or dissolve into Light. Both processes mean that Light is manifest. Most recently you encountered a stubborn aspect of ego, a polarity that held much resistance. But you crossed the line and you embraced ego with choice and as you know, choice is Love. You were able to dissolve ego because you remained in balance and you acted from Love, not fear."

"So if I'd become aggressive and not been centred, fear would've had an opportunity to feed off my conflict?"

"Indeed. You would have resisted your healing and joined in with your ego against your true nature."

"And that would've meant more drama and complication and I would have to dismantle those attachments before I could attempt to dissolve the original polarity."

"Yes you would."

I paused to consider. "This could add up to a slog so I'd probably think about doing it later, if at all."

"Indeed. These understandings are flowing well. For ego, these trapped polarities in your Light nature are mainstays of limitation. They are the lines you think you walk between; the ceilings that keep you thinking you are limited. Ego guards these polarities jealously, thinking they will keep you under ego's thumb. But on your path of discovery, as you continue to raise your consciousness, these aspects will rise to the surface of you. It is up to you how you deal with them. It's always a smoother transmutation if you face what is in front of you in your Now, but there can be temptations to face it later. But later will make your resistance appear larger and your transmutation more difficult."

"So it's my choice."

"Of course. It is always a matter of choice."

"Well, I feel wonderful, like I've made a real difference. It's like a hint of the invincible, though that isn't quite accurate."

"Invincible is ego but unlimited is heart. You are feeling the empowerment of balance and the energy that is released in the transmutation. Remember, you aren't fighting ego, just choosing to release your attachment to ego. And before you are seduced by polarity, remember that not all extreme transmutations are shocking or threatening."

"What do you mean?"

"Ego wants you to get attached, so it's methods are not always as aggressive or shocking, they can also be seductive and charming."

"And a charm offensive can be just as effective?"

"Indeed. It is all attachment. The pendulum swings of ego may appear to be bad and good but in truth they are simply imbalances, either side of centeredness. The greater the imbalance, the greater the ego influence. Your experience was of great polarity but you embraced choice, even when there didn't appear to be any. You didn't assume your ego was right and that the **E**-xternal **G**-overning **O**-fficer was telling you what to do. You were courageous, you remained balanced and you listened to your heart truth. And your alchemy of change is coming to an end."

Merlin clapped his hands and the oak room dissolved into a spin of panels radiating the glow of achievement. I thought I heard children laughing, angry debates, raucous parties until all emptied into a sense of intense grief. As the torrent of feeling subsided, we arrived at a place I thought I knew but didn't really recognise. It was like a flavour that kept evaporating. But from where?

"Time for a holy-day," announced Merlin.

"Don't you mean holiday? It's changed a little since you were last in embodiment. Anyway, I thought holidays were for people who didn't like their job?"

"Actually, holydays are for those who recognise the wholeness flowing through all time and space. Shall we?"

A Tale Of Two Cities

The sun was as strong as the pungent odours coming from behind what I now realised was a very high wall. As my vision adapted, I found myself outside a busy market complex with all kinds of alleys arriving at doors positioned at regular intervals as far as I could see. I was in a stencil of terracotta, its simple earthy texture somehow breathing in harmony with its inhabitants.

Merlin had done another of his disappearing acts, but I was becoming used to acclimatising to the unfamiliar. Besides, I knew he'd return when there was learning to discuss.

"All's well that ends well. Let's unravel this; see where it goes," I muttered to myself.

I started walking, conversing with my absent teacher. "Merlin, I know you'll come back when it's of service. There's plenty more guidance, wherever you come from." And as I looked out of the corner of my eye I could see him resting on his staff and his knowingness of heart.

The terracotta corridor snaked its way through a collection of buildings and narrow streets. I skimmed a finger along the wall, creating a puff of orange as I approached the first doorway. I pushed open an ancient door made of as many cracks of daylight as panels of wood. A rowdy and vibrant marketplace assaulted my ears. I was astonished. How could this commercial cauldron not have bubbled over the wall? I stepped back into the narrow lane. There was silence. I stepped back through the door again into the market scene. Bedlam. Silence, bedlam. Bedlam, silence.

I began to laugh... two cities so near and yet so opposite.

I felt a tap on my shoulder and the promise of a discussion. "I wondered when you'd show up. Quite some contrast, eh Merlin?"

I turned around to face Merlin but was greeted by a man in a turban and traditional Indian dress. "Oh, sorry! You aren't Merlin, are you?"

"No, I represent a different school of learning. But when it comes down to it, we are all one. It's all a joint effort. Simple, really. Just like these walls; a simple framework that cradles the richness of our learning, inside and out."

"But why can't I hear what's going on in there, out here?" I asked, completely perplexed.

"Why? Because you think they are separate. One is the box known as market, the other is the terracotta corridor. Definition keeps you from flow and from connecting fully with your world. Mind is playing a game with you, a game called all-or-nothing, limited-or-unlimited, conditioned-or-chaotic, here-or-there,"

"Wait a minute, slow down. This is all passing in a blur, like mini rockets through space. Slow down. I can't cope."

"You can choose to allow the flow for it is Now. But there is your mind which is still trying to control what it cannot understand. Perhaps it is time to stop competing and surrender to what is."

My new guide continued to unfold a concept my mind thought was quickly taking over everything. Nothing made sense but I had the feeling in my heart that it would be perfectly proportioned, every piece with a purpose, once it had come full circle and completed a unity. It was time to practice allowance.

"Are you in the know or in the feeling?" continued the guide. "Do you allow the unfamiliar or seek to protect yourself from it?"

I was dazed by each word. I knew they all made sense but I simply couldn't put them into understanding, they just kept on gushing over the sides. He was speaking a language I knew but I couldn't piece together.

"Hmmm. Working it out instead of working it through? The habit of many lifetimes."

"It's so tempting to dissect your sentence but that's what's tripping me up. When it falls into pieces, it makes no sense at all."

"The mind has no answers, just questions. It thinks it understands all and yet it is not capable of embracing unity."

"But I thought it was helpful to question."

"Oh yes, it is. When you question, you are the seeker."

"Now, that's beginning to make sense."

"But you are required to source your answers in your heart. Your true nature is Love. You are feeling more deeply into this stubborn ego habit. But it is gradually being overwhelmed by simplicity. Remember, questions—head; answers—heart."

I repeated. "Questions—head. Answers—heart."

"It's not figuring out the magician's trade that matters, it's believing in the trick in the first place; believing in the magic of possibility and its endless nature. Masters never conquer, they converge. They meld with the process; become one with their experience. Then, when the next leap arrives, the process simply flows on, not because you figured out where it was going but because you believed it was endless."

"My holyday is full of wholeness."

"Yes. And now you are embracing allowance so that you can appreciate the wholeness."

The man prepared to sit in the alley on the ground. I was just about to say 'But you can't sit there, it's dirty' when my companion looked up at me, hearing my thoughts.

"Do you see dirt or a floor made of Earth?"

I looked down. "A floor made of Earth," I replied as I sat down next to him, "because everything is simple if you allow the flow."

"And so it is. As you listen to your heart, so the simplicity rolls out before you, just like a magic carpet. When you allow your understandings to be heard, when you allow your creations to unfold then they do just that—unfold. And with simplicity you become as light as a feather. You recycle some of your dense resistance and embrace the true nature that you seek. You glide through your world rather than trudging through density or tripping up under the weight of ego suppression."

"So simplicity can take me where I want to go?"

"Simplicity is always where you are. But it's up to you if you want to be there. Simplicity is for the balanced and the honest."

"And if I bring ego along for the ride, I could fall off the magic carpet?"

"Actually, simplicity simply won't take off with that weight!"

"Then I undergo detachment so I can be in simplicity?"

"Yes. And you undergo detachment so that you can see simplicity. There is a thread of simplicity in all experience but few people believe it is worth tracing. Most lose the thread, thinking that it holds no benefits, no results, no-thing when actually it is a state within which all can be seen—the unity and the attachment; the detachment and the separation. It's all in there, layer by layer, understanding by understanding."

I was dazzled by each syllable that came from his lips. Their sound radiated out in all directions as if self-magnifying. But there was no projection, no force, no apology or manipulation. Each word came from I AM Central.

"Your words have so much meaning, so much depth and yet they're so simple."

"They are born of balance and that is the empowerment you feel. In essence, they have an unending energy because balance magnetises balance. Balance is part of that unending cord of simplicity that unites all. This is the place of subtlety, even though at first glance it appears to be of great contrast or even great insignificance. What can you learn when you're on the outside, away from all the action?"

"What indeed?"

"You relate to calm as being silence and bedlam as having no peace, but are these balanced truths or conditioned habits?"

"I suppose, if you look at it from that angle, then I'd say conditioned habits. With the help of my senses and mind, I think that inside the market is bedlam and out here is serene peace because there's only the sound of energy. But if everything's linked then there's peace over the wall and, for that matter, there's activity here." I stretched my arms out as wide as they would go.

"And so it is," he said. "You are finding the unity in your experience and this is of great service. When the reflections meet, you can create what you require to maintain balance, not through the physical or intellectual nature but through your feeling nature. All unifies through feeling. Not through the dramas of your mind nor the imbalances of polarity but through the sensing of your heart. When you are in balance, you will always sense the sound of Love; you will always hear the nature of simplicity. Nothing is excluded, nothing is separate, nothing is either-or, all-or-nothing."

"So why did I sense the contrast so keenly?"

"Because that is what you've been conditioned to do—feel the contrast, the imbalance, or even the extreme; feel what it is to be separate from the unity and take it as natural. Many in your world have never felt balance. For some it would be too painful to reinstate balance so they are numb to it. Balance is present in all aspects of your world but often it isn't the first place you look, nor the first place you find."

"Are you saying that ego trips us up with a rush of physical senses? Got to feel better, got to feel productive so we rush around doing? Not many people say 'I am choosing to be balanced' or 'I am choosing to feel what it is to be balanced.'"

"Correct. Balance has been buried under layers and layers of attachments. Ego has tried to convince all those in physicality that the more imbalance you have, the more useful and beneficial it is; the more activity, no matter how meaningless, the more things there will be. And yet do these things have value?"

"Well that depends."

"On what?"

"On the intention behind their creation and the foundation of it?"

A Tale Of Two Cities

"Well observed. So if the foundation is scarcity and the intention imbalance, are they of increasing value?"

"No. So I suppose that's why the more people have, the less appreciative or discerning they can become."

"Yes... an ego trade mark. More and more quantity, less and less balance, less and less quality experience. Whereas the cosmic perspective is that the more balance you create, the more effortless your experience."

"And that's where detachment and simplicity come in?"

"Yes, yes. And the flow that you have now embraced. Continue please." My companion extended a hand, lowering his head gently to encourage me on.

"Well...if we go out of balance within our all-or-nothing world then we can stop feeling. That means it's easier to think about our lives, making improvements and changes, but not really do anything about it because we aren't used to applying and feeling what it is to make change. So then the illusion of change begins to become normal. We comfort ourselves in the mind, believing we can exchange actual experience for just the thought of it. We can believe we have real experience because we've been through it in our mind, not experienced it through our heart.

"So we can't learn from only thinking," I continued, feeling centered in my truth. "And that's why we continue putting pressure on ourselves, literally winding ourselves up in increasingly tighter knots of imbalance. The more we think things through, the more ego can lead us to conclusions that make us a victim of our experience. The mind is never the place of real learning, only the beginning."

My companion looked me straight in the eye. "If you flow with the unlimited Universe, you move from your mind to your heart for the practical creation of your life. Through the heart you can learn because the heart encourages you to expand, to risk and to change."

"But there are so many people," I suggested, "who'd

think that such statements as *be in your heart* and *follow your heart* and the like are just impractical, or for people who don't want to experience the tougher side of life."

My guide took up our discussion. "Their observation comes from the mind, though, not the heart. They are observing the hardship and struggle of ego, not the allowance and flowfulness of heart. Ego doesn't want anything to be easy because that is not its experience. Ego doesn't want anything that is different to itself. But when you look through the eyes of heart there is always a way forward, as you have found. But creating from heart requires courage. It is creating the struggles and imbalance of ego that is weakness."

My guide paused and I lay down on the earth as if I'd been rolled out by this powerful observation.

He appeared completely at peace and continued. "You have reached for the tool of courage and have used it well. When you first felt the imbalance of your attachments to scarcity you were bowled over. Literally. But as you built awareness and understanding, you started to use the tool of courage. It is easy to feel pain, feel adrift, feel disorientated at the thought of co-creating with your heart."

I sat up. "So ego has done a great job suppressing feeling and selling us just the impression of feeling, not to mention the impression of truth!"

"It certainly has. Such is your journey. And with courage, and now simplicity, you get to see just how much of your world is fulfilling. And with guidance, you can change and create the fulfilment you seek. Only ego says you have no choice."

"So genuine courage isn't the choice to fight but the choice to create; create alternatives, allowance, understanding. And return to balance."

"Yes. To create from Love, not from fear."

"And ego hasn't really ripped us off with its impressions, we've just been learning limitation."

"Yes."

A Tale Of Two Cities

"And I suppose the same goes for feeling. Ego says that drama, getting attached to the endless ego conflicts in our world, living through others... all that stuff is feeling when really it's just an illusion that becomes real because we put our energy into it."

"Correct. Drama comes from the mind, not the heart. Complication, expectations, assumption... these are all types of attachments ego uses to make the world of the mind appear to be so much more."

"So how do I unravel the conditioning that, until very recently, has stopped me feeling?"

"Through simplicity. One step at a time. See each of your moments as infinite learning and expansion. There is no need to project towards 'more' or become depressed because there isn't any more. All you require is there in the moment. Your moments are much more precious than you could have ever imagined. When you allow the infinite nature of the Cosmos, it is your infinite nature that shines through; the wholeness that you are."

"Then how do I dissolve the habit of analysis rather than creation?"

"Do just that. Dissolve your attachments to the supposed securities of your mind—the facts of life that ego loves to tell you are true when actually they are just the limited version, courtesy of ego. Question what you think you see. Probe the depth of your experience. If it is built through Love then more and more meaning will be revealed. If it is built of illusion then you will see more and more attachments and recognise the attempts by ego to create meaning.

"Realise that when you are Now, in your heart and with simplicity, you can easily recognise the clutter of ego projections and falsehood. And in that moment you can unify your heart and mind."

"As I understand it then, when mind is in fear and heart in Love then I'm dissolving a conflict that ego seeks to keep going. Just like when we feel something deeply inside but the reflection in our world is the opposite; if we remain calm and in simplicity, we'll see the separation between the inner and the outer dissolve. The impressions and falsehoods will be transmuted through Love and the two reflections become as one. Is that the same as saying heart and mind become unified?"

"Yes. The rights and the wrongs of your mind are, as you know, simply different. When you use simplicity you are able to feel the difference rather than perpetuate the conflict. Ego will do all in its power to occupy you, whether it is fighting or charming."

"So keep the path simple and loving and then you'll always see the difference?"

"Quite. And you will learn the value of unity. You can always choose to be in unity but, as always, when you apply your choice in experience, you learn where you are. Is there a large honesty gap between who you think you are and who you are being? Or are you being what you seek? Are you being your true self?"

My companion paused. I felt a huge rush of energy through my body and felt my heart filling with words. "So when a person like me asks the big questions such as *Who am I? Where am I and what is my purpose?*, I should first ask *Am I being myself? Am I being honest in this moment?*"

"Yes. Embracing honesty brings your whole nature towards balance. You see how much you are spiritualising your life and allowing your Higher nature to manifest in your world."

"To be your higher nature, or not to be your higher nature? That is the question," I mused.

"Indeed. The question for eternity," my companion agreed, and glowed knowingly.

I felt myself unifying with the haze of light, adapting to the feeling of expanding out in all directions.

"Honesty and truth," I pondered. "They're so relative."

"An elasticity that allows you to learn. To collapse what you have known as truth all at once would not support you, plus you would not have the fuel to expand beyond what you have known."

"So it's up to me to allow the experience of truth to expand, just like I am now, through the teachings of guidance." I inclined my head towards my guide. "And through my Higher Self."

"Yes. Grow into truth just as you are growing into eternal life."

"Well that's still a bit of a stretch but I am becoming more comfortable with it. It's just that when I'm on my path and I bump into ego definitions and attachments, they bring me back to density and into that feeling that form is more real than the inner truth. I know in my heart this is just ego trying to draw me back into the limited truth with entertainment detours and easy short cuts to what I think I want, but I am getting better at staying in my centre and maintaining balance. Like you said, this is a path of seeking, not a path where we get told what we want to hear. Or, I might add, what our ego wants to hear."

"And so you are listening differently and more clearly. You are hearing the unravelling of the voice of ego and the messages of the heart. They have been tangled up with one another ever since you arrived in limitation but now the heart is no longer being drowned out by ego. The heart message is becoming louder as you choose to listen."

"That sounds like progress," I said. I paused, settling with my new level of honesty. "Ego can always justify, remaining attached and goad me into acting from fear rather than love but I can choose not to listen. And I am choosing to listen to my heart more and more, even when it takes me some time to understand. I want to unravel this. I want to see how chaos makes cosmic sense."

"And so you are and so you will. It is all in the flow and the allowance of that flow. Ego is always interested in finding the conflict and the separation. Ego always asks 'What's in it for me?' whereas the heart seeks awareness, expansion and reunification with the unlimited flow of love."

"So that's why Merlin said we were going on holyday?"

"Yes. A new space dedicated to the experience of unity."

There was a resonant pause that was so deep it dipped our conversation in pure harmony. I was tingling with peace.

"The dimensions are totally different here," I replied to the sensation.

"Because this is a whole new dimension of yourself, a whole new flow of being and a whole new being of flow. Much is coming together and you are feeling a greater sense of unity. You get to celebrate with parts of yourself that you were unable to recognise previously."

"Thank you," I said, feeling slightly uncomfortable but honouring my truth.

"And your capacity for receiving is also expanding. You are seeing that becoming more expanded doesn't mean you encounter more difficulty. You are beginning to appreciate that the more experience you have of expansion, the more you are able to adapt to it."

"Thank you. I AM allowing it." I emphasised the familiar phrase that opened my direct line to the greater Universe.

"And so it is. Being within the unity and simplicity of each of your moments means you'll have a juggling act for the time being. Ego will continue to project the importance of your mind but the choice to feel will become stronger. There will be plenty of surprises and joy. You are shifting from a nature built on imbalance into one built on balance. The greater the contrast, the greater the imbalance. But, equally, the bigger the transmutation opportunity."

"I am my own fuel, right?"

"That you are. And all you are required to do is believe

in the process. Keep flowing and you'll keep going. Progress is process and process is progress. Simplicity makes your experience easier and easier while attachment and mental control fall away. Simplicity supports you in seeing what is genuine balance, then you can identify your learning more swiftly. Then you can command the accelerations that, until very recently, you found so disruptive."

"If I can stop you there… This energy is beginning to come full circle. It's as if we've had this conversation before, like an energetic echo. You've said I've been making progress but I'm beginning to feel like I might've missed something or I need to do something again to properly understand."

"You are hearing the echoes of scarcity attachment through the fear that you aren't getting it right, that you've missed out on something. You are moving to greater depths of yourself and as a result you are seeing that aspects of your attachments appear to have returned. But we encourage you to perceive these feelings as recognition of your increased transmutation ability. The more you embrace simplicity, the deeper your transmutation efforts can become. That is why you are sensing echoes of aspects of yourself you thought you'd already dealt with. When you become more unified, you feel the same attachments at deeper levels but you also have greater capacity to transmute them."

"So just allow these echoes as they come up?"

"Yes. Make your choices as if it were the first time you encountered these sensations. Remember, every moment you are a new, more expanded being, not a soul caught in the nostalgias of passing attachments or the projections of ego futures."

"I see."

"Moreover, your ability to transmute is becoming relatively effortless as you apply your awareness and increasing clarity."

"I'd like to believe that but I can't really say that the journey is effortless just yet!"

My companion paused as if preparing to prod the depths of my scarcity a little more.

"What I mean is," I began sketching a justification, "I want it to be effortless and, yes, the way I've been healing and experiencing has improved. But things can go really well and then they appear to get bogged down and so it's a bit of an intermittent experience of effortlessness."

He smiled as if receiving his cue to continue.

"To understand effortlessness, you need to unravel struggle. To unravel struggle, you are required to go back through struggle to rejoin the effortlessness of your true nature. Your attachments to struggle are the fuel in this process."

"So don't struggle with struggle by trying to make it more than it is?"

"Indeed. Recognise and appreciate how your ability to transmute is increasing. And also that you are able to embrace yourself with much greater depth. Use simplicity to help you see when you are making the difference that you seek. Yes, sometimes when you experience struggle or are in pain it will be because you are resisting but other times it may be that you are simply recycling pain so that you may take your next step forward."

"How will I know the difference?"

"When you sense the difference."

"Self honesty again?"

"Yes. And simplicity and effortlessness and all that you have embraced in our conversation. It is all part of the process and of your progress; the unity of the endless support that is available to you. If you do not appreciate your progress then how can you assimilate it into your greater unity?"

"We're back to allowance again."

"But did we ever leave it?"

"Well, you don't. As for me, I still need a little bit of practice so I don't fall down the honesty gap!"

"It's all in the perception," smiled my companion, beginning to fade back into the wall.

Juggling With Possibility

"Are you preparing to leave?" I asked my companion, feeling my balance shift.

"We are always with you but this connection is nearing completion. Believe in yourself. You are achieving what you seek. Each ending will become a beginning. You are reclaiming your true nature."

As the phrase *reclaiming your true nature* flowed into the air it sent out sparks of light in all directions. Four apples rained down from somewhere over the wall. My teacher caught the unexpected missiles in one gentle movement without a blink or a shift in his serene state. "Here. Something with which to start your juggling."

"But..." I stopped before my mouth betrayed my self doubt. "Okay, I was going to say that I can't juggle... but there's no time like the present to start, right?"

My companion nodded knowingly.

I began juggling as best I could.

"Why did you think you could not juggle?" he asked.

"Because juggling is one of those things that keeps on going when your mind tells you it shouldn't. There's too much chaos in juggling and it depends on balance and trust and... well, the mind always thinks there's a scarcity of those."

All the apples fell into my lap.

"The mind does. But what about the heart?"

"I believe the heart would give everything in its truth a go, to honour the unending flow. You can't keep expanding if you keep on saying no all the time."

"Quite."

"Okay, I'm juggling... after a fashion. Please carry on juggling the words. I'll keep up as best I can."

Instead of continuing his lecture, my teacher now embraced a different angle of learning, preparing a neat diagram of gold and silver dust in the multifaceted earth.

"This is a tree of experience. This branch is your masculine side and this branch your feminine side. At the top, where these two branches come together, is your Higher Self. As you are aware, the masculine side of your nature harnesses your capacity to take action, to translate your intentions into experiences. Your feminine side is responsible for your receptivity, your willingness to open and trust the unlimited creative flow and to coordinate your capacity for that flow. When you are playing the game of all-or-nothing, your ego tries to make you rush from one side of yourself to the other—one moment receptive, the next, doing; sometimes a combination. But ego wants to get its way. It wants to expand limitation; it wants greater and greater extremes—the desire to have it all, but to try and embrace that *all* through travelling from one extreme to the other."

"Not very productive," I said, spilling my juggling act in all directions.

"True. It is just a coming and going that leaves you directionless in nothing but fear and control. Then there is the most common state of being in your world which is *doing-without-any-being*."

My companion started to rub out the feminine branch.

"But wait a moment," I cried, feeling an urgent concern from deep within me. "If the masculine side of ourselves starts to control everything, then how can we survive with no receptivity, no incoming fuel?"

"How indeed?" he affirmed, and proceeded to rub out the Higher Self position and wrote *Higher Self* over the feminine branch.

"So are you saying that if we do more and more without any feminine energy then our Higher Self has to fill in the extreme imbalance by substituting for the feminine energy to stop us leaving limitation altogether?"

"Yes. The feminine is still there but it is so faint because the masculine is taking over everything. Form, and the making of more form, becomes the only consideration."

"So ego is taking over, replicating more and more imbalance?"

"In simple terms, that is the case. Ego creates more and more imbalance which, in turn, creates more and more attachment, whether the person is aware of their state or not."

"Surely such imbalance will end up causing the person's whole nature to break down, won't it?"

"Correct. And the power of pain can often be what restores the feminine. Greater degrees of imbalance require greater and greater degrees of effort until even the physicality, as dense as it is, is so concentrated with imbalance that it is incapable of flow. It can take no more."

"And then there's no flow at all? And the result is death?"

"Exactly. Flow is completely extinguished because the Higher Self can only maintain the situation until the choice to rebalance is made. If the soul then chooses to bring their masculine and feminine sides back into balance, the Higher Self will return to its intended position of guidance."

"But some people are so imbalanced, they wouldn't be aware that they have a choice. What happens to them?"

"They cease their learning in embodiment. There is no meaning in their experience and there is no flow. The form of learning ends."

"But surely, for most people, to be in physicality is to learn through pain and imbalance?"

"This is one way within your world. But as you know, it is not the only way. You can experience through abundance, joy and effortlessness if you so choose. You are just required to be in balance to achieve this. If you are in balance then you will see there is peace within the hustle and bustle, just as there is movement within the peace. But, as you are finding out, you are required to go back through the attachments of ego so that you can create the fuel to return to balance, step by step. And your Higher Self and guidance as a whole support you in addressing what is most healing in each of your moments. Call it a little bit of energetic prioritising."

"So if I get imbalanced I may not be able to hear guidance?"

"This can happen. Ego can try to make you blind to alternatives or deaf to change. But if you embrace simplicity, ego has less and less attachments within which to hide."

"So when I get into the bogged down bits of my journey I just need to remember that this is all part of the process; I'm transmuting, going back through struggle."

"Yes. Perhaps choose to tiptoe through struggle rather than wade through knee-deep."

"I'll try and remember that," I pondered, pausing as my awareness caught up with me. "And so that's why I went through what I went through? To get the money to carry on writing?"

"And what did you go through?"

"Well... the scarcity fears, the struggles with receiving."

"Yes. All part of your process. And it has helped you appreciate your writing once more. And also your alchemical skills."

"And you lot... my guidance. I don't know if I could've got through it without you."

"So it is a unity of appreciation as all serve the natural state of being that is Love."

"So because I'm relatively balanced in this place, I can get a guidance intensive, download some new ways of being, then gradually apply them when I get back to my physical world?"

"Yes. What you would call meditation, being in your heart centre, or surrendering to the greater flow are all ways that you can expand your I AM Presence. This helps harmonise your masculine and feminine sides and expands your relationship with ease, balance and guidance."

My juggling appeared to have stabilised. I'd let my mind

Juggling With Possibility

wander off and stopped trying to juggle and surrendered to experiencing juggling.

"So can I ask you... where exactly are we? Where is all this?" I glanced over the wall and around our environment.

"It is an expansion of your awareness."

"What do you mean?"

"It is an exploration of your greater self, your true nature. It is not a place but rather an experience of yourself."

"But it can seem so real, have so many sensations and natures that are like my time in physicality."

"And why do you find this curious?"

"Well, if form is so limited and we're having this conversation in an expanded state of being, why are we in form at all?"

"Because it is of service. Guidance isn't here to shock you out of form and into your unlimited state, it is to remind you and support you in becoming aware of your unlimited nature. You are here because your awareness of self is expanding."

"So what happens to my awareness when I'm back in my other world?"

"Why not see your experience in limitation, your other world, as part of your greater self rather than thinking you move away from your Higher Nature to another place? Call it your magical world when you are learning about your spiritual nature."

"So it's all linked. I can sort of understand that. So what you're implying is that my other limited world is part of my greater spiritual world."

"Yes. And through expanded awareness you can be in two worlds, as you would think of it, at once."

"But I can't actually feel or see my flat, my other physical experience, now."

"Why not?"

"I don't know."

"It is simply a matter of awareness. When you place your

awareness in the limited world then you can experience that part of yourself. When your awareness is within your higher aspects, you can experience them. And you are experiencing the spiritualising of your life more and more. You are talking to guidance as you navigate through limitation and you are discussing with guidance here, as you think of it. You are present in both."

"So we don't really go anywhere and it's all about awareness?"

"Yes. It is always ego that seeks a destination whereas awareness is elastic—you can experience within limitation or you can expand your awareness so that you can be with other parts of yourself. All of yourselves are one, it is simply that ego would like you only to be aware of ego."

"And that's why you encourage me to think of myself as Light with a bit of density thrown in, not the other way around?"

"Precisely. Ego has monopolised your company and conditioned you into thinking that you are only capable of having an awareness of limitation. But now your awareness is expanding, you are beginning to realise that you have both a limited and unlimited nature. This is all part of the process of ascension. You develop your awareness so that you can develop your relationship with your I AM Centre. As you do so, you recycle your attachments to the limited world and your awareness expands so that you may reunite with the unlimited nature that is truly you."

"So is balance the best tool to keep juggling my awareness of limitation and of the unlimited?"

"In truth, it wouldn't be balanced to use balance as a tool for everything all of the time, doing so just because your mind told you it was best. Your experience is just a flow of intention into form. It isn't an equation you can predict."

"Where would be the fun in that?"

"Where, indeed? And where would be the learning?

Equations seek to define your world just as your mind does, boxing it into known quantities. But experience is a flow of unlimited energy and unlimited learning."

"So don't get boxed in? And don't think that balance is best?"

"Simply feel. Sense how you are connected to the Now through your heart truth. Then the experience of shifting your consciousness will be smooth and you will embrace your learning, cooperate with chaos and expand the awareness of unity."

He leaned forward and plucked an apple from my juggling act. "Want a part of this greater unity? Something you can sink your teeth into?" He offered me the apple.

"It's about time I transmuted my juggling act. Thanks!"

"Yes. A successful alchemy creating an expanded truth."

My companion appeared to pause, sensing if all was completed.

"All is fuel, all is unity. Nothing to it, really," he added.

And as I took a bite into the apple, my Eastern wizard dissolved into the wall with a bow and the flash of sapphire from his turban, a lingering souvenir of the allowance of simplicity.

Fast Food

I sat in a haze of fulfilment, almost hovering above the Earth. The apple was the sweetest I'd ever tasted.

"Nothing to it," I muttered to myself. "We are, after all, more space than we are matter; Light with a little bit of density thrown in."

I looked down at my legs and feet to check if I was floating. I heard a whisper. "Not quite yet. But there is always the magic carpet... the unfolding path of experience... places to go, people to see."

I suddenly felt recharged, ready to explore. I was on my feet within the moment. "Now that's what I call effortless," I smiled, setting off in the direction of the nearest doorway.

"Going somewhere? Or should that be, arriving somewhere?" observed Merlin, standing in front of my chosen portal.

"How about both?! Nice of you to join us. Well, there's only me here at the moment but my new companion was most insightful; gave me the keys to my new magic carpet," I said, winking at Merlin.

"Fancy taking it for a spin?"

"I'd love to! It's parked over there," I said, gesturing dismissively over Merlin's left shoulder. "Just required to recycle a few more attachments before I get my licence. You know how it is... Practice makes progress!"

Merlin played along with me. "Oh yes. It takes time to make use of all that hot air. But your experience of your experience has changed, has it not?"

"Absolutely; much more expanded. I never knew there was so much in simplicity. It's like layers and layers of rich fabric. You just want to bury your face in it and get wrapped up in it."

"Excellent. That's the general idea. Keep within that flow and you will feel all that richness and fulfilment. Once experienced, it can take root in the foundation of your new balance and support you when ego tries to complicate and distort your moment. So what do you say? Want to go inside?" Merlin gestured towards the marketplace.

"Of course! I'm curious to see what's changed. I mean I'm curious to see how my experience of this has changed."

"After you and your replete observations, then," replied Merlin.

I stepped through the door into a completely new environment. The market was full of the hustle and bustle of life but I felt part of it. I felt part of the chaos, not dragged around by it or harassed by its desire to capture me within it. It was like floating two inches above the world while still remaining in it.

"You are indeed getting the hang of your Light," smiled Merlin.

"And what a trip," I replied.

Suddenly, without warning, my stomach started to grumble. Grumbles quickly became rumbles of digestive thunder as they moved ever closer. I gravitated towards a steaming tower of corn topped with a garland of onions, tomatoes and fresh herbs. I chose a mountainous helping without thinking how I would pay.

"Allow me," said Merlin, reminding me of receiving.

"Thanks, Merlin," I replied, clutching my simple feast. I began inhaling the food as if I'd been starving for a millennium.

"You could slow down and enjoy the flavour of your food!" suggested Merlin.

"Now there's an alternative!"

I stopped shovelling and began filling my moments with the savour and flavour of my snack.

"Nourishment has never been so simple and it's always there in abundance, as you now know deep in your heart. Your awareness of what is truly nourishing, and what is simple, is growing."

"I was charging out of simplicity and into scarcity for a moment there, until you reminded me. All this..." I couldn't find any word even close to describing it "... this... sense of unity, of flow, of endlessness is exhilarating, almost overpowering. It's hard to keep balanced. I didn't know if I was lifting off or trying to take great handfuls before it ran out. But I'm stabilised again now. I am adapting."

"Indeed, the process is never short of surprises. Each soul allows, assimilates and authenticates differently. That's the richness of the becoming. Each ascension is unique. Some go crashing into their density, others continually rebound from it. And then there are those who simply explode it. But what's important is that the process keeps on flowing and transmuting, and the unity remains. "Grace is an advantage," said Merlin, looking pointedly at me, "but not always the first choice."

"But if simplicity is this powerful, why does it mostly go undiscovered?"

"Because it's normally lost under a great pile of attachments along with balance, and patience, to name but a few. So souls aren't aware of what goes into the state of simplicity. Ego tells you that simplicity means *in simple terms; on the surface; superficial.* Though that is only one perspective, it's been a popular one. People fear simplicity because ego says there is nothing in it, when really there is nothing to it! No attachments, no controls, no limits. People think they are missing out precisely because simplicity doesn't have the attachments they are used to, when in truth they are simply missing out on ego... which, as you know, isn't missing out at all.

"And so simplicity remains a mystery for most. It's when you go below the surface of yourself, reclaim some of that density, restore some balance to your nature that you see through different eyes. Your experience changes. Your experience of experience changes."

"Simplicity and balance go hand in hand, then," I ventured.

"The state of balance supports the state of simplicity. They are mutually supportive but independent," replied Merlin, accentuating the subtle difference.

"So when our world is simple, it isn't missing anything? For example, people often scoff at those who have simple tastes. They say they're mean or ignorant of more sophisticated alternatives. Ego says 'Oh you poor thing, you're missing out because you can't afford the best.'"

"Ego," Merlin clarified, "sees the simplicity that supports balance as less. Ego always believes more of ego is better."

"But that's just more imbalance," I added quickly.

Fast Food

"Yes. And although it may appear simple to you now, it was not long ago that you fought simplicity."

"Because ego said it wasn't enough."

"Yes. And it will not surprise you to know it is never enough for ego. And it is often the limited nature that predominates. But that is changing. The state of simplicity helps you embrace what you create and appreciate the abundance of your true nature. In each moment you can allow an open heart and an open mind and discover that you are never lacking anything. Simplicity helps you learn to a new depth from the moments you construct. Your moments are sacred and yet there are so many who willingly cast them aside in favour of the disposable society of ego."

"What an irony that a lack of learning now seems a waste to me when, only a few years ago, standing my ground and resisting learning would've meant being right and achieving something."

"Indeed and you have managed to transform your perception so completely by embracing and deepening your connection through a new state of being."

"What's that?"

"Well, in truth it is not new, it has always been part of your transmutations, it is just that now you are able to begin to recognise it."

"And so what is it? Simplicity?"

"Partly. But what keeps you going through your transmutation when its nearly at an end but your ego tells you it's time to give up?"

"Trust?"

"Yes, you embrace trust but you also embrace…"

The word was on the tip of my tongue.

Then it came to me.

"Grace," I said. "That's the word. But what does it really mean and how can it help?"

"Grace is a period when you surrender fully, you transmute any lingering doubt and you believe that what you are moving through is bringing you rewards."

"But my conditioning associates a state of grace with a period of great difficulty."

"But that is ego talking. Grace is a period of great opportunity. It is a chance to demonstrate and benefit from your learnings, to show that you can command the tools and awareness that you are earning."

"So it's a last chance for ego, then; a last stand against expansion."

"In a way. Let us use the example of your financial healing. There was a period of grace within which you realised that struggling, being dramatic or getting depressed didn't help. So you gave up fighting ego and surrendered so you could cooperate with your greater unity. You weren't necessarily comfortable but you allowed your expansion. You unravelled your attachment to scarcity and you transmuted it into abundance. Grace gave you the opportunity to appreciate your shift from scarcity to abundance. All the cycles within yourself synchronised your grace period. You could not have achieved this if you were rushing around in doingness."

"No, I wouldn't have been able to surrender. My healing, which I would've called illness, was actually my vehicle of grace."

"Indeed," smiled Merlin. "Grace has no speed, no time limit. It is a wonderful way to see the meaning in your experience. Grace is the state when the rain falls more slowly, when there are wrinkles in time, where ego thinks nothing is achieved and yet for a moment you are connected fully to your greater self so the adjustment you choose can be made."

"So I sneak past ego and I am complete for that moment?"

"Let's just say ego is so occupied with what isn't happening, its scarcity of doing that it can't recognise the power of grace. And, as always, this is perfect."

"Perfectly simple!"

"Yes. And thus we unite in simplicity and our ending becomes our new departure point. So tell me, practicing alchemist, where exactly did you park that magic carpet of yours?"

It's All Relative

When I awoke the next day I felt as though I'd be run over by a bus-shaped Universe.

"What do you call this, Higher Self? A Light hangover?"

There was no answer.

I stretched out to the bedside table and fumbled around in search of my watch. I took a long hard blink before I could focus on its face. It was already 9:30 a.m. I should've left fifteen minutes ago.

"There's no point in starting your day short of what you think you need. Bring your heart and mind into balance with a new perspective; there will be plenty of those today," encouraged my Higher Self, smoothing out the lumps in my awareness as I returned to physicality.

"Alright, we can continue this conversation when I've stopped feeling the weight of my limited self," I retorted, leaving no doubt about my bumpy transition.

"Don't you mean the passing transmutation?"

"Yes alright, alright," I replied curtly, clearly not in the mood for insight. "Whatever it is, I feel dog tired and, if you don't mind, I've got to shuffle my uncooperative physicality around so I can flow into action, hopefully even punctuality."

My Higher Self appeared to take a larger than normal step back as my grumpiness projected itself clumsily. Bringing my spiritual acceleration together with my physical awareness was like carrying too many items in a supermarket—you hold just those few things you need, bend down for the last one and drop one of the ones you were carrying. Then, as you pick that up, another falls. And so on and so on. As I felt myself caught between reluctance and resentment, I knew I was at that bit just before you realise you need a basket, and what you thought was only a quick errand becomes a much longer journey.

I decided to reach for a temporary structure in which to put everything I'd gained.

"Help, Higher Self! I didn't mean what I said just a moment ago, I just feel a bit overwhelmed. Or is it my mind? Anyway, I can definitely say I'm mixed up and I don't think I can keep this together at all. Why am I feeling this way?"

"Just doing the last part of your present cycle—authentication. That's the bit when ego first tells you that you can put all your new tools and new awareness through your mind but you find it actually won't fit. Then you return to your heart. But you are all flustered by your mind and ego. You can't slow down enough to see that you are perfectly capable and just need to take time out to gather up your new tools in your I AM Presence. So then ego butts in and starts to complain about all the disturbance and tries to tell you it's simpler to go back to what you already knew; drop that shopping there and then and come out empty handed, as it were."

I was irritated with myself. "A return to all-or-nothing, eh?"

"Dissolving all-or-nothing," added my Higher Self. "There is always another way, it's just seeing through those ego blind spots."

"But why didn't I see that?"

"Because you were blind to it; occupied with your ego's disturbance rather than consolidating what you've created."

"Alright. Ego set me up, then."

"Actually, you set yourself up by choosing ego reaction instead of patience. But this is another moment and within this you are choosing learning through self observation…and so your

It's All Relative

path unfolds. Each moment is different, as you are finding out. You can choose to define yourself by your perceived mistakes or you can simply learn from them. You are starting some spiritual multi-tasking, acknowledging how the inner nature can overlap and unite with your outer world. Your inner processing is just being reflected in your outer world. It is ego that is complaining not your true nature. It's ego that doesn't want you to keep the unity between your inner and outer worlds."

"Too late, ego," I said. "I want to balance the outer with the inner, not compound the superficial with the separate. I enjoy seeing Andrew and ego isn't going to change that."

"Excellent. Let me help you with your transmutation while you get on with your Earthly transportation."

"You've got yourself a deal. I AM transmuting my grumpy dissatisfaction smoothly."

"Wonderful," replied my Higher Self. "That's all the invitation I require."

As soon as I'd clarified my commitment, I felt lighter and more present. My physicality became more flexible and I was ready to leave in what appeared to be no time.

"Keep going," I thought. "Next comes *flowing into an expanded perception of time*. I have all the time in this world, and any other world for that matter," I affirmed. "I AM creating a smooth journey to the George and Dragon."

I sensed my Higher Self nodding, encouraging me in my new approach.

As I locked my door, the front door opened. One door closes, another door opens, I thought.

It was the gas man. "Ahh, I'm glad I caught you. You're 1A, right?" he asked.

"Yes, that's my flat number."

"Can I read your meter please? Yours is the only one that isn't outside."

"Can you be quick? I've got a meeting at eleven."

"It'll only take a minute."

I unlocked the door and the meter man disappeared behind the armchair for what appeared to be a mini ice age.

"There you are!" he exclaimed, as if he'd found an errant hamster. "Can you just hold the torch there? It's really dark round the back here. I can't quite see the figures."

My patience was wearing way past thin as the gas man moved at a glacial pace. But I knew complaining would make things worse.

"Of course," I said, reluctantly taking the torch. "Can you see now?"

"Yes thanks. Just getting the reading now."

Isis appeared at the window but jumped off the sill when the gas man re-emerged, startling her.

"If that's it, I'd better get going," I prompted.

"Let me just give you the paperwork," he smiled. "Now, when you look at your bill, there'll be an estimated reading for the last time your meter was read and then the recorded reading here. So that amount you paid last time will be adjusted to your actual reading this time."

I was now close to bursting as he explained the billing procedures, which was probably welcomed with a mug of tea by those with few visitors and a lot more patience. But my hospitality was close to hostility as I hurried him out. I was astonished that such a simple exercise could cause so much stress.

Finally, the gas man had disappeared towards Mrs Daley's and I was free to get to the station. I saw a bus going off in my direction as I came out the front door.

"I suppose it'll have to be a cab," I huffed, letting out a big sigh as I waited at the kerbside.

What was the probability of no cabs passing in ten minutes in the middle of the morning? I was finding out. Meanwhile my Higher Self was chuckling gently as my irritation continued to stretch and distort my Now.

"There's no need to laugh, you know," I complained, feeling rather sensitive.

It's All Relative

"But you've got to admit, it is funny... thinking you are running out of time when you are actually staying in the infinite Now so that you can finish recycling your attachments and move to a new cycle of learning."

"But how can I be moving ahead if I'm stuck here?"

"Exactly! Quite the joke! You can move ahead by allowing being here; by going with this flow, this authentication of your learning instead of resisting it."

"Not from my direction. Not at present, anyway. And don't use my own thoughts against me." My ego was feeling bruised.

"Just observing... That's some stubborn transmutation. Why won't you let it pass; let it flow through and be gone?"

"I didn't know I was stopping it," I replied.

"Disengage from ego and then you won't work against yourself. Surrender. Be in allowance of your situation and the wrinkles in your current time will all shake out, you'll see."

"Easy for you to say. You don't experience time."

"And that's why guidance is possible... there is no limitation."

"Alright, message received. Over and out. Hopefully, understanding it fully isn't far behind," I said, shrugging off what was left of ego as best I could. "I AM allowing the transmutation of this attachment. I AM surrendering to arriving at the George and Dragon in the perfect moment."

At that moment a taxi came around the corner. I took it as a reflection of my transmutation and finally the first grin of the day spread across my face. I wanted to laugh out loud. Ego had hidden in my resistance and done it again; it had got me to fight and struggle my way through another transmutation. But at least, with the help of guidance, I was beginning to see where I went on my detour.

"Charing Cross Station, please," I said quickly as I jumped in.

"Traffic's heavy but I'll do my best."

"Thanks. I appreciate it. But if I get any later today, I could even be early!"

"Miracles can happen, eh?" smiled the cabbie in his mirror.

"I'm counting on it," I replied.

Charlatans Or Visionaries?

As my taxi drew up at the George and Dragon, the church clock tower was showing 12:30, an hour and a half late.

'That can't be right,' I thought.

I checked my phone as I jogged up Church Walk. It was two minutes to 12:00. 'Wow! I've made up nearly thirty minutes in a few paces. Just need to make up another hour between here and the Public Bar.'

"Well, here goes," I said aloud as I arrived, my head brushing the top of an ancient and slightly tipsy door frame.

I scanned the bar but Andrew was nowhere to be seen. I ordered a tea and spotted a booth near the fireplace, close to the main door. As I sat down I began to laugh, first in short chuckles and then full laughter.

"What's so funny?" said Andrew as he blew through the door like a solitary leaf, "I'm only an hour late."

"But that's what's funny, Andrew. So am I! That makes us both on time!"

"But why are you laughing?"

"Because I've been rushing into the future instead of enjoying what's in the Now."

"Well I'm glad we've got that straight! I'll just go and get a pint and catch up! Sounds like you've already started drinking! What's yours?"

"Nothing, thanks. I've got tea coming."

"So I can't blame the grog for your twaddle, then?"

"All in the perception, you know."

"I'll just go and get that drink so I can lubricate my perception. Be back in a tick."

My tea arrived and Andrew joined me with a pint in each hand.

"Now that's what I call efficient, Andrew!"

"Yep! And what do you think of my local, then?" he asked, looking around the room. "Might as well be five hundred miles away, the few times I've been in here. But the beer's good."

"I'm happy to see you, Andrew, even if it's because you're off on sick leave." I raised my cup of tea. "Here's to widening perspectives and better health."

"Cheers!" he smiled.

"So... tell me from the top, headline and all. Why are you at home and what's this about collapsing at work?"

"Well, I was in the office looking at some possible Sunday features and I started to feel dizzy. Next thing I remember, I woke up on the floor next to my desk with half of Editorial standing over me. They were going to call an ambulance and insisted I go to the hospital."

Andrew took a sip of his drink.

"And did you?"

"Not exactly. I felt better in about ten minutes and persuaded everyone that I'd had too much beer at lunchtime but promised to take a few days off and get some tests done. I went to the doctor the next day. My yearly medical's coming up anyway so I had a similar set of tests done there and then."

"And how do you feel now?"

"Well, I haven't had any more dizzy spells, which is a relief."

"And...?" I always knew when Andrew wasn't telling the whole story. "The truth, the whole truth, and nothing but the truth, Mr Andrew Davies."

"Okay. I got the tests back yesterday and... you know the

cholesterol you're not meant to have? The bad one? Well I've got lots and lots of that. Plus I've got blood pressure to match."

"So, high blood pressure and high cholesterol. What else?"

"That's it. Everything else is normal for a man of my age, whatever that really means."

"So what are you going to do about it?"

"Apart from the obvious—eat less and drink less? I don't know, really. I find it all quite depressing, to be honest, because if I take eating and drinking away I don't really have much in my life apart from a great house with matching mortgage. Not my ideal companions at this point. But then, of course, there's always you!"

"And that, *of course*, makes you feel a whole lot better!" I teased.

"Actually, all jokes aside, it does. I'm approaching premature middle age and, if the truth were known, I've got nothing to show for it but a beer belly and a demanding career that leaves me no time to enjoy myself. When I came to again, after collapsing on the floor in the office... for a moment I thought I was dead. And in that brief moment, I panicked thinking 'I'm dead and I'm still in the office working myself into an early grave and nothing's changed!' Funny and sad, all at the same time. Everything since then has been a bit of a blur. I can't even remember our last conversation. Though I can remember how I felt after it."

"So what are you going to do now?"

"Like you always say, that's up to me... isn't it? It's about what I choose, right?"

"It certainly is. And what do you see your choices being?"

"Now you ask me. ... I think that's why I wanted to talk to you. I don't know. But for the first time in my life, I want to find out. And you're the one who strikes me as having done a lot more research into the weird and wonderful than I have. So where do you think would be a good place to start?"

Charlatans Or Visionaries

"Here and now is always a good place to start," I said. "But remember, I'm not going to be behind you nagging you along. Whatever you want to change, talking about it is a start, but going beyond that takes the four Cs—Choice, Commitment, Courage and Confidence. Plus a huge sense of humour, which you've already got!"

"Okay, I need to choose to change. No one else can do it for me, right?"

"Right. And talking about it is fine but the most important thing is that you practice—put your changes into action. Then you'll see the real benefits."

"So how do I do that?"

"Let's start with your health—your physical body, okay?"

"Yep."

"Well, there are three other bodies that make up you. There's your mental body—thought processes, logic, analysis, desire to control, administrating your world and trying to live in the future.

"Then your emotional body—your feelings, creating, expression and your desire to be a victim and live in the past.

"And then there's your spiritual body—the *Why-am-I-here?-How-am-I-connected-to-the-Cosmos?-Am-I-a-seeker?-Can-I-find-purpose?* part; Your Higher Self; the guidance that has some pretty handy hints when it comes to change."

"Okay. I've got four bodies in one."

"Exactly. And in very simple terms, you're made up of Light and density. Some parts of you are more flexible, allowing and open to alternatives than others. Basically the dense bits of you are made up of resistance—resistance to change; the desire to keep everything controlled and mistrust alternatives. So, Andrew Davies, let's see how much of your density is running your life. How would you describe illness?"

"Being in a state of ill, I suppose. I know it's come from abusing myself, eating lots of the wrong food, and drinking too much."

"So you need healing."

"Oh, hey, I didn't say anything about healing!"

I seemed to have hit a nerve. Andrew became agitated, taking refuge behind a wall of resistance.

"What's the matter with healing?" I asked, confused.

"I'm not some weirdo trying to give up responsibility for my life. I don't need healing, I just want to get well."

"But healing *is* getting well."

"No it's not, it's experimenting with charlatans and freaks who charge a fortune for thin air and expect to be treated like demi-gods."

"Hey, come on! Who are you and what have you done with Andrew? You know... the open-minded one that was investigating change?"

Andrew turned bright red. "I slammed the door on him, right?"

"You positively bolted towards some pretty radical conclusions, leaving me far behind!"

"It's just all that New Age stuff... We've had so much of it at the newspaper; so many people looking for miracles, wanting to be healed and ultimately being taken for a ride."

"But Andrew, do you really believe that the press presents a balanced view? Or do they rely on a sensational angle?"

"Bit of both, I suppose."

"So why can't healing and the New Age be a bit of both, too? I think we can agree that there are charlatans in any profession, right? What about all those upstanding professions that've fallen flat on their faces in scandal and deception? Why is it that, all of a sudden, people apply different standards to healing and spiritual development? Why do people get over some official ripping off the general public for hundreds of thousands with a shrug of governmental cynicism but then, if someone is unscrupulous in a New Age business, immediately the regulators move in and the whole of the sector suffers?"

"Because people don't like getting ripped off, especially

by something that doesn't work. At some point in our lives we've just got to learn to live with what we've got, learn to be realistic about how much we can change and how much we can trust. That's just the way things are. There are too many people who just trust too much; people who put their hopes in things that aren't going to change in a decade of Sundays, let alone a month. It's simple: people don't like change. Once a lifetime maybe, but not regularly. Where would we be if everything kept on changing?"

Andrew's open-mindedness appeared to be closing very rapidly. I was shocked at how quickly he'd begun defending the status quo.

I glanced up from our discussion and saw a man in his late forties sitting at the bar gulping his pint quickly, well on the way to his next.

My Higher Self whispered to me, "Your environment is always here to help you."

"Andrew, hold that thought for a moment. Take a look at the bar."

He glanced up and out of his defensive rant. "Yes it's a typical bar. What are you getting at?"

"Do you see the man slightly hunched over at the end of the bar?"

"Yes. What about him?"

"What do you see, Andrew?"

"A man enjoying his beer and his own company. Seems perfectly normal to me."

I smiled.

"What? What are you getting at?" squirmed Andrew, agitated as he grappled with his inner disturbance.

"Look with your heart. Andrew. Put what you think you see aside and tell me what you feel you see."

Andrew's lips parted, ready to voice his reaction at my sudden request. But he stopped. In that moment, he turned to embrace the Now and the feelings he'd been fighting. He glanced over towards the bar, then back at me, and then looked down at his drink.

"I see an unfulfilled man washing down his disappointment with one too many pints at lunch time."

"And why do you suppose he's doing that?"

"Because his ego's conned him into believing that he doesn't have to feel. He can avoid what isn't happening or what is happening in his life by blanking it out in one simple lunch hour."

He paused for a moment. "But more and more beer isn't going to change what he's feeling. He's the one who has to choose to change."

Andrew looked me straight in the face. "Because ego is a con artist and a con artist takes someone who wants something for nothing and gives them nothing for something. Ego just keeps on taking, draining that someone until nothing is left. Ego has control of everything and there's no change. And all that *nothing* you've been investing in means you haven't got a life."

He paused to ponder again. "I'm sorry. I was a real cynic just then. It's been a tough week but that's no reason to take it out on you. Although I'd love to say I'm getting back to normal, I don't know what normal is any more. And you stopped me with the perfect life-size example. The man at the bar could be the perfect reflection of where I could be going. If I keep listening to my lazy cynic, that is. Make that my proud, lazy cynic who thinks that he can overcome anything and doesn't need anyone. If I stay with that conditioning it's like going back to the con artist hoping next time will be different; that next time I'll feel differently, I'll get fixed and everything will change as if by magic."

"Well, change can be magical, Andrew, it's just that you've got to create your own brand of magic and embrace your personal alchemy rather than wait for the Universe to wave a wand and fix you."

"So... no more letting conditioning tell me. Even if I think I can keep this going, look where it's getting me."

"You said it."

Andrew stared into what was left of his beer.

I leaned forward and placed my hand on his arm. "Remember, ego is lonely. That's why it works so hard to keep you. Ego is a victim boxed in by fear, control, lack and loss. It's not bad, it's not good, it's just a way of experiencing limitation. But now you've decided to live differently, it's up to you to keep on choosing to believe that you can find the rewards of living beyond the limits of your own mind and ego. And you will find what you're looking for, so long as you're willing to choose; willing to experience the change."

Andrew let out a long sigh. Still facing his beer, he brushed away the tears that were welling up in his eyes. "I do understand what you're saying. I could easily become the man over there. I can keep on listening to that limited logic that says 'This is just how it is. Deal with it.'"

He looked up. "But I'm glad I came here today. And I'm glad that you're here to help me see when I'm sliding back into what I know instead of staying with what I feel. Deep down in my heart I understand why there are no guarantees in any changes that we make because then there wouldn't be any change. Guarantees define our world, they don't embrace change. And I think the reason those who represent change get such a hard time is because everyone has fear, and when their security is questioned, most people defend the safety that fear creates rather than being honest about what they really want to change. So the New Age is a sector that most are prepared to criticise when secretly they wish they could trust and embrace a little bit of that personal alchemy; feel some genuine inspiration rather than the hype of passing fads. You're right and I'm sorry."

"Andrew, just put being right or wrong aside for a minute. As you've just said, your whole world has turned upside down, literally, in one week. And along with that, your security and your comfort zone. I'm not here to zealously convince you of anything, but what I am here to do is help you channel this disturbance into some kind of sense, some kind of understanding that can help you move forward in the coming weeks. The New Age isn't going to save you and nor are the doctors for that matter. It's up to you. One doctor could look at your test results and say you're a prime candidate for a heart attack before you're forty. Another could say that's totally incorrect, and another could say it's up to you. Your health depends on their experience and on their perception of you. So who's right and who's wrong?"

"It depends."

"Precisely. Depends on what you choose. So answer me this: Are you happy with the sum total of your current life and what it's brought you? Or do you want to change it? Others' opinions can't change your state, only you can."

"You mean, if I'm judgmental and closed then I'm not going to get anywhere? Least of all, find alternatives?" Andrew looked decidedly uncomfortable.

"Okay, no need to be harsh on yourself. But that's a start. So, are you going to start inviting change in or are you going to get a few second opinions so you can find a doctor who tells you what you want to hear? A closed heart can't receive. Judgment makes expansion really difficult because it's like attaching yourself to a certain place on your path—when you want to move on, it becomes difficult because your judgments have fused you to a rigid way of living. And so you take one step forward and see you're caught, and you can't move on. You just end up going around and around in circles."

"Okay, not all the New Age is rubbish. So tell me what you think healing is."

"The capacity and ability to rebalance. Illness is simply a sign that you've got out of balance. The bigger the imbalance, the more serious the illness. When you're younger, you've got less toxins—which are accumulated imbalance—and so your physical body can adapt more easily; it can remember it's way back to balance and well being. But the more your toxic one-offs become regular habits, the more your path of balance gets clogged and your body finds it harder and harder to get back to balance. It forgets. It loses its way because the natural pathways of balance are no longer flowing freely and your body becomes increasingly conditioned to ill health. And it can happen in all your four bodies, not just your physical one. So healing is helping you find your way back to balance."

"That means I could be physically fit but still have imbalances in my emotional or mental bodies?"

"Yes, that's possible. But remember, the physical body is the last port of call, as it were."

"What do you mean?"

"Healing is a flow of energy. The energy flows through the non-physical parts of you—your Light presence and your mental and emotional parts—and when it gets to your physical body, if you've ignored the signs of imbalance in, say, your mental state, for example, and you drink more to suppress the work stress you are under, then the imbalance turns physical and that's much harder to reverse.

"Sounds like I've let all this go on far too long."

"It's all relative but, yes, you've been listening to your ego that said you could put up with this struggle; you could even withstand pain, because you'd just be giving up if you didn't."

"So now I've had a wake up call and I've got to pay attention and be open to healing? And I can get healing from a doctor, a natural health practitioner, or a faith healer? I assume they're all able to advise me on how to bring the wellness back into my life and, just like anything, it's my choice. Nobody can make me do anything. It's advice, not force."

"Absolutely. For some, wellness simply means not feeling pain; that is, not feeling the discomfort of their imbalance. So they take something for the pain symptom and don't think or aren't interested about the actual cause of the pain. If they don't feel the pain, they think that they don't have a problem."

"You mean, taking medication to block out the pain? But you know how I hate being dependent on anyone and or anything! It took me two days to make that phone call and ask you to meet me. I thought I could work it out but the only way I could see, until we started talking, was the doctor, and he's recommending long term medication. I really do want to change, but I certainly don't want to get into taking pills all the time."

"So use some of that money—the money you say you don't have time to spend—and start investing in being balanced and enjoying wellness. That's what healing's all about. Look in your own newspaper. There're plenty of new therapies featured every week on the health page. See what inspires you. Maybe you can find a doctor who's happy to combine conventional medicine with natural methods. It's up to you. Anything and everything is waiting to be discovered."

"But how do you know? How do you really know? You speak with such... I don't know... authority, conviction... whatever it is. But how can you be so certain?"

"Andrew, I just feel it and I trust in that belief in alternatives. There're no answers in the mind, only in the heart. If you want to find your way back to balance then you're going to need to seek out the alternatives that build your path back to balance. Seeking in your mind is just looking at a level that you already know. There isn't any expansion in that; no genuine newness. If you want to find change then you're going to need to look into the unknown. Do and be something different. If what you're doing and being has got you to this place then have you really got anything to lose if you try something different?"

"I could lose twenty-five pounds!" said Andrew, attempting some nervous humour.

"What about recycling some of those self destructive habits? Then you'll start to create the recipe for your return to balance as well as lose the twenty-five pounds!"

"I guess it's seek-and-ye-shall-find-alternatives, then?"

"Yes it is. Ye will definitely find, but it's up to ye to do something with what ye unearths, not just stare at it saying 'Oh that's nice, I found an alternative.' Journey over!"

"Turn the corner and keep on going, then?"

"Absolutely. If it's a choice made with self loving and self healing intention, it can easily unfold into a path that leads to a permanent change and reinstates balance."

"Not like the corner I was turning before, off into the 'I-don't-care-about-myself' oblivion," he said despondently.

"Exactly. If you're honouring balance then 'I-don't-care-about-myself' isn't a road you choose to go down."

"Am I turning a corner now?"

"I'm choosing to believe that, but do you believe it? What's important is that you actually keep going; keep your momentum up so when you hit the sticky parts of ego and it protests against the changes you're making, you have enough momentum to get through into new phases."

"Okay! Rush at change like a bat out of hell, then!"

"No, not at all. Just be open and willing to change and work to keep your balance while you're applying your chosen change."

"So gently does it, then?"

"But gentle doesn't mean weak and ineffectual, which is what your ego has led you to believe. Gentle can be very supportive and very effective, particularly for someone who's got high blood pressure and cholesterol!"

"If I choose gentle... and I don't actually remember what that feels like... but if I do, then there's no reason why it won't help?"

"No reason at all. Rushing at change can often mean that you try to do too much too quickly and then you simply give up because you use up all your reserves of willingness. But if you do something differently, with balance and honesty you can make a permanent change. For example, if you exercise three times a week but eat four times as much then maybe you won't lose weight. But if you exercise regularly, be honest about the amount you eat and keep balanced as best you can, you'll probably start losing weight. And after you've adapted to the initial change, you might even grow to enjoy it."

"So start as I mean to go on?"

"Definitely. Start with a balanced intention, then you'll create a new phase of balance. It doesn't matter if you work with a personal trainer, a healer or a nutritionist, none of them can fix you, Andrew, nor will they hand out easy pills."

"Okay, but I still don't understand what a healer actually does."

"A healer can help the four bodies that you are made of get back into balance. There are many different kinds of healing. It depends on where you are in your healing process as to which kind of healing you attract. Take weight gain. Sometimes being overweight is related to how much you eat, but other times it's related to how comfortable you are with yourself, your level of self love. Sometimes it's related to your conditioning, your habits and the way you think. What's important with healing, just like any service, is that you respect who you choose to work with; you believe in what they offer and you make an effort to learn. Even if you don't understand everything they talk about, you allow the process because your intention is to make a difference in your life. What you think, what you feel and how open you are to change will all contribute to your physical health."

"Okay, okay. I understand a little better now. And I'll concede that not all healers are crazy weirdos with few words and expensive promises. But answer me this: Not all people have got a physical problem like me, but they still go to healers. Why? There's nothing wrong with them."

"You'll be glad to know that imbalance comes in all shapes and sizes! Also, just because imbalance isn't physical doesn't mean it doesn't require care. Being angry is an imbalance but it isn't physical. Having low self esteem is an imbalance too but it's not physical either."

"Oh, that's really cheering me up. All these non-physical imbalances to contend with, not just physical ones?"

"Yep!" I smirked, patting him on the back. "The reason you have an illness is that you didn't listen to all the non-physical signs of imbalance that developed before your collapse."

"Those being?"

"The stress in your mental body of the pressures from forcing yourself into longer and longer working hours. The pressure in your emotional body when you feel what it's like when you've created what you've been striving for all these years but you can't enjoy it. The confusion and lack of guidance in your spiritual nature because you've done so much *doing* that you've lost sight of any real purpose or fulfilment. Those imbalances, for starters! We've all got some, Andrew, and they're unique to each individual."

"Oh, *those* other signs. Okay... I've seen them on and off but they haven't really registered until now."

We both fell silent. Andrew pushed away his second pint and called for a menu from the bar. "I'm feeling really hungry. Shall we order?"

"Great. Works for me."

"The wheels in my head are going around. You know, what you're saying is beginning to make sense. Admittedly in a very odd sort of way. It's not what I thought."

"Andrew, it never is! It's what you *feel* that counts."

"Well there's a twinge of something somewhere. Maybe I've pulled my back? Just kidding. Seriously, though, I think that perspective, that lens is pulling out; more of a wide angle shot than a close up. Something is happening."

"If you can relate to that feeling in all four parts of

you and realise that this is a heart-centred change, not a mind game, you can easily create a lasting change that'll mean you're in the land of the living and learning for a long, long time to come."

"You really believe that?"

"Absolutely. But that doesn't matter. What matters is what *you* believe... Anyway, I'm going to have the soup and the veggie bake."

"I suppose I shouldn't have the steak pie then," Andrew said, looking at me guiltily.

"Now, don't look at me like that! I'm not the food police, you know, just an innocent bystander chatting with a friend who tells me he wants to make a lasting change in his life. Well, that's the rumour, anyway!"

The waitress came over to take our orders.

"Okay... Can we have two soups and two of the veg bake, please?" asked Andrew.

"Certainly. Any more drinks?" the waitress asked.

"No, I think we're fine thanks," replied Andrew, holding fast to his commitment to change even though the waitress hesitated slightly as if waiting for his *real* answer. "We're fine, thanks," he repeated.

"Okay. One food order coming right up," replied the waitress, moving quickly down the worn steps to the kitchen.

"That was simple, right?"

"No," replied Andrew with a smile. "Actually, it really was surprisingly easy! When she came to take our orders, I couldn't see anything else on the menu. It was a sign!"

"You'd better not be mocking me or I'll sing!" I threatened.

"Would I do that?" Andrew replied sheepishly.

"Yes." And I drew in a deep breath as if preparing for a powerful note.

"Oh no, not that! Please! Anything but that!" Andrew slid about in the booth faking his own death.

"Alright," I replied, letting out my breath. "I'll let you off. Because I care."

"But seriously," he continued, "I'm curious now... When does all this healing start taking affect? And why does it sometimes get worse before it gets better?"

I could see Andrew the journalist pressing for answers.

"I'm not completely ignorant," he said. "I have actually read some of the articles, you know."

"Nothing is set in stone," I said. "There's no knight in shining armour ready to rush and save you from your own impending doom, nor from your healing. Everything is up to you. The more flexible you are, the smoother your change will be. But sometimes, the bigger the imbalance, the bigger the adjustment in the beginning and that's why things appear to get worse before they get better.

"Perhaps it'd be more helpful to see change as changing all of you a little bit rather than fixating on just one area, such as your diet. If you look at changes in those four bodies that make up you, you could see how all these parts of you are working together to support you in gaining a better quality of life. Yes, the choice to heal, to rebalance, could affect your weight but also your self love, your attitudes and your perceptions. Every part of you could benefit, not just your physical body."

"So how do I do that?"

"First, look at what you've got to work with. I choose to believe that whatever you call it, the Cosmos, the great big thing..."

Andrew interrupted. "Now you're getting all technical on me."

"Andrew, I'm serious."

He sat up straight in his booth. "I'm all ears. Please continue."

"Anyway... that unlimited flow out there is Love. And I believe it's always supportive, it's just that from our limited perspective, and through the eyes of ego, it can appear to be the complete opposite."

"You mean we could think that *Out There* isn't helpful, it's conflicting and wants us to fail?"

"Yes. If we've been investing in denial and resistance, it can seem like the Cosmos is giving us a hard time and we're a victim of our circumstances. Then giving up on our health and accepting limits can easily become our normal."

Andrew's face intensified as the meaning of my words began to sink in. "So if I really want to change," he began, "then I've really got to start helping myself instead of thinking that I've got so out of balance that there's no point any more... and that I've got to die of something?"

"With those assumptions, it's not really surprising you collapsed on the floor at work!"

"Do you really believe I have the ability to create that?"

"Absolutely! Because you're part of the Cosmos. Just because you have a physical body and you're 'down here' as it were, doesn't mean to say that you aren't in some way joined with All-That-Is."

"But how?" insisted Andrew. "Your spirituality can be really deep but in simple terms, how can a beginner like me work with this... Love, this... All-That-Is?"

"By realising that you have a choice. Everyone has a choice, it's just that it's easier to think that there isn't anything else other than this physical world that we're wrapped up in. It's by realising that you and I are fundamentally the same. You have an unlimited part and a limited part. The difference between us is our awareness, and how we experience our world. But we're equal when it comes to our spiritual nature."

"But you've got to be more spiritual than me; look at all the time and effort you've put into it; how much you know."

"Look, the amount of time and the amount of knowledge doesn't affect your spiritual path. It's about the conscious choices you make, the practice, the willingness to learn from your life and the way you create. We are equal, it's just that your choices and your experience of life are different currently. Ask yourself honestly, Andrew... Why have you had your episode and I haven't had such an episode? We are the same age, we've both done sport in our lives and we're both married to our work. What's the difference?"

"Choices. I've chosen differently, I guess."

"Exactly. So we aren't better or worse than each other, we've just been looking at our experience from differing perspectives, with differing awareness. I'm not saying you have to look at life the way I do. What I'm saying is perhaps if you're not deliriously happy with the way your life is to date then maybe it's time to choose differently. There's an unlimited number of ways to change and there's plenty of help to make those changes. You aren't alone."

"That sounds a bit scary. Does that mean green spacelings or men in white coats are going to take me away and make it all better?"

"No, Andrew, it doesn't. Nor does it mean you're going to let go of your flippancy!"

"Okay, this personal empowerment is serious stuff."

"Serious in the sense of giving-you-a-better-life serious... yes, definitely. Serious as in I-am-going-to-turn-into-your-mother-nagging-you-every-time-I-see-you-ill... No, certainly not. If you want to create another health crisis, go right ahead. I can't stop you."

"Understood. Please carry on."

"Well then, when you choose from Love, you don't get fixed, you learn to cooperate with the greater Universe, your intuition and the reflections in your world. Slowly but surely you live a different way that creates more joy and, in your case, good health. You learn what it takes to take care of Andrew."

"So what would you advise? If there's one thing I should start doing to expand my awareness, what would it be?"

"Use the phrase *I AM*. It helps you develop your

awareness because it calls upon the connection to the unlimited Cosmos; helps you communicate your creations more clearly and helps you realise that you are co-creating with your outer world, not competing with it or struggling to survive. Let's take your example... If you believe you want to change and you want the unlimited flow of love to help you then you can confirm your commitment by saying *I AM creating new ways to rebalance my health*, *I AM believing I can change* or *I AM being honest about what brings me joy*. But you don't use the I AM if you don't believe in what you're saying."

"So basically, be careful what you ask for. And don't ask for anything you aren't prepared to receive."

"In simple terms, yes. It's not to be afraid of your unlimited ability but to realise that the Universe doesn't judge you. So if you ask for something in one of your cynical moods then you could easily create it. Be loving, be honest and be clear about what you want and don't be too attached to the form."

"What do you mean? I thought this way of creating worked," Andrew said, confused as though he'd missed a step.

"The Cosmos has a lot more ways of creating than we can hold in our limited minds so sometimes we're a bit simplistic or limited about what we imagine our creation is going to look like. So don't have rigid expectations, otherwise you could really slow down what you want to receive."

"How?"

"By being too controlling. By controlling the unlimited flow through your expectations."

"I shouldn't get my hopes up too high, then?"

"I'm saying not to become too rigid about the journey you go on to learn about creating what you want. If you have fixed ideas, you could easily frustrate your process. Many people miss what they ask for because they have complicated assumptions or expectations that just deflect what they want rather than magnetise it to them."

"So go with the flow and believe it's working with you

to bring you what's helpful. You'd say self loving is right and supportive?"

"Basically, yes. If you don't see yourself as co-creating with the Cosmos then you'll never see what a great creator you really are. Ego isolates us, telling us it's never going to work and so settle for what we've got. Or even, as you said, you've got to die of something. But that's just ego talking, and maybe the real Andrew doesn't actually agree with ego. But if you don't work out what your intentions are and start exploring those intentions with the support of the Universe, how are you ever going to know?"

"Okay, I hear you loud and clear. The in phrase is *I AM*, right?"

"Yep. It's more about cooperating with the Cosmos rather than a spiritual fad. But I know what you mean. When you use I AM, you go straight to your guidance and to the unlimited energies that are available to you in that moment. The more you use the phrase, the more you learn what you can create and how the All-That-Is co-creates with you."

"Okay," said Andrew, now charged up and ready to go. "I've made the choice to change. That's one C. Commitment is creating the I AM statements that describe what I want, what I want to change at present, etcetera. The Courage is to deal with the reshuffle that happens when I start moving back into balance after I've been in the habit of imbalance for so long. And I assume that's where the Confidence comes in?"

"Confidence is about the capacity to allow trust. *Con*, meaning 'with' and *faïence*, meaning 'faith' or 'trust'—with faith, or with trust."

"And why do I need trust?"

"Because you're walking away from what you know and that makes your ego, the limited and controlling part of you, very nervous. But a few of the moments you spend in change will always be unknown because if they weren't unknown, there wouldn't be any change."

"So confidence helps me keep going when everything feels unfamiliar; when ego could tell me I've made a mistake or that things aren't going to work out."

"Exactly. You're getting the hang of the unlimited already! Looks like you're a natural. A natural healer!"

"Now watch it there! I can spot a charmer and ruse a mile off! And if what you said is the cosmic truth and the unified truth, then we're all naturals!"

"True, but few make their natural ability a normal part of their life."

"Because they don't have the awareness of what's possible?"

"Precisely. But it's always available."

"Just hanging around?"

"The opportunity to learn is always just hanging around. And it looks like you've taken the Universe up on its offer of a new perspective. So without further ado, I give you... yourself! Arise, Sir Andrew, knight of the returning realm of balance."

Embracing Nourishment

All our food arrived at once. The waitress was very apologetic.

"I'm so sorry. We're frantically busy so I was hoping you wouldn't mind if I brought all your food together. The plates are really hot so it should stay warm while you finish your soup."

Andrew, always happy to complain at the first sign of poor service, smiled to himself but remained calm. "Just put it all here and now, we're starving," he replied, welcoming the food enthusiastically.

He slurped his soup and ate vegetables as if he was a career vegetarian. We laughed at how we'd struggled through our recent changes as if they were caricatures from a book entitled *Surviving in Existence, and Other Cartoons*. But now, what had seemed so intense, even shocking, was starting to look like a way forward. This book of experiences wasn't full of episodes of ego resistance, it was full of all the ways we'd chosen to process change; chosen to change our minds and exchange ignorance for the willingness to learn. As we talked, we realised we could even laugh about how we'd struggled with the obvious and avoided the helpful!

"I don't remember it like that!" I laughed.

"That's your choice, and probably just as well," replied Andrew through a mouthful of cauliflower, laughing at how we'd arrived at this point in our lives. "So, going with the momentum of change, tell me, how's your other book going?"

"Unfolding and unravelling."

"All at the same time? That doesn't sound very stable. Don't you have an outline or a plan?"

"Not with this book. It's been quite confusing but I'm getting the hang of it now. I learn something new and then, practically in the next writing moment, it's happening in the book. It's all about flow not logic."

"So you're writing a travel book but you haven't gone anywhere?"

"Well... yes and no."

"But aren't you short of material?"

"No. I'm not short of material, it's just that the material is coming from a different source, that's all. So, as it turns out, I'm too busy to travel in the conventional sense but the book is getting written."

"So, if we stretch the truth a bit..." probed Andrew with a smirk. "You get out and about in other ways, right?"

"Okay, you investigative journalist, yes. I've gone off on a few interdimensional jollies; a few conferences with my cosmic colleagues! And those trips are amazing. And it's coming together perfectly, even though most of it has been a complete mystery until it landed on the page."

I could sense that Andrew had an issue with something I'd just said. He leaned back, putting his hand behind his head.

"Hey, you're a great writer, I'd agree with that any day, but how can you say it's perfect? Even the most confident of people would hesitate to use the word, *perfect*."

"Why?"

"Because it's... well, perfect; the best; without flaw. You know what perfect means. Stop pulling my leg."

"Andrew, I know what perfect is commonly assumed to mean but that's not what I'm talking about."

"Oh, don't play semantics. Perfect is... well... perfect! Isn't it?" Andrew was baffled. "But... maybe not? By the way you're looking at me, there could be another perspective? Another answer? Perhaps I've been nailing myself to another of those judgments that will restrict me by the time you get to your reply. So what do you mean by perfect, then?"

"I believe perfection is a state of being, not a judgment or a standard. Perfection isn't the illusive target that most don't reach, it's a state that keeps on being, keeps on flowing. It's a challenge to define because that's just it... like fulfilment or joy, these are all states that are dependent on awareness."

"So you're saying fulfilment, perfection, joy... they're all dependent on your perspective rather than a fixed definition?"

"Yes. You clearly have ideas about what perfection is—maybe it's a target or a standard that perhaps you don't think that, by rights, anyone should ever admit to, even if they do reach it. But what if we take ego out of the equation and the perception? What if we say it's not all about us, it's about us being flexible enough to see how we fit in with the cosmic flow, the greater Universe, All-That-Is?"

Andrew's mind was clearly buzzing with imminent criticism but he just couldn't seem to get the words out.

"Andrew, you of all people... stuck for words?"

"Ha ha. It's the weirdest of sensations. I can't put it into words because there don't appear to be enough, or the right ones. But I sense there's another way of looking at this, even if it's cooking my brain! Are we being outside the cube? Could I

Embracing Nourishment

be floating in the greater Universe and looking into our little world of limited experience?"

"Why not? Isn't that what thinking outside the cube is all about?"

"I suppose so. But I've never really done it like this before. The only thinking outside the cube I've done is daydreaming. I was a specialist at that, tuning out of boring lessons at school. But this is completely different. It's like two ways of experiencing are unfolding together but they're diverging. It's like speaking in pictures. One perspective is saying that to use the word 'perfect' is bigheaded or arrogant, not to mention impossible..."

"And," I interrupted, "I'm the first to say that could be so. It all depends on your personal truth and what you feel."

"Yet this other way, the way that's all pictures, is prompting me to believe there's something different."

He paused. "But that means there isn't a right answer. The equation doesn't work. A plus B doesn't equal C. But it's not because I know it, it's because I sense it. Is this awareness-expanding?"

"Sounds like it. But how do you feel, though? It's your experience."

"Different," he smiled, gliding from side to side as though floating in some kind of 1960's flower power time warp. "It feels strange... as if I've suspended the normal parameters of life just for a split second so that my awareness can expand... and my mind can't react quickly enough to stop it. It feels very liberating. Who'd have thought I'd get my first really spiritual experience in the George and Dragon?" Andrew seemed genuinely overcome.

"Why not?" I challenged.

"Why not, indeed. We are in the company of myth and legend and there is, after all, no wrong place to start living your life. So if I explore, letting this feeling run, what would you say is the real nature of perfection? The expanded version, as it were? What does it feel like to you?"

"If each moment we're in is part of the state of perfection then, whether ego likes it or not, the only aspect that alters is the way we experience that moment. Perfection just *is*. We have the capacity for it and it is ever present, but most of us are too wrapped up in ego to experience it. Just because we want to experience a limited version doesn't mean the true nature of perfection is diminished in any way. It just keeps on flowing."

"Okay, so the Universe always gives us what we require but we don't often recognise it," Andrew observed, appearing to be coming back to Earth.

"Exactly. Ego tells us that it isn't good enough, it didn't come on time, it's too early, it's too much or it's too little, or too late. The list of rejections, projections and disallowance is as long as our mind can make it to keep us limited. And, for the most part, we listen until we've shoved the experience, even the possibility of perfection, right out of our lives."

"Exit, stage left," said Andrew, and pointed to the door.

"Yes. Or even out of sight completely. Then ego says this is the proof that we have to believe in our limited state because there isn't anything else. Have you ever noticed that, for most people, being perfect is only something you can achieve after you're dead and someone else recognises it? If you acknowledge it while you're alive then it becomes some kind of exaggeration, not a normal part of life. So as we said, you've then either got a head bigger than Mount Olympus or you're deluded because perfection doesn't exist. Yet it's actually there all the time, ready to be discovered and embraced.

"I understand that being told you have high blood pressure and cholesterol wasn't what you wanted to hear but... it's perfect. Why?"

I paused, realising Andrew was about to go into full flow.

He took up my question. "Because it's the perfect reflection of where I'm at in my life right now. I'm perfectly

Embracing Nourishment

imbalanced and so that's what had me falling from the edge of life, albeit briefly. And if I hadn't collapsed last week, we certainly wouldn't be having this conversation. Although my ego would love to disagree, it is a perfection I'm willing to acknowledge. The Universe is doing me a huge favour."

Andrew paused, as if his surge of awareness had been fulfilled. "And on top of that, I'm going to change my view of vegetables. That meal was great! Who says you haven't had a proper meal if you haven't had a steak? Plus, I don't feel like falling asleep."

"So you're not bored to death yet, then?' I probed.

He paused again, feigning deep consideration. "No, not yet. I'm finding out there's simply too much to be discovered and, at the ripe old age of nearly thirty-five, it's about time I went on some journeys of my own so that I can reshuffle into balance in a less shocking way. Discussions like these start me seeking the life I'm missing out on, the life I actually don't have. Not a great place to be but, hey, what do they say? Most people actually don't know what they want but they can tell you what they don't want because they've usually lived it. So it ain't pretty but I'm working backwards through what I don't want so I can arrive at what I do want."

"*You're working your way back to you babe, with a burning love insi-i-ide,*" I quietly sang.

"I thought you weren't going to sing! I've just found a reason to live and now you go and do that!" Andrew joked.

"It's up to you how you experience this journey but always remember: while you're recycling your denial and lack of self love, you're creating what you want... all at the same time."

"You know what?" he interrupted. "I think I'm doing just that. Perhaps I've finally seen the light at the end of our conversation."

We both smiled and paused as our new beginning found its end.

"Shall we get the bill?" Andrew suggested.

"Yep. I've got incoming," I said, pointing to the top of my head.

"What do you mean?"

"Another chapter's bubbling. Better get home and commit it to screen."

"Okay, I understand. It's perfect. And it's our *The End*... for now, anyway," smiled Andrew.

"Yes, the end to a perfect new chapter. I'll just go and write what comes before that."

"Hey! You're scrambling time again! But why not? It's a very over-rated concept, time, eh?"

"For sure," I replied. I put on my coat and gave Andrew a hug.

"I'll see me soon on the page, then?" he replied cheekily. "And don't worry, I intend to feed you lines for a long, long time to come."

"I'm very glad to hear it," I smiled, narrowly missing the low doorway as I honoured a new creative beginning.

Balancing With Now

Along my return journey, I scribbled into my latest notebook and arrived at Charing Cross just before the afternoon rush hour. As I returned home, I was met by a vision of Merlin standing at the door to my heart room. "I know this might appear a little rushed," he said, "but your Higher Self has suggested that you make a renegotiation."

"I understand that our path's about trust but how can I agree to something I have absolutely no idea about?" I replied, taking off my coat and glancing around the kitchen.

"Through pure heart feeling,"

"Okay, let me find my connection." I sensed a small tremble in my heart. "And what happens if I don't do this?"

"This is a heart choice," prompted Merlin as I edged closer

to analysis. "There is no judgment in the higher realms, you know that. Your choices are your own. We are simply here as a guide."

I felt an enormous surge of upliftment without the slightest hint of worry or limitation, as if I were out of my body. I sat down in the armchair and took a moment to rebalance.

"Okay... feels wonderful. I AM embracing my renegotiation, whatever that is. After all, it's perfect. I feel balanced and in the middle of Now."

"And so it is," said Merlin, radiating joy and purpose.

We stepped forward in unison and pushed open the heart room doors together. I had no idea of the place that awaited me. I felt empty of definition; neither impressed nor disappointed. My heart and mind were completely silent. I closed my eyes as if the renegotiation was a birthday present. As I opened them I was greeted by absolutely nothing. All was pitch black; complete darkness. I couldn't make out one form or distance, and there was no sense of gravity or momentum; no sense of being attracted or repulsed by anything. I was adrift in nothing...

There was a small tremor through my whole being. Then another. I knew immediately that the tremors were coming from ego's office in my mind. It was begging for attention; demanding and needy as divisions and limitations were being discarded one by one. Nothing could be measured in nothingness. Nothing could be defined or controlled. There was no comparison or description, there was no form. Ego was shaken to its core as it tried to force the nothingness into form.

I reached for feeling, remaining in my heart and allowing the process. Ego tried a new direction, sending out projections of shadows in the remotest parts of my memories; gathering all the attachments, limitations and fearful conditioning it could find and endlessly presenting it at the centre of my mind, hoping I'd become desperate for the habits I once relied upon. But there was nothing to do but surrender to the unknown; the lack of definition, certainty and safety.

Glimpsing a stream of my recent transmutations like a

flashback, or forward, I didn't react, I just continued adrift in nothing. Detachment, spontaneity, synchronicity, assimilation, perfection, authentication—they were all there, everything was allowed, anything was possible.

Ego had gone quiet, somewhere past assimilation. In this complete stillness there was no desire to find out what it was or wasn't doing. Floating had become normal. There was no force, repulsion or attraction, just flow.

"Now you can return from whence you came," whispered a voice, energised with pure balance.

"But I don't know the way," answered a panicked voice in my head. "I simply don't know the way."

I was shocked at the reply. That wasn't me, was it?

"You are a unified individual," came a voice from within me and within the darkness.

"I am," I replied, startled by the response. "I AM. Inner Authority Mentor is the way. My nature is Light, my nature is Love."

"You are both freedom and unity. They are not separate for there is no separation."

"I AM embracing unity. I AM," I confirmed, repeating my commitment.

The silence was deep and endless as it leaked into my sense of self. Or was I leaking into space? There was no direction, there was simply everywhere. There were no limits, no known quantities.

I began to hear a song. *"You're everywhere and nowhere baby... that's where you're at... going down a bumpy hillside... in a hippy hat..."* The song floated away but then returned. *"And so it's hi ho silver lining... and away you go, now baby... I see your sun is shining... but I won't make a fuss, though it's obvious."*

What on Earth...? I began to laugh and laugh and laugh. Now I understood how I'm going to get back—look for the silver lining, eh? Believe the Light is always there. Be your own Light, even if there doesn't appear to be a spec in the whole void. Be the Light, see the Light. Be the Light, see the Light. I was now chanting my way through nothingness.

As the intention passed through me, the dark began to ignite with a collection of stars as if someone had switched on a billion fairy lights. They converged into a symphony of implosion and expansion. I tried to shade my eyes. As the intensity grew, it became more and more uncomfortable until a door of white opened in on itself and a familiar cloud of purple mist rolled around its base.

"Ready?" asked Merlin.

"Yes. It's getting really bright in here. I'm just not built for this degree of intensity."

"And yet you have adjusted much. And we see that you are working on it. New architecture. Not as physical as you used to be, eh? Conducting yourself differently."

"As you always say... everything is relative, just depends on how current I am. Don't want to blow a fuse now do I?"

"Indeed. These are the days of the endless extraordinary; the space in time that allows you to peek into the other worlds you occupy and see how your awareness stretches to embrace both your limitation and your infinity."

"I think you've just flown past me, Merlin. But I can sense how this energy is rejuvenating me from the inside out. And if I find myself back in that place where I think I'm scraping the bottom of the barrel of infinity, I'll start singing my way out!"

"That's the spirit that you are. Neither here nor there, but all. You are choosing to expand your awareness, out like a giant bubble, from the highest of Light to the darkest of density."

Merlin's description struck a cord within me. "But how can I span such a polarity?"

"You didn't so much stretch across polarity as unify within it. You recognised the illusion of ego and you trusted your true nature that is Light. There was no need to know, no need to conflict, control or fear loss. You recognised your core nature when your environment could have dictated otherwise."

"I could've thought I'd run out of Light or even been abandoned?"

"Indeed. Ego could have convinced the Light Being you truly are that you were only the dim limitation of ego. You could have allowed your lack of Light to be you, rather than being the abundance of Light you really are."

"So... my renegotiation is completed?"

"Indeed. Renegotiation achieved. You are arrived at the new you."

"And after the complete darkness? That was the Light?"

"It was. And also the Light that resulted from the transmutation of some dense dimness!"

"So transmutation can only occur in Light?"

"Yes. This is why the reconstruction of your I AM Presence is so important in your ascension. The more transmutation you achieve, the more your I AM can stabilise and support you. The more your I AM is stabilised as the balanced unlimited centre of your world, the more you can re-engineer your experience so that you return to your natural unlimited state. The voyage of discovery and density you've just undergone gave you the chance to make a core upgrade."

"That being?"

"You consciously chose Love instead of fear. You made your first pure heart choice. Great cause for celebration, I might add, even though it appears so..."

"Like nothing!" I interrupted, as my heart filled with encouraging words.

"We were going to say that it appears so unified, without contrast. You could call it early days yet but you are in allowance of the concept."

"One question, though, Merlin. If you're guiding me along with the other guides, didn't you know I would achieve this? Didn't you know I was capable of it?"

"Oh indeed, we were aware of your capability but, contrary to the influences of your limited mind, nothing in any universe is guaranteed. All is a flow and that is perfect. Perfection would not be possible if the flow were fixed. You are listening to the echoes of destiny, not the true nature of your ascension."

"So I could've failed?"

"Put it this way, you could have chosen a different path, a different way of making the shift. You know, all choices and moments are sacred. You choose to learn from them as you perceive them. There is, in truth, no failure, just choices to learn. If you had chosen differently then you would not have been judged, but also this discussion would not have been relevant nor would it be taking place.

"Each lifetime, as you would think of it, has different possibilities. There is no destiny in the sense of events being preset but there are aspects of yourself that you wish to explore. In some lifetimes you evolve more than you anticipated, in others, less. But you are not rigidly set into a timetable of realisation."

"But I chose to stay with my ascension? To keep raising my vibration and merging Light with density?"

"Indeed you did. You chose to stay in embodiment because you believe its limited nature can be transmuted. You chose to believe you can flood the density that has been enmeshed within your true Light nature with detachment and love. Guidance supports you in this becoming so that you can continue to transmute your dense aspects. But also be aware of their fragility. There will come a point when you are Light and you have completed your re-engineering into Light. That is when you ascend. When you return to unified loving consciousness then you can choose your form and your expression.

"Great! When does that happen?"

I realised the futility of my question. "I'll answer that myself... Not in my near future because I'm the one still attached to outcomes and time. Correct?"

"Something like that. But it's all perfect and all a part of the unity that you are."

Baby Steps

For the next couple of days I struggled with my new expansion and wrote next to nothing. I felt disconnected from my world; expanded but unplugged. The weather seemed to taunt me with moody overcast skies and sudden downpours.

"Why can't you share some of that flow with me?" I muttered as I traced the path of bulging raindrops down my bedroom window.

No sooner had I asked than the sun came out and with it Isis, pawing at the window. "Am I glad to see you," I exclaimed, stroking her com-pletely dry coat.

Isis looked at me blankly as if to say "I'm nothing but extraordinary; each moment a new Goddess".

She kneaded my duvet into a satisfactory bed, tucked in her feet and tuned out.

"Oh that's just great! You arrive and then take your awareness somewhere else."

Isis remained motionless, purring.

"That's your ego talking," said my Higher Self. "Obviously feeling a little abandoned; left in the lurch with an ever expanding Light. Density just isn't what it used to be, eh?"

"Okay, I admit it! I don't seem to be adjusting very well to my core upgrade. It feels like I've pulled the plug, not increased the current. Perhaps you've seen directionless and adrift before?"

"Yes, but this is more expansion with ego adrift. It's all in the perception."

"Easy for you to see! You've got 360 degree surround-vision, and more!"

"Your true nature is not lost. On the contrary, you are gaining more and more awareness and learning to balance at higher and higher levels of consciousness."

"What's missing, then?"

"Your ego, actually. It used to be much closer to the

centre of your world. That was when you had things under control and you could simply get back in your mind and reign in your life. But now, all is different… emphasis on the *all*.

"With expanded awareness, you are beginning to see how far you are unravelling ego control and expanding beyond limitation. You are also seeing that you are Light in nature but you still have density to consider. The Light nature is beginning to shine through but ego will still try and pull the wool over your eyes from time to time, telling you that its limited perception is more important, rather than being insignificant."

"Ego hates being insignificant, doesn't it?" I mused.

"Ego dislikes anything that it cannot control, insignificance included! But forget about ego because that's all about ego! Really, this is all about unity. You are feeling what it is to expand and to cope with allowing yourself to flow as a unity."

"Keeping myself together?"

"It's more a question of keeping balance flowing and being aware when certain changes in your overall self—higher self and lower self—require patience and processing space."

"So I'm not adrift, then, I'm just processing?"

"Exactly. You are processing; expanding beyond where you thought you were."

"And, of course, I wasn't really there, right?"

"Here, there and everywhere is all relative. When your awareness expands, so does your understanding of your self, your experience and your guidance. Just because you have an I AM Centre doesn't mean you automatically choose to create from I AM. And sometimes, the denser parts of ego want to trick you into believing that they are running your experience and controlling you."

"But I don't seem to be able to lift my disillusionment. Ego is telling me it's not worth it. If this is the core rebuild, the big expansion, then where's the roll on the drums? Where's the dramatic change, the flow of ease? Is this it?"

"Yes, this is it. And that is it and all is it! All you are

hearing is ego realising that there isn't anything in it for ego. There is no limitation in expansion and there isn't any drama. There isn't any loss or conflict and there's no destination. Expansion is... expansion.

"Ego, not your heart, is let down. You're finding out that the greater Cosmos isn't built on results or comfort zones. If you want to find inspiration then you are required to recycle some of your lack of inspiration willingly. There is no point in blaming the outside world or joining ego and doing yourself down. Your outside world is your inside world. The separation is becoming thinner and thinner and that is one of the reasons your ego is so depressed. Existence just hasn't lived up to its expectations! Ego thought it could control you but you made other plans, and what's worse for ego is that you acted on them. You arrived, you learnt, you detached. Your ego, though, would have much preferred that you left, you hid and you succumbed to what it says is the obvious and real."

Once again, guidance was shining a light into my dim perception.

"You're right at that spot, as usual," I observed, "that little piece of risen perspective that can be so hard to see sometimes. It's very easy to slip into criticism and feel that ascension is hard, especially after those moments spent in pure expansion. After those, everything appears to be such a let down! That feeling of euphoria that happens when I'm connected with what seems completely unlimited, I feel like I can achieve anything. Then I land back here and it's back to tunnelling through density, recycling fear and resistance. It just seems relentless."

"It seems relentless because, you guessed it, it *is* relentless! But you can change how you feel by weakening the gloom of the past few days."

"How do I do that?"

"Remember your magic carpet. Remember that your life is a flow of experiences and allow them to unfold. See

Baby Steps

yourself as going on a journey of exploration, not carrying heavy burdens of resistance from one destination to another. You aren't experiencing in order to get the conditioned results of the mind, you are experiencing unconditionally so that you can appreciate the rewards of the heart. They are the wisdoms that will serve you for eternity."

"I'm listening. Ego still has one foot on my magic carpet but keep talking and I'll find my balance again and then we can take off."

"These are only temporary attachments but to make sure ego doesn't turn them into something a little more stubborn, what about an outing?"

"You mean, get away from it all?"

"Not really because your transmutation is always with you. When you run away, it will still be right there waiting for you when you get back. What we mean is, don't stick at what isn't flowing. See the flow as it really is, multi-fold. If this stream has turned into a trickle, find another one; join another part of the unending flow while the resistance dissolves. If you are truly embracing your unlimited nature then there is no time to lose. There is no time. So why not step back, invest in a different angle, a different approach?"

"But that's my problem—I'm not particularly inspired to find a flow. That's why I can't."

The phone began to ring. "I'll just get that, Higher Self," I said out loud with the hint of a smile.

"Hello?"

"Hi, it's Andrew. Have I caught you at a bad time?"

"No, just a grumpy one. I haven't been able to write since I saw you last."

"Maybe I'm your lucky charm."

"We all create our own luck, Andrew, charming as you are."

"Charming enough for you to help me this minute?"

"That depends."

"Oh, come on. I've never heard you like this."

"I've never felt like this."

"Come on, get your other lovely self to make a come back; a permanent one!"

I felt my ego stiffen and I knew that ending the conversation would lengthen my time in disallowance.

"Okay... I've got rid of the grumpy me and this is the new improved version speaking. So how can I help you?"

"Good. I rang to say that I have a short list of therapies and I wanted your advice as to which one to choose."

I was speechless, my ego short circuited. My mood changed instantaneously. "That's wonderful! You've brightened my day!"

"What? Didn't you think I'd do it?"

"I didn't say that. I just think it's wonderful you're keeping up the momentum. So read them to me. What've you got?"

"Well... I've got a Doctor Fong. He's a Chinese herbalist. Then there's Teresa Johnston. She's a dietician. Then there's Janet Gilbert. She's a naturopath. And lastly, there's Steven Henry, a homeopath. What do you think?"

"Great! Have you tried any of these approaches before?"

"Nope."

"Okay. Simplicity works. What do you want to change regarding your health?"

"My weight, my appalling diet and my inability to do anything to improve the fun factor in my life."

"Right. Hold your first finger over the page of names, close your eyes and run your finger down the page. Stop when you feel like you want to stop."

"You're joking, right?"

"No."

There was silence on the other end of the phone. He let out a long breath.

"Okay, here goes," he finally replied. "Just know I'm only doing this because you suggested it."

"Well don't do it then. Only do it because you believe in it."

"Okay, that too."

He began his scan down the list. "Whooow! That's really extraordinary. Heat came up my arm when I crossed Doctor Fong's details and then again when I passed the last name. Who was it again? Steven somebody. Here it is... Steven Henry."

"So there you are... a homeopath and a Chinese herbalist."

"But shouldn't I stick with just one? Do that for a while and then try the other one?"

"You can. It's up to you. But the Yod picked out two."

"What's the Yod?"

"The finger of God. It's an astrological term."

"So you mean it's a sign I should see both of them?"

"The finger belongs to you, Andrew. There's an expanding part of you connected to the unlimited. I'm joking with you, but I'm also asking you to trust the unlimited in you—that spark that's communicating with you. You felt it. You know what I mean. You could've connected with only one of those therapists, but you didn't."

"Okay. So just go with the flow? Ring up both?"

"Yes. If you want to."

"Okay, I'll ring them up then I'll ring you straight back."

I was puzzled. "Okay. Speak soon then."

I put the phone down, unsure as to why Andrew was going to call me back, especially after he'd just made his choice.

"Ours is not to reason why," I muttered.

"And ours is not to assume either," added my Higher Self.

"What's that supposed to mean?"

"Be in allowance of this new flow. The Light is breaking through that stubborn density as we speak. Just be patient. It isn't completed yet."

The phone rang again.

"Hello?"

"It's me again."

"Yeah... I was getting a strong physic feeling... A man... about thirty-five... in need of care... bit squidgy at the edges... Just kidding! How was your telephonic expedition?"

"Well, one of them can see me this afternoon at four because he's had a cancellation and the other one can't see me until next Thursday. How can these people be so busy?"

"Because, Andrew, there are lots of people out there like you looking for alternatives!"

"Well, anyway... Wanted to ask you another favour."

"What's that?"

"It turns out that Doctor Fong is an acupuncturist. I didn't read all of the details. He does the acupuncture treatment then he recommends herbs to help you get better."

"Great! You get two ways combined in the one."

"But I've never been for a session like this... so I was wondering if..." There was a long silence.

"If what? I don't know what you're getting at?"

"I was wondering if you'd come along with me."

"Come on, Andrew, it's really quite straightforward. You're a grown man. It's a piece of cake. You won't feel a thing. You've had scarier headlines, trust me!"

"I do and that's why I'm asking you. I might be a grown man but I'm a scared grown man believing in something I've never done before. But if this can help me heal, I'm willing to give it a try. I just need you to help me out. Just this one time."

"Okay. I'm sorry, I didn't realise it was like that. I'll be happy to come. Where's the appointment?"

"It's about twenty minutes away from you. I'll text you the address. Thanks for helping me. I know it's only baby steps but those are better than stalling completely, right?"

"You never said a truer word, Andrew. Seems like baby steps are the order of the day."

Wayshower

I surrendered to Andrew's sincere call for help and closed the lid of my computer.

"Everything is in the flow. You are helping one another," came the familiar commentary of Merlin. "Just because you help in one direction doesn't mean it is only in that direction. What goes around…"

"…Comes around," I said, completing his sentence. "I'm learning to give without expectation; from that place in the heart, right? I trust what you're saying, and it rings true in my heart, but how can Andrew be helping me if he's the one who's asked for help? I'm confused."

"Your mind is confused, not your heart," began Merlin. "You heard your heart reflection in your world. You heard Light. You heard the flow calling, it just wasn't in the direction you expected. The soul you know as Andrew is using his Light nature, not reaching for his conditioning. He is allowing flow. There is a flow of Light between you and a flow of service, and your ascension is all about honouring the Light that is your true nature, within and without."

"So Andrew's call for help reflects the Light within me?"

"It is reflecting your willingness to support Light nature within you."

"And there's no separation so it's all the same Light?"

"Indeed. You are, we are, beginning—a joint effort as always—to guide within the limited world. You are Light bearer, wayshower. You are supporting another in a collective truth which is the truth of the heart. The soul you know as Andrew is supporting his true nature and you are there to show him the way to honour that process as he takes those first few conscious steps. Once he begins his path, it will become… first nature."

"So we're sharing the Light that we have in common, Andrew and I?"

"Indeed. And you are deliberately radiating your Light because you are consciously choosing to honour that Light by serving Andrew. Ego tells you service is a process that happens when you can't cope—someone just takes over and tells you what to do. But this is not service, this is control. Service is a tool like detachment or discernment. When you choose to serve, it comes from the heart. You are honouring that person's path of discovery without expectations. You are equals.

"Many see service in a polarised master-servant, controller-controlled kind of way. But in truth, service is the ability to support Light and in so doing support the Light unity that is your true nature. Think of service as cooperating with the greater Cosmos to create empowerment. And you are worthy of the task."

"What do you mean by *worthy*? I know the dictionary says it means to be good enough, but if we suspend the limited definition, what's the bigger picture, the Light understanding?"

"That depends on your perspective, but how about this: **W**-orking **O**-penly, **R**-esponsibly **T**-o **H**-elp **Y**-ou. The expanded you, that is. Sometimes that means you receive and sometimes it means you serve. But both receiving and supporting are part of the flow of love and they are equal."

"So because I'm becoming more aware, I can serve my higher aspects and my world simultaneously?"

"Indeed. A little bit of spiritual multi-tasking."

"But won't that ultimately drain me if I end up helping lots of other people like I'm helping Andrew?"

"Why would that be the case?"

"I suppose that's my conditioned assumptions talking, not my heart. Service is often portrayed as, to be frank, a worthy cause that leaves those serving with very little, even to the point that they become martyrs of their service. They can't do anything for themselves, just keep on doing for others... as if looking after others becomes their service opium; the exquisite downer that just keeps on draining them but they can't give it up. As a result, they just get more and more run down, run over by the selfish demands of an ungrateful world. People say that's good but I just can't see it. Where's the joy in that?"

"As always, your perceptions are for your learning. Each individual has their perception and their learning. So it is to ask your heart whether or not you believe in that experience of service."

"In my heart, no."

"So is it part of your heart truth? Is that a balanced observation of service?"

"No."

"So do you think your ego is influencing it?"

"Probably. So it's limited, and it's exaggerated by ego so that I'll be put off experiencing the joyous part of helping people. So ego is trying, yet again, to limit me."

"You seem surprised. Why? Would you have thought anything else of ego?"

"When you put it like that then, no. Ego thrives on limitation."

"As usual, ego reaches for conflict, not balance. Ego tries to complicate and dramatise rather than clarify and feel what is happening. But it is up to you to recognise this falsehood. When you hear strongly imbalanced views, when you realise you see only half the picture, then you know this is not your true nature, it is just the shadow of your former self."

"You mean, ego?"

"Indeed. Whether your experience is extremely *good* or extremely *bad*, you can see that it is not balanced. If it is not balanced then ego is affecting your perspective. Therefore, in this case, ego supports service that is imbalanced and distorted. Ego tells you that if you help someone then they will drain your energy; that there will be nothing left over for you. But this is a scarcity manipulated by ego. Can you run out of energy given that your true nature is unlimited and unending?"

"No. Only ego runs short of energy because it has isolated itself away from the greater Cosmos."

"Indeed. Therefore, what are you really running short of if you serve others constantly, day in, day out?"

"Balance?"

"Well realised! It is the intention behind your service that is important. And if you are purposeful and in balance with your world then service is wonderful, joyous and unending like any other experience in your world. If any experience in your world ceases to be joyous then it is to detach and reassess your balance point. You understand that pain and struggle are not natural but you are still learning to create and experience without conflict or resistance."

"So if I were to draw up some service guidelines, they'd be... One—Consult my heart and look into the intention behind my service. Two—Serve myself and others equally. Three—Don't try and force service on someone because then I'd be judging what they need and just trying to control them. Four—Realise that giving and receiving are equal and all part of the unity of creation. And... Well, that's about it, really." I felt satisfied with my summary.

"You wield the tool of clarity well," encouraged Merlin.

"Going back to my original comment, Merlin... Do people only feel drained because when they undertake service, their heart isn't really in it? Or they start out with a judgmental rather than a balanced intention?"

"There are many different angles of perception and understanding and all bring learning. Ego distorts purposeful and balanced service for its own gain. Ego says you help someone because they are a victim and need someone to take control of their life. Ego tells you service is the need to be needed. Ego looks for victims that it can encourage to remain victims and then it encourages you to help them maintain their victimhood."

"I can see that gives ego *power over* rather than empowering the person and guiding them into taking responsibility for their choices and their changes."

"Precisely. Then there is the ancient ego favourite—It's better to give than to receive."

"But that must be imbalanced from the outset."

"Yes, but for many this ego habit is so ingrained in their world that they can understand or accept nothing else. They are blind to ego and ego helps them nurse their blind spots." I was enjoying dismantling the service attachments of ego.

"Okay," I continued, "on the same theme of *Service misunderstandings ego has used*... What about *Service is an obligation, not a choice*?"

"Oh yes, that old chestnut; suggesting that if you claim to serve then you have to help everyone, irrespective of their situation or the requests they make? In your heart, though, you now understand that service is, just like anything else, a choice. You don't *have* to do anything but you can choose with awareness and now, hopefully, with balance. As you are finding out, the flow of experience isn't an exact account of giving and receiving, nor does it always have a monetary value. But it is always worth something, tangible or intangible."

"Like the service Andrew asked of me... I can't measure support but I know I'm creating it by being with him."

"Yes. You are valuing his steps of change and that is truly priceless."

"So one of the reasons why service can be abused is because many don't register its intangible value? They assess their experience through the material, tangible cost and that's all?"

"Correct. The sum total value of their world is what they can see, what they can control and what they can possess and count," added Merlin.

"But as I see it, in really simple terms, as that dynamic equation between tangible and intangible value tips more towards the tangible, ego, rather than love, becomes more valuable in the limited world."

"Indeed!" enthused Merlin.

He paused knowingly. "The obsession of possession," he remarked.

"What do you mean?"

"Ego can't truly value something unless it has control of it. Control can easily become fixation; the only thing... an obsession. If ego does have control then it will start to fear losing what is under its control. Ego will need more and more energy to keep the control it thinks it needs."

"That must be why ego just consumes and consumes without balance... so it can keep this obsession of possession going."

"Indeed. Ego must have more because that makes it feel secure. It creates more and more attachments so that it can complicate and stop you from learning the principle wisdoms of your physical world. The more obsessed your world becomes with control, the more it will be under ego control. The more your world expands into love and the awareness of change, the less ego can control you because you are less attached to what ego represents."

"So ego always wants more?"

"Ego always wants control. Whether it is control through lack or control through hoarding."

"And it all comes down to fear, control, lack and loss."

Merlin nodded in agreement.

"I suppose if I apply this understanding back to the concept of service, this must be why you can't help anyone if they don't want to change."

"Go on," he encouraged.

"Because that would be control, not service."

"Precisely. Those who choose pain over change are still within ego's obsession of possession. They are turning in on themselves, either looking for someone to fuel them through pity or avoiding the opportunity to change because ego tells them they will lose control."

"So service is a choice both ways; a choice to give and a choice to receive."

"Indeed, a choice to give love and a choice to receive love. Something that is always worthy of a heartellectual."

Merlin stepped back, drawing a huge circle of silver-violet light with his staff. "And so, heartellectual, it is time you walked your talk."

I was still a little hypnotised by the dazzling circle. "What did you say?"

"It's time to fly. Enjoy your homework. Think of it less as a service charge and more as a service choice!"

And with that, Merlin opened up what I'd come to think of as The Purple Corridor and was gone.

Returning from my inner world, I glanced at my phone clock and realised what he'd meant. "Time flies when you're having fun. And now it really is time to fly," I muttered to myself.

Servings Of Wisdom

I met a rather pale Andrew outside the herbal centre, exactly on time. Andrew was never on time for anything. I was beginning to see how important this excursion really was.

"Ready?" I asked, opening the door for him.

"Well, I'm willing. I don't know about ready, though."

"Willing means the rest will just take care of itself. In we go."

We took our seats in the reception area, surrounded by boxes of herbal remedies and softly spoken conversations in Mandarin.

"I hope they speak English," said Andrew, appearing to turn an even lighter shade of pale.

"I'm sure they'll have someone to translate if they don't speak English."

Armchair Alchemist

"But how can they consult if they don't know the language?"

"Andrew, Chinese medicine is about consulting your body, not just your mind. They'll take a look at your skin, your tongue and then feel your pulses for each organ group. Then they'll understand how to approach your rebalancing."

"You mean they don't want my medical history?"

"I'm not saying they wouldn't be interested but, as I'm sure you'll agree, your medical history is written all over your body."

"You are what you eat, you mean?"

"That's part of it. And also it's to remain open when you experience new approaches to anything. Just because it's different doesn't make it bad. So just because this isn't the approach you've been used to, that doesn't make it bad or inferior. You're the one who said you want to give this a go. So do just that. Give it a go! Let the practitioner work with how you feel; reach the core of you, not just touch the surface."

"So I suppose there isn't really a language barrier, then?"

"No there isn't. It's all about listening to your body; understanding how all the bodies we've spoken about harmonise together. Remember, your physical body reflects how you're feeling emotionally, how you've been treating yourself, what your beliefs are... well, I could go on all day. So by feeling, you can take into account the unity between all the different expressions of you—the emotional, mental, physical and spiritual. It's not looking at bits of you in isolation."

Just as I finished the sentence, a petite Chinese lady appeared through the curtain that divided the reception area from the consultation rooms.

"Mr Davies? Is this your first time for treatment?" she asked Andrew.

"Yes," replied Andrew. "Can you tell?"

The assistant smiled. "Please fill in this form and then Doctor Fong will see you."

Andrew was beginning to break out into a sweat as the reality of his choice landed in his mind. He froze temporarily.

I heard *Choice is love; service is a choice* going around and around in my heart room. I applied it as best I could.

"Do you need a pen, Andrew?"

"You're asking a journalist if he's got a pen?"

He fumbled in his inside pocket. "Sorry. Do you know what? I actually don't have one."

"Here, borrow mine," I smiled.

Andrew spidered his way across the page in his left-handed scrawl. It reminded me why he'd become such a good typist.

I sat with him as he continued to process his agitation. He was frightened about where his imbalance had pushed him and yet knew he couldn't stay there. I was silent, visualising a purple unity from my heart room into the herbalist's clinic.

Andrew handed the form back with some added droplets of sweat.

"Ready?" I asked Andrew, standing up as the lady opened the curtain and gestured for him to proceed.

"Would you mind coming in with me?" he asked.

Andrew now looked more nervous than ever.

"Not at all," I replied. "I'll just stay with my friend, if that's okay," I told the lady.

She smiled reassuringly and opened the curtain wider.

Andrew seemed visibly taken aback by Doctor Fong. He could easily be in his late twenties but in reality he was probably closer to forty.

"Do you think he's got enough experience?" Andrew whispered under his breath.

"He's perfect, Andrew. And older than you think. Not that that's got anything to do with it. Just trust the process. Remember, age doesn't equal wisdom, just linearity. It's not how long you live, it's what you do with your moments that matters."

Andrew grimaced, perched in what appeared to a very uncomfortable position.

"Are you preparing to run away at any moment?" I asked in low tones with mock sarcasm.

"Yes. I mean, no!"

"Well make your mind up. If you're staying, why not relax? There's nothing to worry about. Really."

Andrew laughed nervously just as Doctor Fong looked up from reading his form.

"Show me tongue, please," said Doctor Fong. His assistant hovered at his side in case translation was necessary.

Andrew obliged. The doctor scribbled on his notepad and then asked his assistant a question in Mandarin.

She began to translate. "Mr Davies, has your blood pressure problem increased lately? Have you had any serious stress?"

"Actually, I have had some dizziness lately... but only once. I'm not on any medication, if that's what you mean."

The assistant turned to the doctor and translated his answer in what Andrew seemed to think was too few words.

He nudged me, "Do you think she understood everything?"

"Yes, Andrew. And she can understand you right now! You'll be fine. Just surrender. Allow your healing," I replied in reassuring tones.

Andrew went quiet.

"Please put your hands here," said Doctor Fong, pointing to the small cushion on his desk.

Andrew placed his hands palms-up on the cushion. The Doctor felt different parts of his wrist and wrote notes.

"Your body have shock. Your blood pressure high and your liver sluggish. This weaken you. You need to calm down. You okay with acupuncture?"

"Yes," said Andrew, looking round at me with astonishment.

"Please take off your shirt and trousers and lie on bed face down," he said, indicating to the narrow consulting bed alongside the wall. "I come back soon."

Andrew looked at me, folding inwards with embarrassment. "I don't even let my mum look at me in underwear, let alone a herbalist I've never met before!"

"Oh, Andrew! He sees people all the time. It's his job."

Andrew started to undress.

"Not looking," I said, shielding my eyes.

"Okay, okay. But does he have some herbs to cure terminal embarrassment?"

"Probably," I giggled. "Why don't you ask him later?"

Andrew smiled reluctantly at my answer. "But I have to hand it to you, you said he'd know about my condition. I just can't get over it! No tests! Just the touch of my wrist!"

"Remember, this is all constructed from ancient wisdom that carries an eternal truth. Nothing needs to be complicated to make a difference. Simplicity is a lot more valuable than you might think."

Andrew didn't answer, distracted by the what-if's and what-could-be's rushing through his mind at high speed.

"Shall I wait outside?" I offered nudging him gently out of his preoccupation.

He was torn between commanding his situation and falling into victimhood. "You're just outside, right? And you can't do this for me, so... I'll see you when it's over, right?"

"Absolutely. Just relax and see this as getting over the emotional and mental barriers just as much as rebalancing your physical body."

"Okay, I'm going to close my eyes now and open them when it's all over," Andrew said, lying down on the consulting bed.

"Fine. Whatever it takes to be relaxed. I'll be waiting right outside for the new you, okay?"

Unconditional Change

A flushed but refreshed Andrew appeared almost forty-five minutes later and nudged me gently. I was miles away, flying through a landscape of sunflowers and deep blue sky. Andrew cleared his throat, hoping that would hasten my return.

"Oh, I was miles away, having a dream of a day. What about you? You look different. Much better! How was it? How do you feel?" I bombarded him with enthusiastic questions.

"Better than I thought. No... Actually, *much* better than I thought."

"That's great! So you'll have no problems next time."

"What do you mean, next time?"

"You are going to sign up for a course of treatment, aren't you?"

"Am I?"

"Hopefully, yes."

The assistant smiled at me as she opened the appointment book.

"Andrew, you're not going to return to balance if you don't get on the road and stay there. Treatments aren't one-offs that fix you until your next dizzy spell. Everything you're going to do for your health in the coming weeks needs to be contributing to balance consistently. Healing is investing in the path that leads you back into balance. How out of balance do you think you are?"

"Massively! I haven't felt this good in years."

"So don't you want your *normal* to feel more like this?"

"Of course."

"Then you're going to need to work at making your old massively-out-of-balance normal into a wonderful-energised-in-balance normal."

"This treatment certainly seems to have helped me understand the energy I've been missing out on because I've been treating myself so badly."

Unconditional Change

"Great. The treatment has started unblocking you."

"What do you mean?"

"All the abuse has numbed you. You've been blocking yourself up with too much booze, stress, bad diet and more and more extremes. It's easy to get imbalanced but then it can be even easier to keep on going and get progressively more blocked... until you have a major health problem because your body can't cope any more. Sound familiar?"

"That sounds a bit harsh. I can cope, but I just don't *live* any more. I've got no quality of life, even though I've supposedly got everything that should be making me happy."

"The obsession of possession," I muttered to myself.

"What did you say?"

"You're back to your think-style, Andrew. You don't have a lifestyle, remember? That's what created your collapse."

The assistant stepped away from the book, trying to avoid eye contact as our discussion became more intense.

"Okay, okay. I was slipping back into ego habits, trying to justify my imbalance. So where does that leave me now?"

"More aware, Andrew. That's a start. But you've still got to apply that awareness if you're going to make a difference. So is your equation of life going to add up to big, juicy, fat, meaningless imbalance? Or are you going to invest in change and feel the benefits on a regular basis? The choice is yours."

The receptionist tried to look like she was elsewhere, embarrassed at our public display and yet intrigued by our honesty.

"Can I call a friend?" Andrew grinned, attempting a joke to deflect my concerned-but-borderline-zealot intensity.

"You already did, remember? That lifeline was me. And you aren't trying to win a million, you're trying to win your life back. If you want a direct answer then I'll tell you right here and now that I don't want to get any more phone calls about you collapsing at work."

"Okay, okay. I might be a thick skinned fleet streeter but

Armchair Alchemist

I know the truth when I hear it. And it's okay, the truth doesn't hurt any more now, it just makes me feel uncomfortable and weak. Maybe there's some progress in there somewhere?"

The receptionist stepped forward as if an appointment schedule was imminent.

"Look, taking the abuse your ego has been dishing out over the past six or eight years isn't weak, it's just plain daft! But I know what you mean... when you've done something for so long, it feels unsettling. But that doesn't make it wrong, just different. And you feel better, so why not build on that feeling? You don't need to settle for steady physical decline. Do you want people to say *Look, there goes fat balding Andrew*?"

"Oh, please, enough of the charm. What you really mean is I'm too fat for liposuction," replied Andrew with a forlorn frown.

We both started to laugh.

"No, you're too great a soul to give up on yourself now," I encouraged. "You've got a chance at genuine change."

"Really?" he replied.

The receptionist took out her pen, ready to write.

"Yes, really. So are you going to make one giant leap for Andrewkind and sign up for a series of sessions?"

"Do I have a choice?"

"You've always got choice, Andrew."

"But you can't make it for me, right?"

"Right. And I wouldn't. And that's my cue."

"What do you mean?"

"Time to honour the creative process, my friend. The keyboard is calling."

"But you can't go! I haven't finished yet."

"No, you haven't finished yet, but I have," I replied gently, standing ready to leave. "You'll be fine. I've got faith in you. Perhaps at this time, a little more than you've got in yourself, but that'll change. All you need to do is make the choice that's in your heart."

"But how do I know?"

"You don't, you feel your way. And you practice so you can feel even more. And before you know it, you're feeling your life and finding your way back to balance."

Andrew's mouth hung open but he could form no more protests. I hugged him and walked out into the changing light of dusk and the growing acceleration in my heart.

The Space In Time

When I arrived home, it seemed I'd been away for weeks, even months. Everything was as it had been only a few hours before but it all appeared so distant. I made a pot of tea and slide into my armchair, hoping the confusion I felt would dissolve.

"You won't find what you're seeking there. No point reaching that far back, it's almost ancient history!" said my Higher Self.

"I didn't know it *was* the past."

"You're trying to reconnect with the old angle, the old truth... but everything has changed; pulled back. You've got a wider angle now, more detachment, increased vision."

"Seems like blurred vision to me. I don't have a clue what you're talking about."

"Just feel and listen to the sound, the vibration the words are making, then you will understand. You have enabled, embraced and now you are empowering."

"You mean I've allowed and now I'm assimilating so I can authenticate?"

My Higher Self continued without answering me. "The mind always thinks it knows, but feeling is the gateway to progress. If you think you know it then it is highly likely that you are bouncing off what your ego and mind are telling you is happening rather than feeling and flowing with what is really happening."

"Alright, I misunderstood where I was. You showed me that I was going back to familiar mental patterning. Guilty as charged."

"We would call it charged with self observation."

"Okay, so now that I'm listening from my heart rather than trying to put this into a logical progression of the mind, what were you saying about an old angle, an old truth?"

"As you are observing, the conditioning of the mind is strong. And so it will drag you around as it tries to work everything out when in truth it is only fragmenting your progress into little pieces so it loses it's integrity."

"So don't try to work it out. Got that."

"Exactly. Because in this process, the measuring nature of your mind is being challenged. Linear logic tells you that you have to think in terms of a sequence and a set of consequences—you did A so logic assumes that B will follow. You haven't done X so the consequence is you can't have Y.

"But now you see things differently. You aren't limited to the controlled way of logic. You know the order of chaos is just that, a flow. And so although we sketch the cycle of processing to support you, the order is not what supports you. It is the openness and allowance of the cycle of rebalancing. You don't have to work it out logically from one point to another. You don't need to be secure to expand. You don't need known quantities to be fulfilled. Your vision was temporarily blurred because you are relating differently. You have a new learning architecture."

"So, I'm allowing my perception to adjust so that I can get a new angle instead of forcing the old one which hasn't enabled any progress."

"Yes. And you have not looked in this way... in such a comprehensive manner, so it is taking some moments for you to adjust."

"So let the old architecture of learning go. It's achieved what it was meant to. I'm not starting all over again, I'm just creating differently; new framework and new way of relating to the unlimited flow. I am building on all the progress I've made."

"Indeed. So much can be achieved in your world if you remain in your heart and you allow. This is one of the most powerful simplicities of your ascension. It also helps dissolve the nagging objections and manipulations of ego that can easily slow your progress up your curve of ascension.

"So... let's look at the service you gave today through your newly-expanding perspective."

"Okay."

"Serving unconditionally was a new experience. You learnt that, just because you serve and support another, does not mean you miss out on your own path. Service is a unity that honours the paths of all involved. Service doesn't stop you being you because it is part of you."

"All part of the service," I joked.

"Yes, all part of the multi-directional service. When you help someone, you aren't only helping that person, you are also helping yourself and sending the intention of support out into the humanity as a whole."

"Wow, that's three directions already. But, hey, who's counting?"

"In truth, until very recently, ego was counting. It was asking *How much? Is it worth it? Will I look weak?*"

"But that's three projections."

"Precisely. For ego, these projections are valid and important. They help you conflict and attach to your experience. They help ego add up it's big equation so it can prove to you that you are alone, that you don't have energy to spend on others and that, when it comes down to it, the only aspect of your life you can rely on is... you guessed it—ego!"

"But service is a choice. Unconditional service doesn't ask *What's in it for me?*"

"Correct."

"But if a person is assessing consciously the intention

behind their service, what are the Light questions that would be helpful? For example, instead of asking *Is it right?*, I could ask *Is it loving? Is it supportive of myself and others?* And instead of asking *What's in it for me?* I could ask *What's the feeling?* or *What's my intention behind my service?*"

"Correct. And where would you find your answer?"

"In my heart. I'd sense if it felt supportive to do it. I'd feel the rush of purpose or that sense of connecting with progress and expansion. Like I felt today."

"And you would also feel the unity."

"In what way?"

"Hopefully, in all ways during these moments. Instead of asking your questions with a defined result in mind, you are now embracing many different perspectives. Is it of service to me to help? Is it of service to the person? Is it of service to the greater community? Am I honouring my personal truth? Am I controlling? These are just some of the intentions you could explore."

"That's a lot of service. Feels heavy."

"The only reason you are feeling heavy is that there is so much Light within all of these directions. All directions unite. Your mind does not have the capacity to engage or embrace this unity so it simply repels it or resists it. Resistance is dense and that creates a dense, heavy sensation. It's this that is weighing you down. The mind says that multi-directional creation has no point because the mind isn't prepared to allow this perspective and the growing creative flow."

"And that's the limited bits of ego trying to convince me they are me."

"Quite. And as you know, the mind will never give up being right."

"Because that would mean ego would be giving up control?"

"Exactly," said my Higher Self, then paused. "So how do you feel now?"

The Space In Time

"I feel much more comfortable with my expanded perspective. Ego is still trying to regain control by saying this is wrong, and that I've overdone it; saying that helping Andrew like that was irresponsible when I've got a book to finish. You know how ego can be. But I'm just allowing all of that to flow on by. If you'd told me that I was going to serve in lots of different directions today, I simply wouldn't have believed you. But I understand now. I've been through my experience; I've allowed it from the heart so we can discuss it.

"I know you don't withhold the truth of these experiences but to understand them, I need to go through them and sometimes it's only afterwards you can give me guidance. It's like having an ego blind spot. I just have to trust that I'm going through the resistance even if I can't see it. Trust the heart more than I've done before. Both Andrew and I have had faith today. In a way, we've both believed that something completely spontaneous, something beyond our control and out of our normal experience, can make a difference. It's so simple, even obvious when you can see it. It's like everything stops for a moment to unite everything in love."

"It is simple to allow the unlimited flow so that ease, joy and effortlessness become obvious." My Higher Self's words descended into the sentence like small feathers falling on the gentlest of breezes. Meaning echoed throughout my heart room and I felt a flash of brilliant light holding me in a euphoric embrace.

"That's some authentication," I gasped, feeling as though my heart could burst with such a sensation of peace.

"And a new architecture of learning," smiled my Higher Self. "Your mind was, until very recently, having a very busy day trying to control your progress. But now you are allowing a greater truth."

I closed my eyes and allowed the flow of images from my Higher Self. First a stream of words floating through countryside gaining more and more momentum. Then a spray of white water as the words fall through a cascading waterfall. And then a rushing sound as the flow tumbles through rapids, gushing towards the sea.

"And truth is no different than the flow you see. The words balance gently with each explanation. But no words can ever describe all angles of truth. So it may be easier for you to see truth as an ever expanding flow of love, not facts or words."

"I understand," I relied. "It's just that ego always tries to put a box around my heart truth in each moment because it uses limits as its foundation."

"Well observed. But now that limitation isn't the foundation of your world, you can become more and more at peace with the constant expansion of flow and an expanding truth."

"And trust there is a way, even if you don't know where it is and where it goes."

"Yes. Trust leads you through limitation so that you may be wayshower. Trust enables your alchemy and helps others see their own path." Guidance was beginning to fade. "Trust the flow of love and the understanding will come. Trust the flow of truth and you will understand your next healing."

Fellowship Of Chaos

I awoke the next day in a distressed turmoil of sweat and bed clothes. A night of dark dreams had been anything but sweet. My left eye refused to open and I could feel it was inflamed and stuck tight with the residue of sleep. I felt a wave of mild panic through the whole of my body as I tried to focus through my right eye.

An impatient Isis pawed at the window. I stumbled as I caught my foot on the end of the bed. As I opened the window she meowed and purred as if she'd found me all over again. Or maybe she understood I was in need of some healing company.

"I'm very glad to see you, Isis, even if it is through only one eye." I welcomed her in, still trying to loosen my matted lashes.

Although I wanted to go back to bed, the pages that were stuck behind my other eye were calling to me. *Let us out! Let us out!* they pleaded. "I'll write you down when I can see," I replied, distressed at my sudden lack of vision.

Isis didn't make her usual comfortable resting place in the bed clothes but followed me into the bathroom. I recoiled at the strange sight in my mirror. Who was that? I didn't recognise myself.

"I'm surprised you came in, Isis," I said, bending down to stroke her. "I'm looking at a case of mistaken identity! Perhaps ego is tired of this ever expanding truth and has decided to retaliate with a left hook."

Isis continued to rub against my legs as if everything was as it should be. I knelt down beside her and we bobbed foreheads as tears began to well up in my eyes. I leaned against the radiator, overcome with a desperate downpour of frustration.

"I can't see," I sobbed. "Why can't I see?"

Unperturbed, Isis curled up in my lap. As the surge of emotion eased, I called for help.

Merlin dissolved back into my awareness. "You aren't alone. This will pass soon. And you are correct in your observation—ego has been disturbed. But there is nothing wrong; you are healing. You are just required to remain neutral so all this entrapped limitation can find a way out. Stabilise your Light and then the transmutation will be completed."

"I don't know if I can," I cried. "I can't see what you mean."

"But you can sense it. Just centre on the feeling then the limitation will find its way out. There is always a path for detachment, always an answer, just allow it to flow. This is the least disruptive way. Honour your capability. You are worthy."

Merlin's words flowed with a gentle but profound

strength and my descent into self pity halted. I began to feel the flow of Merlin's words, stopping at the word neutral.

"What do you mean by neutral?" I began.

"Neutrality is an energetic state that supports your transmutations and stabilises your initiations, particularly at higher and higher levels. It supports smooth transmutations when ego is trying to give you the impression that all is crashing down around you or that you must fight to maintain your level of progress. Such situations are illusions but ego has some talent when it comes to creating an illusion."

"But this illusion of real seems pretty tangible to me."

"That it may. Ego has even chosen to give you the impression that your left eye and your left brain are not functioning; the impression that they have no vision. But return to neutrality and you will allow this residual resistance to pass. Then you will not become attached to what is barely left. Shall we join together in the intention of transmutation in the silver-violet light of change?"

"Absolutely," I replied with a sense of purpose that took me by surprise.

"Remember, ego is not fighting you. Ego is not wrong, it is just leaving this part of you. You are remaining neutral and reclaiming your true self."

"I AM neutral. I AM transmuting my resistance to my new vision," I announced, and woke a sleeping Isis who looked up and immediately began to purr.

I closed my right eye and started to embrace clouds and clouds of silver-violet in my inner space. I invoked the empowering flow of transmutation in my heart room and in my physical abode, creating a unity of Light within and without."

The frustration of conflicting ego turned into the grief of passing ego.

I returned from my meditation slumped over a cheery Isis who was now rubbing her face against mine, tickling me intensely.

"Time to rise and shine," said Merlin.

Rubbing the tickling away, I opened my right eye. My left eye followed.

"The tears of frustration were useful after all," observed Merlin.

"Transmutation is, after all, one hundred per cent efficient. Or so you keep telling me. But eye wash could have also done the trick!"

"But you don't have any," replied Merlin.

"No. As you obviously can see, I don't even have the appearance of eye wash in this limited world. But as you always say, what you require in each moment is right in front of you," and I stroked Isis as she prepared to jump off my lap. "And for that, I'm becoming truly thankful."

"And so are you also thankful for the dreams you had last night?"

"I'm working on appreciating the flow. But you appear to be saying that those nightmares are helpful. I'm not so sure I can be thankful for those just at the moment. One minute I was sitting on a beach and the sun was shining and I was feeling really relaxed when, next minute, a massive wave was rushing towards the beach and I knew I couldn't get away. All I could do was watch it arrive. The sky was completely obscured by the wave. There was nothing but wave. I was scared out of my wits!"

"What purpose do you think the wave had?" probed Merlin, ignoring my ego's attempts at dramatic blame.

"Well, as I understand it, water represents emotions, flexibility and fear of loss. I read it in a dream book once upon a long time ago. So I suppose this was related to the transmutation I've just gone through, the one you guided me through."

"And what part of you fears unlimited flow? What aspect fears a flow that has no description, no dimensions and cannot be defined by anything that is familiar in your world? Something so massive that it embraces all in its path?"

I sensed a response. No thought, just a wave of energy that I could put into words.

"Ego."

"Indeed. And what does a wave of true unlimited power bring?"

"Chaos?"

"Indeed. And why did you feel such overwhelming fear?"

"Because ego didn't want me to feel it was possible to cooperate with chaos. It didn't want me to feel what it was like to be within that flow, that unlimited flow."

"Bingo! And so ego tried to define the wave in its limited terms. In one way, that meant there was no hope, no possibility to reclaim limitation or control. You felt the fear of ego when faced with unlimited capability. You also felt the disallowance within your own mentality and the fear of loss within your emotionality."

"So ego was grieving because I'm creating a new sense of the unlimited?"

"Indeed. You are beginning to understand within your heart that there are initiations that you are required to undergo when you encounter them. You cannot talk yourself through them, as it were, nor study how to behave and respond. You learn in the moment, otherwise they wouldn't be initiations.

"So from time to time on the path of ascension, you will encounter aspects in your world that have been buried within you for what your ego might consider an immortal length of time. They have been there forming the cornerstones of your limitation from the beginning of your descent into physicality. So when you undertake to transmute these aspects, the disruptions are without precedent because they have never been achieved before."

"But you can guide me when I go to these deep levels of limitation?"

"Yes. We can always guide you through change but, as we have previously discussed, guidance does not know all there is within the world of limitation. Guidance senses the limited and unlimited aspects of you in any moment. We cannot predict the way your ascension will come to pass because the manifestations of ego are as varied and unique as there are souls in your physical world. This is why it is to trust the process."

"You wouldn't want to predict, anyway."

"Indeed. It would not be of service. We do not predict your path, we allow your path and your learning so that you may develop your alchemical skills."

"And that's why you reminded me about being balanced, being neutral and not to re-attach to ego by thinking I was fighting or that ego was wrong?"

"Indeed."

"And also, from what you've said, I now understand why Higher Self said that when I'm asleep, I'm actually awake. That's because when I'm more aware within my other selves, like when I sleep, then I shift my awareness in a certain way that I can't do when I'm in my physical state. I suppose what I'm trying to say is that I'm more flexible when I don't have a physical body to consider. My conditioning says that nothing much happens when I sleep but that's because ego doesn't see the more conscious parts of my nature as contributing to anything."

"Ego doesn't see them at all, it just has an idea of them," added Merlin.

I was encouraged and continued.

"In a way then, the nightmares are just as valuable as the initiations here in the physical world because they're all contributing to change that can help my ascension."

"Indeed. Dreams are a much more flexible medium for transmutation because they have less of the appearance of attachment. But ego underestimates their impact in your general ascension because it disregards anything that is not within form."

"So the more adept I become at using the tools you

teach me, the smoother my transmutation process will become in my physical experiences."

"That is so. It is always important to undergo the initiation and we would not support you in transmutations that would undermine your materiality. If an initiation is in front of you then you are worthy of it. And whether you crash through it, struggle through it or laugh your way through it, what is most important is that you do flow through it."

"Okay. From now on I AM transmuting, when possible, the imprint of belief that I have within me that says that if it's a struggle then it's worth more. Because I still think an aspect of me is influencing some of these less-than-elegant transmutations."

"And as you ask and give your commitment, so we honour your intentions and guide you through your healing."

Merlin paused and I got the distinct impression he was flicking through my energetic layers.

"Merlin, are you browsing through my attachments again?"

"Would we do that?"

"Yes. You're probably working out how much ego is still lodged in there."

"Analysis is of the mind. But, as guidance, we are able to observe how much of your true Light nature is functioning. It does not serve to linger on limitation."

"Well do you mind stopping? It's making me nervous."

"Perhaps it is the wayshower in you embracing the truth of the Ascending Master in the Physical.

I felt another all-embracing flow of emotion and tears followed. "You really mean that, don't you?"

"You do not require the approval of your guidance to complete your ascension. But embracing support can be uplifting."

"I do feel it from time to time. Like when Mrs Daley helped me with my finances and when I helped Andrew and when I'm writing from my heart. All those times I feel the rushes of euphoria and purpose. It's as if I get a sensory glimpse of what it would be like to have no limitation, to return to true nature. It's like everything is working. It's effortless and all makes perfect sense."

"And these are all parts of your ascension. As you transmute your path in bite-size pieces, so do you feel in bite-size pieces what it is to be eternal. But we don't want you getting carried away with euphoria and not finishing the job, now do we?"

"Being carried away on waves of euphoria is tempting from time to time but it's ascension I'm seeking and ascension that I'm completing. So to maintain balance, I'll stick to your guidance. If bite-size pieces is what's required then that seems perfectly digestible to me."

My stomach gave out a long grumbling plea for food. "Time to fuel the physical, Merlin. I'd ask you to join me, but..."

"Thank you for your invitation. We would be delighted to join you, a slightly different stream of nutrition however."

"As you wish. The more the merrier."

Just as I walked into the kitchen, the door bell rang. It was 8 a.m. Who could that be? I glanced through the spy hole in the door to see Mrs Daley, complete with rosy cheeks and a top-o'-the-mornin' smile.

I opened the door with, "Good morning, Agnes. How are you?"

"Wonderful," she said expectantly.

"Fancy a cuppa?"

"Love one," she beamed, continuing her momentum towards the armchair.

"What about a community breakfast—Isis, you and me? A ring of Light consciousness eh? What do you say, Isis?" She blinked a smile as Merlin winked from within my heart room.

"Perhaps, since I invited myself in," began Agnes, "I can

cook breakfast. You look like you've been through a big shift again. An' p'haps some emotional restructuring?"

"All of the above, Agnes. And I had the most disturbing dreams last night. A huge wave was heading straight for the beach I was standing on. I woke up with my left eye all inflamed. Couldn't see or think. It's better now, though."

"Distressing it may be, but everything 'appens for a reason. An' sometimes it's not important to know why, it's just important to feel differently."

"That's very wise, Agnes."

"Thank you. An' I hope Isis has been giving you healing. She's so good like that. Always turns up when you could do with some healing company."

"Yes, she arrived first thing, right on cue to help the distressed human."

"So what've you got in that fridge o' yours? If I know you, it'll be nothing. But, hey, miracles never cease."

"Funny you should say that. I've turned over a new reality recently, Agnes. No more *cupboard-is-bare*, I now shop regularly and nothing 'grows' in the fridge. So this morning, I'm in the position to offer you a full continental breakfast, even with eggs of your choice, if you wish."

"Well, there's a turnaround! Looking after yourself, now? Whatever next?" she smiled. "I'll 'ave scrambled eggs an' tomatoes an' toast, then, please."

"One scrambled eggs on toast with tomatoes coming up. And Isis? Your order is?"

Isis looked up at me while she purred around Agnes.

"Was that sardines I heard you say? One sardines coming right up."

We all sat in what appeared to be a larger kitchen than usual, talking of the days of experience that'd now flowed into late summer. Agnes slapped my arm playfully as I teased her about her gentleman friend. He was surely a computer hologram hanging out in cyber space because I'd never seen him. Of course he didn't exist. Agnes promised she'd introduce him soon, sending a wave of endearment through me as she now called me one of her trusted friends.

"So, 'ow are those pages coming along?" she probed.

"It's a real tale of Neptunian proportions. It never rains but it pours, and then it's a drought, and then a tsunami."

"Easy does it! I'm feeling a little soggy… But the peaks an' troughs of the waves are productive, aren't they?" encouraged Agnes, concerned for my creative welfare.

"Yes, I believe they are. The end is nigh, if that's what you mean."

"An' so these are, of course, the times of mastering the flow; of rising above the limitations of our collective drudgery so that we can realise the empowerment we seek."

"Bravo, Agnes! Yes, we're sailing the high seas of transmutation and making a difference in our collective experience. We're members of the fellowship of choice, seekers, wayshowers and ascending masters in the physical." And with that, I began the second order of scrambled eggs with creative flare.

"Oh, I like the sound of that," said Agnes. "Ascending masters in the physical…" she mused. "Sounds like we've got friends in 'igh places an' the power of alchemy at our fingertips."

"Well, I'm choosing to believe we have, Agnes. But as we know, with empowerment comes responsibility, not to mention the ability to maintain balance while we practice that alchemy. So in the last couple of days I've been looking at things through different eyes. Today was the practical," I smiled, "and all that practice has helped me appreciate perfection… creating with purpose in each moment. Talking of which, what are you going to do in your moments today? Made any plans?"

"Yes. I plan to be spontaneous all day long," replied Agnes with a bizarre resoluteness.

"Let me get this straight. Your single plan… is to have no plans?"

"That's right."

We both laughed.

"That's wonderful, Agnes. Sounds like you're allowing chaos."

"That's right! When I got up, I saw your light on. You're never up at this time so that was my chaos lead! Then I thought *Why not invite myself in? Come and have breakfast with you?*"

"And so you did, and here you are," I replied enthusiastically through a mouthful of food.

I was distracted by my phone ringing and I crammed the last morsel from my plate.

"I'll just get this," I said, gesturing at the phone. "Please make yourself another cup of tea, Agnes."

"Top o' the mornin' to you, Erica! What can I do for you?"

"Cheery little soul, aren't you? How's my masterpiece coming along?'

"Work in progress and process. But there are pages... There are definitely pages."

"And pages and pages?" she persisted, both serious and inquisitive.

"Yes. Quality and some quantity."

"Good. Today you're doing really well on the abundance front because I called to tell you I've got a royalties cheque for you, sooner than expected."

"Wonderful!"

"Those in high places have decided that your book has performed so well in the last two months that they'll give you your royalties a month earlier than planned, to help with the money they aren't paying you now."

"All gratefully received," I said, winking at Agnes.

"Would you like to come into the office and pick it up or do you want me to post it?"

"I'm in the flow at the moment so can you post it, please?"

"Okay. As you wish. I'll just shuffle paper in my ivory tower until you've finished your chapter and have time to see me, then."

"Erica? You are joking, right?" I couldn't tell if she was joking or serious, her comment was so unlike her.

"Yes... but it would be nice to see you, all the same... You know... catch up... stoke the fires of inspiration a bit."

"Okay, I'll see you when the current episode is completed. Everything's alright, though?"

"Yes... ish. Nothing much to report really. Looking for some purpose, I suppose. The general hubbub is doing what it does but it's the vision and direction that concerns me. Doing things without direction often means things carry on in the same old circles, around and around. The board has de-stuffed themselves somewhat. Don't know if it's going to be enough to rebuild everything but there are signs of change."

"Well, if it's inspiration you want then perhaps you should also meet my neighbour, Mrs Daley. We're just having breakfast with her cat."

"Sounds cosy."

My attempt to include Erica in our Light Community seemed to have the opposite affect.

"Pen pushing calls, I'm afraid. Get back to me when you can. Any time next week is fine." And with that, she hung up.

"Was that your editor?" asked Agnes.

"Yes—Erica. She's been really supportive and it turns out that the big wigs there want to give me some royalties after all; keep me happy, perhaps. My contract is up next year so perhaps they're concerned I won't renew."

"Well, who knows? You might not."

"Exactly, Agnes. Anything is possible, right?"

"Absolutely anything. In every moment we're surrounded by potentiality as far as the third eye can see, an' beyond!"

My phone started ringing again. Agnes began putting on her coat.

"You don't have to go," I said.

I glanced at the phone and saw Andrew's number. "It's Andrew," I mouthed. "Could be a while."

Agnes gestured to leave. "See you in the flow. I'll see m'self out," she smiled, closing the door gently.

"Hello Andrew. I'm having a densely populated morning. People, people, people."

"Hey, you might find you've graduated from antisocial to social-light! I can see the headline now... Successful hermit has coming out party!" he teased.

"Oh, ha ha ha, very funny. Okay here's a headline for you... Editor drops twenty pounds and tailors his own new line!" I retorted, laughing.

"Close. More like, editor rings to moan about the toxins he's been wading through as he returns to balance," Andrew said in a slightly more serious tone.

"Oh, you make me laugh. You've actually rung up to moan about your progress? Isn't that a little contrary?"

"If you call that kind of pain *progress*."

"It's all got to come out from in there where you've been storing it! And it's not that bad really. I bet if you were willing to admit it, your general energy levels are fantastic, right?"

"Yeah, alright, I'll admit it. Things are getting better. And the headaches I've been getting are actually the perfect diet because I've been eating less when I don't feel well and going home from work early."

"There you go, then! Everything has its purpose. And on top of that, you've managed to start doing all the things you wanted to do, even though the method leaves a little bit to be desired. After all, Andrew, everyone has headaches."

"But mine are worse than everyone else's because I'm special, you know. You've got to feel especially sorry for me!"

I greeted Andrew's attention seeking with silence.

"Hey, stop practicing what you preach," he pleaded. "It's

me... Andrew... your best friend. Make that your only friend. Aren't I even allowed to exaggerate a bit? Steal a bit of your inspiration through pity?!"

"Not listening!" I laughed heartily down the phone. "Keep going Andrew because this zealous friend has actually paid for a private detective to follow your every move so I know where you've been. And I have it on high authority that you're transforming from Andrew-the-Wreck into Andrew-the-Salvaged."

"You haven't really got someone to watch me... Have you?" He actually sounded worried.

I laughed even more. "Of course I haven't. I have better things to do than get attached to the drama of Andrew's healing. But on a serious note, I am supporting you. I really want you to do what you feel is going to get back command of your life. And it'd be nice if you joined me in that state of being called self belief!"

"Actually, I'm happy to inform you I've invested in a little bit of that self belief—I've signed up for a minimum of ten sessions of acupuncture."

"Great! That's definitely one giant leap for Andrewkind!"

"So now I've chosen progress, can I start moaning?"

"No you can not! This is an inspiration zone. It's moan free!"

"But what's the point in making progress if you don't moan about how hard it was getting there?"

"I don't know, Andrew, you tell me."

"Okay, no point in moaning," he conceded, finally letting go of his flagging self pity.

"And what about your other therapist? Did you go and see him too?"

"The pincer movement, you mean? One on each side prodding me into healing?"

"Let's say the two dedicated professionals supporting you in your return to balance."

"As a matter of fact, I did. So now I'm surrounded!" he replied theatrically.

"And...?"

"Well, the scoop is... I cried a lot and then I felt better."

"Good!"

"Good? I wouldn't necessarily say paying someone so you can cry is ideal, but I do feel lighter. Plus, I'm not revealing any secrets at this stage but the scales may also indicate that change."

"Great. So out with the prematurely balding old age with no one but alcohol for company, in with the new Andrew."

"But there's always... you. I've always got you. You need me because we're in this together, right?" replied Andrew, feigning adoration.

"Gee thanks. That makes me feel a whole lot better. I know old ladies who'd put you to shame. One in particular who's the youngest old age pensioner I've ever met. And she's a friend, I'll have you know, so you aren't my only friend. Then there's Erica..."

"Okay, okay," surrendered Andrew. "I might have to make an appointment to see you because now you've got friends! I think that's enough expansion for my insecurity to take! My fleet street persona can see where this is going—the big headline... There's no point in highlighting struggle."

"None whatsoever. You'll just attract more. And you don't want to be that dense, right?"

"No. Density isn't all it's cracked up to be. I should know, I've been there, done that and been investing in struggle far too long."

"But that's changing," I encouraged. "Getting better means getting back to where you came from."

"And where was that?"

"Balance, Andrew. You came from balance! You weren't always as blobby at the edges. It's just self abuse and neglect, that's all."

"I know. You're right. I believe in all our conversations. It's just that honesty can be quite a change. I used to be in control, you know. I could laugh off any serious meaning or purpose. And now look at me! I'm in search of it."

"Sensitive New Age guy, then?"

"Yep."

"Could do wonders for your love life. Lose weight; have a charm makeover; invest in alternatives and flexibility; give up the stubborn victim… They'll be swooning in the George and Dragon. Has the acupuncturist found that point that helps you lose twenty-five pounds yet?"

"Oh, you mean the one where I deflate while flying around the room like a farting balloon?"

"Yeah, that's the one."

"No he hasn't. But I'm working on that. And you watch it, cheeky! You're disturbing my very sensitive nerves!"

"Okay. Well make sure you ask at your next session. And if there are no more revelations, I'll look forward to seeing your inner and outer beauty at a later but soon-ish date."

"Line four's flashing so I guess I'd better get back to being an editor."

"Look after yourself, Andrew. We'll catch up soon, eh?"

"Yep. Don't call us, we'll call you. It's a promise! Bye."

I hung up and boiled the kettle, made a fresh pot of tea, and sank into the armchair, my arms draping over the sides.

"Haven't seen that much social activity since… well, forever," I mused. "It felt like the middle of the day when it was only quarter to ten. Hey, maybe *I* was the old fart that had been dangerously close to turning into a hermit until Mrs Daley rescued me!" I smiled to myself.

"Well, Merlin, that was some company!"

"Was it not of service?"

"Yes, actually. That social vortex was exactly what I required. Funny that," I smiled. "Do you know what, Merlin? I think my capacity for joy is increasing."

"So the more truly is the merrier?"

"Yes, you're right, as always."

"Let us settle for Light rather than right, for it is wise to be merry and you are merry to be wise."

"And so it is," I said, bowing my head to my master guide.

"All in good time," replied Merlin, "all in good time."

Come Together

Weeks of intense writing were punctuated with friendly encouragement from Erica, Andrew and Agnes. The community of guidance was expanding and unifying in a seamless flow of support. Andrew was the champion of transmutation; Erica's courage helped me get out of my creative cul-de-sac; Agnes was always there to contribute humour and practicality.

Even if they weren't aware of it, each of my fellow ascending masters in the physical was providing a strand of collective truth that brightened my day and enriched my pages where their echo increasingly left its impression. My Higher Self introduced me to an enriching flow of guidance that enlightened me on up-to-date internal angles and bridged the gap between my inner discoveries and outer creativity. As our Light matrix moved towards completion, I realised it was the week before my publishing deadline.

In the middle of one of our higher consciousness discussions, the phone rang off the kitchen table, vibrating its way across the floor towards my feet.

"One moment, Merlin. I'll just take this call. Hold that thought, would you?"

Merlin raised the eyebrows he didn't have.

"Okay," I said, smiling as I moved to retrieve the phone, "you don't control and you don't think... but you know what I mean."

Come Together

The phone was displaying Andrew's number.

"Hi, Andrew. How are you?"

"Great! How about you?"

"I've been swimming in the middle of an ocean of letters."

"And?"

"They've now rearranged themselves into a book. Well, almost. I'm just in the last phase now."

"No longer the spiritual worrier, then? Sounds like you've arrived at that place you arrive at when it's all over. Creative peace, I mean."

"Now that's quite some spiritual observation. And yes, I am nearly arrived... the spiritual warrior. But I can hear in your voice that you've got something urgent to say, so fire away. This wouldn't have anything to do with the dietary warrior, now, would it?"

There was silence.

"Come on Andrew, you're dying to tell me. What's the winning number?"

"More like the winning combination. New attitudes, new intentions and new work ethic... which all adds up to... thirty-five pounds!"

"Congratulations! Your Higher Self must be very proud! Can I buy you an organic soup to celebrate?"

"Actually, I'd like to buy you lunch. If it weren't for you I wouldn't be this new, vastly improved Andrew. And you've almost got a new book, so why don't we make it a double celebration?"

"Thanks. I'd be delighted. I'm happy to help. But also remember to give yourself a pat on the back because it's you who made the changes."

"Okay. Thanks for the vote of confidence. And I did that because you showed me that I was more interested in what I can't do and moaning about it. And then you got that honesty weapon out and I had to surrender that stubborn ego stuff and begin believing in what I want rather than pushing it away all the time."

"Hey, it's all part of the journey."

"I don't know if I like the sound of this," Andrew interrupted jokingly.

"We're reflections for each other. You gave me some of my best material, along with Agnes, Erica and the inner crew."

"There'd better be a jolly big disclaimer in there! Sounds crowded," he teased.

"I did change the names and the waistlines, if that's what you're worried about! But there's always magic in fiction because it's all the bits of life we wouldn't believe if it weren't made up, right?"

"I think you've got something there. We've lost magic because we're too busy with the mundane, nailing down life instead of letting in a bit of chaos. That's why we end up pushing up daisies. When we die, we realise we should've promoted growth rather than trying to keep it to a minimum."

"Yet more material, Andrew. I feel another book coming on."

"Before it does, meet me at midday at the organic place just opposite work."

"Your wish is my command, oh Ascending Master in the Physical."

"What did you call me? Oh, never mind, you can explain later."

"Will do. Midday it is."

As I joined the midmorning momentum, everything appeared to be moving in slow motion. Perhaps I'd been out so little in the past few weeks that I'd forgotten what busy-ness looked like.

"Perhaps you've forgotten what rushing into the future, forcing change and resisting progress was like," suggested my Higher Self.

"What do you mean?"

Come Together

"You are detaching from the desire to force the flow; to make it into something; to make yourself be something. Instead, you are creating, not trying. You are flowing, not forcing. You are cooperating, not conflicting. When you've been through a major shift in yourself, your observations change. You experience differently, in a more detached way. As you are sensing, you have more space! And you know in your heart that you aren't missing out on anything, you're beginning to see how enjoyable balance is."

And as my Higher Self's commentary was completed, I caught sight of Andrew as I crossed the road to meet him.

"Perfect timing, eh?" said Andrew and my Higher Self in unison.

"As always," I smiled with a mixture of joy and astonishment. "You're looking wonderful. Really great!"

"Thanks. My heart thinks so too. I've just got my tests back and I'm well on the way to getting healthy. And what's even better is I haven't had to kill myself to do it."

"That certainly has its advantages," I smiled.

"You know what I mean. This combination of treatments working on mental, emotional and physical well being have made it much easier than I'd ever thought possible. So let's get some food and we can sit down and have a good old chin wag."

We piled our plates high with steaming hot food and settled at a corner table away from the noise of the main restaurant.

"So... you're a walking miracle, then," I began.

"Well, I'm certainly walking in the land of the living now. I've been walking a mile a day before work. Five weeks now. Before, I could barely get out of bed but now I'm excited to say I actually enjoy it. And all these feelings I've found, my body is actually feeling again instead of being this big block of stone. It's quite disconcerting sometimes just how much you can feel."

"You're a total New Age guy, now!"

"I'll take that as a compliment because it feels wonderful and also...." He hesitated.

"And the truth will out, Andrew. Come on, what's the story?"

"I've got my eye on this cute dog walker. She's got a chocolate Labrador she walks every morning before work. I'm currently getting up the courage to ask her out."

"Well, well, congratulations... ish. So what do you mean, working up to it?"

Andrew looked at me as if I had a secret guaranteed solution.

"Why not ask her?" I suggested.

"Oh, I thought you were onto something then... a secret recipe... or easy pills or something. You see, I'm looking more for the *How to ask a woman out and guarantee the answer is going to be yes!* solution. I'm terrible with rejection."

"The secret recipe is... Start!"

"I was afraid you were going to say that."

"Look what you've just been through. All that change is a permanent courageous change. Why stop there? Start on relationships while you're at it. Think of yourself as recycling the old Andrew in favour of the new Andrew. You're becoming an Ascending Master in the Physical... because you're doing just that. You're detaching from your limited ego that says you've got to moan about your life and make it harder until you end up in sub-zero joy. Also, you're mastering what it takes to be genuinely empowered. You're rising out of struggle and beginning to command your power. You're taking responsibility for you creating through love, not fear, and going through the changes that make that a reality. That's genuine empowerment and all the empowerments you undertake add up to mastering change—mastering the alchemy of change. Which is why you're becoming an Ascending Master in the physical world."

"But an Ascending Master in the Physical? That sounds

a bit grand. Can anyone do and be this? Take that man over there," he said, pointing to a man queuing at the counter. "He could be an Ascending Master in the Physical too, right?"

"Yes, he could be. Anyone can be if they choose to. It's not an hereditary title, it's created through the ability to change. So why couldn't it be you?" I asked, gesturing at Andrew with my spoon.

"Okay, let's say this alchemy is growing on me. What's my next step?"

"From what you've said, you've already got your next step."

"What's that?"

"Expanding into a new area. Honouring your flow of truth brings you to the dog walker. Ask her out. Or are you content with becoming a stalker rather than a walker?"

"Oh, ha, ha! But when you talk about actually facing her, I feel like I'm grinding to a halt. Why, if it's something that I really want, can't I just go ahead and do it?"

"Because you aren't used to experiencing what you want, remember? You've spent years going against your heart and doing what you *think* you *should* do rather than feeling what you truly want."

"But now I've changed?"

"Yes. But you still require fuel to keep that change going."

"So that's my current alchemy of change?"

"Basically."

"So I've got to convert some of the resistance I built up before I changed?"

"Yes. And that's why you feel like you've ground to a halt. Well, you haven't, actually, you've just started tunnelling through some of your resistance. You're recycling the old so that you can make this next new."

"So why does it feel so difficult?"

"It's just difficult for your ego to let go of hardship and

struggle because that's what it values. All these attachments are precious to your ego but that doesn't mean you believe they're valuable. So just because things might be challenging for your ego doesn't mean they're hard for the real Andrew."

"So don't assume it's going to be difficult?"

"Exactly. Be with your alchemy of change. Do and be what's necessary to release those attachments so that you can move forward. See this new stage of creation following on, contributing to all the changes that you've already made."

"Okay. That's a bad habit of mine, I admit... always thinking it's going to be difficult. Leave the best til last because all the other stuff is so hard to get through!"

"It's all just conditioning. But you're changing, rebalancing into ease, right?"

"Yes, that's what I want to do."

"So start giving the new Andrew bigger projects to manage. Promote yourself and your dreams. If you don't, who will?"

"So it's down to facing rejection?"

"Let's say it's down to being willing to believe you can find a relationship. And, yes, part of that is facing rejection. But be joyous about what you want to create, not weigh yourself down by becoming absorbed by what's standing between you and it. Nothing is set in stone so don't go about fulfilling your ego's objections by believing in them. This lady doesn't have to reject you. Just like you, she has a choice. And you're not going to crumple in a heap if she isn't interested."

"So don't get attached to my ego's expectations?"

"Exactly. That's the spirit. Be detached and balanced because if Labrador Lady sees the Andrew I've seen blossom into balance in the past few months then of course she's going to love you."

"But you're just biased!"

"No I'm not, I'm honest. You're a walking inspiration. You're a master alchemist in the making. It's just that ego's got you suspended over the honesty gap—what you think you should do versus what you really feel you want to do. Mind or heart? Logic or magic? So I'm giving you a push out the door, as it were. I'm suggesting you stop holding on to your emotional security as if it means something to you. You know it's nothing in comparison to that warm fuzzy feeling you now believe can be yours. You are the sensitive New Age guy, after all."

"So don't walk up to her thinking I'm already defeated, walk up to her without any expectations."

"Yes! You've got it!"

"But that's difficult."

"No, Andrew, it's just different. Just be yourself—the genuine article. Ego can't compete with that because when you are you, there's no shadow. You shine brightly and purposefully, whatever you do."

"Okay, hold your poetic horses! You're getting carried away now. And if you're such a relationship guru, why the hell don't you have a partner in life?" he challenged, his ego pushing him onto the defensive.

"But I have," I said smugly.

"You have? So why didn't you tell your best friend then? Been keeping it all to yourself?"

"Oh no. No cloak and dagger. It's all out in the open."

"What do you mean?" he protested, not knowing whether to feel hurt or confused.

"The biggest relationship in my life at the moment is the one with my spiritual learning."

"What kind of relationship is that? Bit of a get-out clause there, eh? It isn't even real. How can you have a relationship with thin air?"

"Just because it isn't physical doesn't mean it isn't real. And more importantly, I'm working with my flow of truth. I'm not saying it couldn't change in a moment. You don't have to be alone to be spiritual. You don't have to be or have anything specific. Nothing's set in stone, nor in physicality for that matter!"

Andrew was listening intently.

"But," I continued, "it does help if you're honest about what you do want so that you can create it and learn from your experience. It's called surrendering to the flow, Andrew. Surrendering to the empowerment of love and simplicity. And, perhaps most importantly, it's awareness of self. You could say I've been blissfully unaware, coming and going and missing out on a relationship all these years. But what if I've been joyous and fulfilled with travelling and writing? What if my heart has been full of these projects, just not a relationship?"

"So you haven't really been missing out on anything?" mused Andrew. "It's just my ego that says that because I want a relationship, so everyone else should want one too."

"Maybe. Or perhaps it's the conditioning of society that says you can't be fulfilled on your own; that you have to have a relationship and you shouldn't die on your own. What's important here is what your heart tells you. Your heart and your guidance want to help you learn. What's the point in presenting something to you that isn't relevant? If I'd wanted a relationship and I'd been putting it off all these years then I'd be in denial and resistance. But if I try and force something that isn't my truth... how can I learn from that?"

"You can't, I suppose. And, in general, you're that happy-go-lucky bohemian getting paid for what you love doing, so I'd hardly call that denial."

"So, Mr Davies, what's important is that you nurture what's in your heart so you can learn from it, empower yourself and allow love into your life, whatever form that may take. And at this point for you, it's Labrador Lady. That project is one that's closest to your heart. And currently, my Higher Self and my friends are closest to my heart. The flow of creation is simple. What's calling to you right now is what counts."

"As long as it's loving and contributing to balance?"

"I'd certainly recommend you put your energy into

what's loving, balanced and joyous, but you can also choose to reinforce ego. Either way, you'll learn."

"But if I want to create easily then I've got to take responsibility for what's loving, balanced and joyous, right?"

"Yes."

"You always make it sound so simple."

"That's because it always is. Ease and simplicity is the natural state of being, it's just our mind and ego that bring in all the possible ways we can detour from what we really want and, as a result, miss out on it."

"But I keep coming back to *What if she says no?*"

"Why, though?"

"Because I find it comforting to worry."

"And how's that helping you contribute to balance?"

"It isn't, I suppose."

"Exactly. Because it's just giving your ego another way to control you. Worry is the desire to control that loving flow of the unlimited Universe that can help you."

"So stop worrying and start trusting?"

"Precisely. What's the point of getting back into the attractive bracket only to spend the rest of your life worrying about whether you attract or not?"

"No, but..." Andrew screwed up his face while he searched for justification.

"No buts, Andrew, they just waste your energy. What you forget is that the Cosmos is an endless flow of potentiality. So if Glamorous-With-Labrador says no, that doesn't mean the Cosmos has said no to you. All-That-Is just keeps on flowing and keeps on going, that's why it's endless. If your intentions are clear, it's only a matter of flow and self wisdom before you meet someone who does say yes.

"It's ego that exists in scarcity saying you always face failure and you've only got yourself to blame. The Cosmos actually says you're worth loving, but it's up to you to believe it. No one, not even the dog walker, can do that for you."

"Okay. You were talking about I AM statements last time we met. You were saying that was a useful way to cooperate with this unlimited flow. So what do I do in this situation?"

"You tell me."

"Well... what about saying *I AM opening up to new relationships*... would that work?"

"Sounds great. You can ask the Universe to cooperate on anything but you need to believe it in your heart centre."

"Maybe *new relationships* is a bit vague then?"

"It's general rather than vague, but it could mean you get a lot of female friends, for example, rather than a girlfriend. Or maybe that you create new work relationships or meet new neighbours."

"I get it. Be more specific about my intention, then?"

"Certainly, if it's what you really want."

"Okay. I AM creating the perfect situation to talk to the lady dog walker."

"Wonderful. Just better hope there isn't some eighty year old lady walking her dog every morning," I joked.

"There's always something else! It's so damned hard to pin down this creation thing. There must be a formula somewhere!"

"I was only joking. You can't pin down the unlimited but you can learn how to work with it. Then you get to understand yourself better and as a result your creations improve. Know thyself and you end up knowing thy creation skills."

"Everything has a purpose, then, right? Even if I can't work it out straight away?"

"Definitely. There's purpose and learning in everything. Every moment a different angle, every moment a different learning."

"So what about saying *I AM creating a girlfriend*? Then if the dog walker likes me, great! And if she doesn't then I've covered what I want to create anyway."

"What about, I AM creating the *perfect* girlfriend?" I suggested.

"Isn't that a bit heavy? Doesn't all that perfection put pressure on me?"

"Perfection isn't a target, remember? It's a state of being."

"I know what you mean but I'm still really uncomfortable with the word, perfect."

"But I don't mean ego-perfect as in stereotypical leggy blond, I mean a flow of energy that's helping you heal and, likewise, you'd help them heal. The person would help you learn about relationships and you'd help them learn too. Perfect doesn't necessarily match what your ego likes, it's what's the most supportive... in this case, to help you understand what a loving relationship is."

"You're saying then that *perfect* could be what I think I don't like but I could actually learn a lot from it?"

"Yes. Hence the phrase *opposites attract*. Some people get the last thing their ego thinks they need and, actually, it works out really well.

"Perfect could be challenging but also very rewarding. Let's face it, you're dangerously close to confirmed bachelordom... so you've got habits, Andrew."

"Ingrained ways of being?"

"Exactly."

"Okay, so... *I AM attracting the perfect girlfriend because she will be the one to help me become more flexible and, as a result, make room for her in my life rather than just for me and my shadow.* How's that, then?"

"Something like that, yes. You could attract someone who won't put up with the greatness of your lateness. Someone who inspires you to start writing again. Someone who loves your sense of humour and your old fart ways."

"Now watch it!" he said, pretending to be offended.

"It's just important to appreciate that when you say *perfect girlfriend*, you could be attracting someone who does things that really irritate you. Someone who reminds you of your mother or adores you and follows you around, doting on you like a lost sheep. There could be plenty of things that they do that you don't like... but you still love them."

"I don't have to turn into Mr Universe, then? Say all the right things all the time?"

"No, you don't have to fake it to be liked, if that's what you mean. That's ego. And it wouldn't last. But when you get into a relationship and you're being honest, there's a lot more opportunities to learn about yourself and to allow the relationship to evolve. And if you've been working to heal your imbalances on the mental, emotional or physical levels, then you'll send out a clearer and clearer message of what you want as you become more and more balanced and honest about yourself."

"And if I sort out what I want, it might be Labrador Lady but it could also be a hundred other women?"

"Exactly. So when you observe it with an abundant attitude, all of a sudden it doesn't look so scary if she rejects you. Also, you're giving yourself space to change, too."

"Basically then, if she doesn't like me or find me attractive or interesting, it's because I'm bloody boring or because I'm listening to my ego talking me out of trusting my heart?"

"Those are two possible interpretations but it could be so many things, depending on your perspective. If you're loving to the best of your ability, then you'll find what you're looking for. You've got yourself back; now you're getting your life back."

"I suppose if I can get back in shape, why can't I get a girlfriend?"

"Why not, indeed. And be honest—you haven't had that much practice in relationships because you haven't had any long term relationships. Apart from your one with work!"

"True. So I can't expect to find Mrs Right materialising out of a puff of smoke with a beer and two tickets to the rugby world cup?"

"You can wish for it, but in the meantime it might be an idea to realise that it's not all about you!"

"That's where the give-and-take comes in?" Andrew smirked.

"Put it this way, relationships are a way to see how love flows. And if you aren't flexible, then love can meet some resistance."

"So relationships are like a sailing boat. I'm being poetic here... They're all romantic, spontaneous, going with the flow and then, from time to time, they can get dashed on the rocks of resistance. So you've got to compromise, yeah?"

"No, that's conditioned expectations talking. Love does not mean there's automatically a relationship. That's why you can fall in love with someone and they don't feel the same way. And then a relationship doesn't necessarily mean compromise either."

"But come on, everyone who gets married has to give up something for their partner. That's just how it works."

"Does it?"

"Well that's how I thought it worked. Am I falling down that honesty gap again?"

"No, but I think you're relying on what your ego has told you rather than what your heart truth is saying. Relationships are about learning to relate. And some people mistake control for love and some believe that to love someone, they have to give up their heart truth when, in reality, neither is necessary."

"So now, as a beginner, I think I'm completely out of my depth! If I don't have to give up anything and my girlfriend doesn't have to give up anything, then where's the give and take?"

"Give and take is flow, right?"

"Yeah, okay."

"So for the flow to be there, for the relating to happen, the foundation of the relationship needs to be love and balance."

"Hmm. Sounds positively idyllic," Andrew pondered.

"And what helps balance?"

"I don't know. Being yourself; being honest, I suppose."

"And do you think that we," I said, gesturing around the room, "as a people, as a humanity, are practicing love, balance, honesty?"

"Some are. But maybe not all the time. Or not a high percentage, anyway."

"So what are we all doing the rest of the time?"

"Arguing and conflicting; playing power games and resisting change I guess."

"Bingo!" I enthused. "And you wonder why people think that our nearest and dearest relationship is a compromise! It's only choosing to listen to ego that makes our life a compromise, irrespective of the situation. Ego will always try to limit and conflict to keep the separation going."

"So it all comes back to choice. If you choose to heal the relationship with self then your relationship with someone else will also reflect that healing."

"Yes, what's out there is always in here, even if it's just the smallest trace."

"So, if I'm honest, I think I'm worried about a relationship compromising me because one of my fears is that I'll end up with a bossy woman who just puts me in my place because when it comes down to it, I'm a soft touch."

"But just because you're a soft touch, as you put it, doesn't mean you're a victim. You can be gentle as well as strong, you know."

"I hadn't thought of that."

"That's because what you want in a relationship doesn't come from your head, it comes from your heart. And, in your mind, going through all the possible scenarios that could wreck or distort your relationship is doing... what, exactly?"

"It's putting my energy into what I don't want instead of cultivating some flexibility so I can actually create what I really want."

"So relationship is an opportunity to explore the flow of love."

"There you go again, being simple!"

"Because simple works, Andrew. Simple flows. Simple enables balance so that you can give your exploration into relationship a chance. Try not to think of relationships in terms of all-or-nothing."

"But isn't what you're saying just a bit idealistic? Say I do create a lovely girlfriend… What happens after the lovey-dovey stuff? What happens when the rose tinted glasses come off and she dumps me because I want to go to rugby all the time."

"There you go again. All or nothing."

"But it's not. I really love rugby and I'm not prepared to give it up."

"And who says you have to? It's not girlfriend *or* rugby, y'know!"

"Oh." Andrew realised what he'd said. "That's the all-or-nothing bit rearing it's imbalanced head, then?"

I smiled. "Ego conditions us to believe that it knows best. It tells us what we want to hear. It manipulates our perceptions so that we end up looking through the eyes of ego, not the eyes of heart. To stop these all-or-nothing reactions you need to choose to keep balanced. Then, slowly but surely, you won't jump to fear when ego pushes you. You'll realise that fear, imbalance and even extreme is a choice, just like anything else. So don't automatically think that the world is against you. Just because you make change doesn't mean you have less choice, nor that you're a victim of how that change turns out. The unlimited loving Universe is here to help you, so stop preparing to fight. Stop thinking *What's the worst that can happen?* and embrace the increased choice… which is really what expansion is."

"Okay, I think I get it now. Ego wants to fight, complicate or push me to extremes and it's up to me to choose if I tag along or not."

"Exactly. Ego wants us to fight ourselves or others so that we don't find out how wonderful Love is. So if you don't listen to your ego, you could sense in that heart of yours that there's the potential to create a girlfriend who enjoys rugby too. Perhaps when you get a great girlfriend and your experience of relationship expands, you might find out that rugby isn't your only love. I can see the headline now: *Andrew dumps rugby for true love!*"

"But what happens if she dumps me?"

"Andrew!"

"What?"

I could feel my frustration rising as he continued to nurse his stubborn blind spot. But one smile from my Higher Self and humour replaced judgment.

"Warning, warning! Doom and gloom alert on the horizon!" I joked.

"I'm sorry, I don't mean to be a pain. It's funny really. You keep guiding me out of this mental maze only for me to choose to plunge back in there for one last look. But don't give up on me now. There's a growing part of me that's courage-harvesting; getting it all in one big heap so I've got enough to do the deed. And that's a start, right?"

"Yes it is. And...?"

"Because... if I don't ask her out, I'll wonder and wonder what would've happened. And that'd be really, *really* irritating."

We both began to laugh.

"So, in a way, I've got to break out and take that chance because I couldn't cope with the irritation!" he said.

"Perhaps irritation isn't quite the intention behind asking Labrador Lady out for dinner, but I know what you mean. Don't live regretting what you *could* have done. Don't live in a nostalgic illusion of how this *would* have been had it worked out."

"So don't let ego con me into being what it wants. Be courageous and then all those loving intentions will add up to something and that something will have been earned so that

Come Together

I can value my creation—in this case a relationship—when it arrives. If it's not Labrador Lady, it'll be someone else. Perhaps I should play the numbers game."

"Andrew, remember, quality is what your heart senses. If you just go for quantity then you're going to be appealing to your ego. It's not *impossible-perfection* versus *anything-will-do*!"

"Only joking!" laughed Andrew. "Got you going, though."

"Oh, very ha ha," I replied, still smiling.

"So to complete this, I need to detach and allow all these mental objections to float by like clouds in the sky," said Andrew.

He paused. "But one nagging thing... The cynic's back but I have to ask this again... What do I do after the rose tinted glasses come off? What do I do to keep her loving me?"

"Andrew, you *are* love, we *are* love. The whole Cosmos is made of the stuff! You don't force love, you just be love. You can't run out of love but you can just chose to turn away from it; fall into control and out of love."

"But how can you be so sure?"

"It's what I believe."

"So maybe the Beatles were right, then... All you need is love?"

"Yes, but that doesn't mean love at any cost or under any circumstances. Just because we are love and our whole world is made from Love doesn't mean any kind of experience of love will do."

"So then, what I need is a quality experience of love?"

"That's more like it! You allow the flow. But that doesn't mean that you agree with just anything or everything, it means you discern from your heart by finding out what you really believe."

"So we're back to honesty and belief."

"And belief is a choice. So it all comes down to choice. You can choose to believe that the Universe is loving and supportive. You can choose to believe that you're naturally loving and that you can create someone who loves you for who you really are. It's all your choice. Just realise that love is a flow and that flow *can* be temporarily interrupted or diverted by your ego. So if you want to keep being in love, then do just that: be in the flow of Love and don't let ego stand between you and what or who you love; between you and the work that you love and the experiences that you love."

"But that all seems so simple and yet fantastical. Isn't being in love for the rest of our life completely unrealistic?" he contested, obviously wanting to be convinced.

"Why?" I challenged.

"Well, have you ever met anyone who is totally 'in love' all the time?"

"I could've but maybe I didn't notice them because I wasn't open minded and open hearted enough. I've only recently graduated from hermitdom, remember?"

Andrew nodded in acknowledgement.

"Just because I've never met anyone," I continued, "doesn't mean there aren't thousands out there. Ego always says that if I haven't experienced it then, of course, it can't possibly be so. But we know that simply is not truth, it's just limitation; it's the ego-centric view of life. Also, we have an image of what 'being in love all the time' should look like and that's often perceived as being soppy, dreamy and completely fluffy. But perhaps it really means being balanced all the time, doing what you love, being love and sharing that love without expectations."

"So being in love is really about being balanced and fulfilled rather than just sex and romance?"

"It depends on you and your experience. I'm just saying that whether it's the whole of your life or just your relationship, perhaps you can be in love all the time but it might look different in different situations."

"My cogs are whirring around," Andrew said, trying to

roll his eyes into the back of his head. "So if love is a flow and I can relate to love through discernment and allowance, then I might find a relationship within which I can be in love. It's not a fantasy built on ego expectations but a relationship built on the relating of love.

"From what I've observed at the office—and yes, I do stop sometimes to look around me!— I've seen the marriages and relationships become control dramas. Everyone seems to be trying to control their partner into being what they want rather than loving them for who they are."

"But it doesn't have to be like that," I hinted.

"So invest in love; forget about the control dramas, compromises and expectations ego is trying to sell me... then my ticker will just keep on ticking?"

"Yes, yes and yes!"

"Here's to loving relationships, whatever form they may take," announced Andrew, raising his sparkling apple juice.

He looked at his glass. "One of my inner demons says to me *What? You're reduced to sparkling apple juice? What's the world coming to when you can't have a few pints at lunch?*"

"And what do you say?"

"I just let it all flow by. I've realised I'm not giving up booze on some holier-than-thou trip, I'm just listening to my choices more closely instead of sticking to habits that just reinforce ego."

"Personal truth is a great place to start and also a great place to stay! Less chance of ego detours," I encouraged.

"Yes, of course. Now I've got a more broadened understanding of choice, I realise how blinkered I'd become with ego. The limiting habit slowly but surely becomes the only choice until you assume it's your whole world. Quite insane, really. But when you're going through ever-decreasing choice, it seems so normal."

"So what's normal now? For Andrew the Balanced?"

"Let me just consult my personal truth!" He paused,

smiling broadly. "Honesty. It's always a great place to start creation. You taught me that."

"And, Mr Davies, I'm going to have to push you for an answer."

"Normal is now weird. Weird is becoming normal. On top of all that, the limitation I've been habitually cultivating is falling apart."

"And falling together in balance?"

"Yes. Falling together with the Universe and that sense of freedom I've been longing for for so long," he mused.

"So let me make a toast. Here's to quality, not quantity!" I said with an artificial solemnity.

I paused. "And here's to quality relationships, wherever they may lead."

The Return

I arrived home on the stroke of five. Now that's what I call a long lunch! I felt a twinge of guilt as I looked at my closed computer.

"You think you should be working," observed my Higher Self. "Your ego thinks you've been wasting your time with long lunches and opinionated chatter."

"Okay, you caught me. Yes, I'm feeling ever so slightly guilty and ego is using quantity over quality saying that it's all about the time I spend writing rather than just allowing it to flow. But self criticism can be tempting when it's my final week before deadline and there's still two chapters to write."

"It's your attachment."

"Yes, and I'm becoming aware of that. But I am a little concerned because currently there's no end in sight! Just teasing; I didn't really mean that. There is an ending, I just haven't downloaded it yet; it hasn't fallen into place. And going out with Andrew seemed so flowful, so effortless and I'm really glad I went."

The Return

"Why are you justifying joy?"

"Because my logical mind says I should be home forcing the end of my book to happen, I suppose."

"But that's not the effortless creativity you want, is it?"

"No, I know. It's just a little more difficult accepting it when you get to the practical."

"But when you remember that every moment is contributing to supporting you, that you designed every moment so you can enjoy effortless creativity, then you stop forcing, you stop beating yourself up."

"I'm getting to that bit."

"What about having that food you aren't allowing yourself?"

"Alright, alright. What's it like, knowing everything?"

"I wouldn't know," replied my Higher Self cheekily.

"Oh, ha ha. I get it, you're just wise to me, eh?"

"That's the idea."

"How can I be hungry? It's only 5 o'clock and I had a huge lunch."

"But are you hungry?"

"Yes."

"So nourish yourself. Nourish yourself from your heart, not from your mind. Logic can never plot the spirals of chaos, only the lines of limitation."

I listened to the wise flow of guidance as I feasted on sardines, soup, toast and salad.

I looked across at my computer to see if I'd get the buzz to write. Nothing.

I heard a muffled sound. I went to the window to see if it was Isis but it wasn't. I realised it was my phone squealing and buzzing from the confines of my coat pocket.

"Hello?"

"The clock is ticking so I thought I'd call in and see how everything was going," launched an anxious Erica.

"Quite well, Erica. Only two chapters left."

"Not the worst news I've ever received. So when do you think the remaining two chapters are going to appear in this realm?"

"If I'm honest, I don't know. This isn't a precise science. But it will be completed for 3 o'clock on Monday, that's a promise."

"So we're both learning trust, eh?"

"Yes. And if you were to rattle around in that elephantessical memory of yours, you'd find that I've never let you down."

"Searching archives." Erica made whirring sounds of cogs in her mind searching for an answer. "It appears you're correct."

"No point in worrying, then, eh?"

"Oh, I'm not worried, I'm actually impatient. I'm eager to read your next installment."

"As always, Erica, you'll be the first to read it when it arrives."

"Great! So what am I going to do now?" She appeared to be squeezing efficiency out of her remaining time in the office.

"What about going home on time for once? Take that husband of yours out for dinner or do something spontaneous for a change. Go to the theatre; call that friend you've been meaning to meet up with. But above all, give yourself permission to let go. It'll all work out just fine!"

"Message received and understood. Looking forward to seeing you on Monday."

"We'll both be there, the manuscript and me."

She hung up as my Higher Self began laughing at my slightly frantic but upbeat tone.

"Just because there's no secrets between us," I said, "and you know I'm under more pressure than I'm letting on, that doesn't mean you can laugh."

"You're only under pressure because you're letting your ego put you under pressure. Besides, laughter lubricates the heart and helps it expand."

"Okay, I'll detach and nip that pressure in the bud."

"An earnest choice, indeed. But isn't it time you got ready?"

"What do you mean?"

"Time to practice what you preach."

"But I thought I was? I've done spontaneity, trusting me with me. So what's left?"

"Letting go."

"Letting go of what?"

"Your target, your deadline."

"I thought I had."

"Not quite yet."

"If you hold on to it too tightly you will shut down your creative connection and you won't be able to complete it. You can always finish a book, but can you complete it? Can you support it into saying all it comes into being to say?"

"Okay, I'll have a relaxing night in, sleep early and then get back to it early tomorrow morning."

"But that is tomorrow. What about now?"

"There's obviously something in Now that I can't see."

"Yes. One last journey so you can come full circle and complete your book."

"And what's that?"

"Go upstairs."

"Where upstairs?"

"Remember 3A?"

"Yes."

"It's time to pay a visit."

"But I don't have a reason to go. You're the ones who always talk about invitation."

"Who said you didn't have an invitation?"

"I don't know who lives at 3A. What on earth am I going to say? *Hi, I live in 1A and the voice in my heart told me to come and see you?*"

"Why not?"

"Because not everyone thinks like us. You know what I mean... Number 3A doesn't know me from Adam."

"Assumption, assumption, assumption. It's time to let go of assumption."

"Okay. Let's say I did go and knock on their door. What am I really going to say?"

"How about *Hello*? Make it up. You're an author aren't you? That's what you do. Make it up from the heart. You could even tell the truth and say your Higher Self suggested it."

"Look, I really appreciate your guidance but I have to live here, you know."

"Suit yourself. But ego has so many assumptions and they take up a lot of space. Take worrying what other people think; worrying there's nothing outside of the famous cube; labelling spontaneity as having no value... to name but a few."

Pacing around the kitchen, I tried to work out how to approach my letting-go challenge and I came full circle. Answers in the heart, questions in the head. Here goes.

I picked up a handful of books, glanced in the mirror and was just about to leave when...

I couldn't find my keys.

I rifled through my coat pockets but they were empty. My frustration level began to rise. Now I'd chosen to let go, I couldn't leave.

The mini-farce continued for ten more minutes as I retraced my steps since I'd arrived home.

There was a tap at the door. It was Agnes.

"You might be needing these," she said, handing me my keys.

"Did I leave them in the door again?"

"Yes, you did. You seem like you're in a bit of a fluster."

"I was staying in and then I decided to go out and then I couldn't find my keys."

"Sounds like your ego's tying you up in knots! But don't

The Return

worry, it'll all unravel soon. It's always like this when you're about to do something meaningful. You always get those last minute ego panics."

"You've hit the nail on the head, Agnes. It's exactly that. Thanks. Good to know I'm not going mad."

"Oh, I didn't say that," she winked. "See you later."

"Thanks. Will do."

I returned inside to pick up the books. And a jacket—I was suddenly feeling cold. Locking the door, I departed on my weirdest and shortest journey yet... up two flights of stairs to a flat I'd never been in, to meet people I didn't know for a purpose of which I was unaware.

I knocked on the door while wafts of a relaxing scent floated onto the landing.

A lady answered.

"Welcome. You've come for the meditation evening?"

"Yes. My Higher Self sent me," I joked.

"Great. Always a good recommendation," said the lady, ushering me in and appearing completely unphased. "Aren't you the author that lives at 1A? We see you talking to yourself outside your door a lot. Discussing whether you're going to float through the door or unlock it, I suppose?"

"Something like that!" I laughed nervously.

"Well, I'm Kate—computer programmer by day, meditation host by night. Make yourself at home. It's a bit crowded these days but the more the merrier, I say. And just when we think we've got no more room, one of the walls expands so it all works out."

"You live in a Tardis, then?"

"Yes, I think we probably do," she smiled.

"Will Doctor Who be joining us?"

"Well, you know the Interdimensional Time Lord... anything's possible."

"But you've got room for some books I hope?"

"Oh yes, thanks. We already have a few copies but there's

a book club discussion group starting so more copies would be excellent. Your timing's perfect, thank you."

I looked around the sea of faces and was surprised to see someone I knew.

"Agnes! Long time no see!" I blurted out.

She laughed. "Yes... It's amazing what you can find on your own doorstep, isn't it?"

"You never cease to amaze me, Agnes."

"Ditto."

As 7 p.m. approached, the room began to fall silent. A flow of relaxation filled the room and the meditation began.

When I next opened my eyes it was 8:30. Animated discussion followed, accompanied by tea and cake.

The next time I looked at the clock it was 10:30. Time seemed to be leaking towards the ground floor.

"Well Kate, thanks for a great evening. I really enjoyed the guided meditation. I'd love to come again. Is it every Tuesday night?"

"Yep, usually. Glad you enjoyed it. See you again."

I turned to Agnes. "I've got a long commute, Agnes, so I'd better get started!"

"Oh, I know what you mean," she smiled. "Won't be too long myself. Isis or I will pop round tomorrow."

"Wonderful. See you then."

Walking down the stairs I could feel my Higher Self right next to me. "Alright, alright," I smirked, "they knew me, even though I didn't know them. There was a familiar face. Everyone was really welcoming for our journey outside the cube. Just because I wasn't aware of the purpose before I went didn't mean it didn't exist. And assumption doesn't make life easier. Have I covered everything?"

"A wonderful summary of your learning."

I opened my door and looked at the computer. The promise of a chapter heading sped past my vision.

"Ready to complete it?" asked my Higher Self.

The Return

"Yes, I am. But one question. Why was it so hard to go to 3A and why do I feel so differently about the book?"

"You let go of your ego's expectations. You stopped piling more and more targets and controls on yourself and you enabled yourself to create in the flow, not just do what logic told you. Logic may appear right and sensible but it is always limited. It is always putting you back in a framework rather than helping you expand from what you already know. Logic cannot prove expansion, it can only define more logic."

"So chaos and centeredness are here to stay?"

"It's up to you. But the more centred you become, the more you will flow with chaos until creation is effortless and you see that you are cooperating with the greater Cosmos rather than limiting yourself to what you know."

"And 3A? What does that represent?"

"That is a place of community. Little by little you have returned to community. First Erica, then Agnes, then Isis, then Andrew and now... The list is expanding. Earlier, you couldn't be spiritual and be with people. You perceived that your path was one of journeying without physical company. But now you are finding that you have plenty of company; plenty of ascending masters in the physical on the same wavelength, even though they have vastly differing life experience and some of them even look quite normal."

"Ha, ha."

"You are all seekers, wayshowers and spiritual masters in the making, wherever the alchemy of balance takes you."

"So enjoy community before it spins off into its next formation?"

"Yes. Enjoy the community you are part of and understand that there is always community inside and out, all you're required to do is seek it out. The invitation is always there but you are required to choose it."

"And now?"

"Now is now. Nothing more and nothing less. It is the

point where all your pasts and all your futures meet. And it is fast becoming your home."

"But the acceleration is up to me?"

"Always."

I felt completely connected, yet there was something I couldn't put my finger on; something near that I could sense but couldn't understand.

"Higher Self, are you planning something?"

"Well, Armchair Alchemist, that would depend on you."

"Another contract?"

"Yes..." My Higher Self was treading carefully. "But not with us directly."

"With whom, then?"

"Your new old best friend."

"Who?"

"Your great friend that has been with you since the beginning and promises to take you to places you've never been before."

"Sounds intriguing. But this new old best friend... Do they help me with the practical side of writing, or the visionary side?"

"This soul can help you create exactly what you require in each moment, from all sides in all ways."

"So when do we meet?"

"It's not actually a question of when, more a question of how. There are many elements involved."

"Do I come to them or do they come to me?"

"Put it this way... you meet in the middle."

"So all I've got to do is find the middle?"

"It's simply a question of staying in your centre."

"So again I'm meeting up in the middle of my centre with a new old best friend that I don't know I've met?"

"Yes."

"Easy then."

"Effortless."

The Return

"I accept. So when do we get started?"

My Higher Self coughed as though there was a part of my commitment still to be made.

"What is it?"

"Your acceptance speech."

"What? You want me to thank the whole world?"

"That would be wonderful, but it is also important to authenticate with your Inner Authority Mentor."

"Okay... I AM embracing my new old best friend in the perfect balance at the perfect moment."

"And so it is."

"And?" I was surprised at my eagerness.

"There is the small matter of completing your current work, and then solving this riddle. Not necessarily, of course, in that order."

"Okay. And the riddle is?"

> *"She's around you and within you,*
> *sometimes hidden but ever seen...*
> *She reflects the inner and the outer*
> *for you know you are a team...*
> *She's a man for all seasons and a mother to all men...*
> *Your reunion is in the becoming*
> *when all your seasons complete as one."*

Silence expanded out in all directions. The flat suddenly felt like it had endless space and I was unified, expanding within it. I felt weightless and yet present, purposeful and yet free of any burden or direction. My Higher Self stood in silent support.

"I AM allowing this, Higher Self. I'm not out of my depth quite yet, but I'm going to need some help."

"And what kind of help would that be, Armchair Alchemist?"

"You, of course. That goes without saying and... The

Merlin kind; the Sananda kind; the Archangel Michael kind; the Djwal Khul kind. I think that's everyone for now."

"Any more? You are unlimited, after all."

"I AM embracing the perfect guidance."

"Perfect."

And with a flash of silver-purple, blue, gold and pearl, guidance opened the door of my heart room as wide as it would go.

"And there we are," I replied. "United once more."

I began to walk towards my friends.

"Yes, united we are. One voice, the voice of many. Ever present, awaiting your invitation to guide and serve the path of self enquiry."

"Funny... I've got a question to ask. It just popped into my head."

"Just one?" answered a joyous chorus.

"There's always one more question, right?" I smiled, with tears of joy rolling down my face.

"We are counting on it," came the radiant reply. "We are counting on it."

More About the Author...

Alexandria presents workshops, seminars and private consultations around the world, inspiring and teaching the principles of the Alchemy of Change in people's day to day lives. These events include:

Discovering the Inner Wizard

A workshop which inspires you to take command of your creativity and experience the benefits of a heart-centered life.

For information, email: InnerWizard@lifeoflight.com

Harnessing the Alchemy of Change

This workshop embraces the powerful process of change that liberates blocked and stagnant energy, recycling it into fulfilling and life-changing progress.

For information, email: AlchemyOfChange@lifeoflight.com

Connecting to Natural Forces

A full day intensive, this workshop initiates you into a deeper relationship with Mother Earth and explains our planet's role in the spiritual development of you and Humanity as a whole.

For information, email: Mastery@lifeoflight.com

~

If you'd like more information about Alexandria's work, please visit: www.lifeoflight.com

If you'd like more information about this and other books by Alexandria, please visit: www.lifeoflightmedia.com